Political Consulta
and American Elections
Third Edition

When it comes to elections, campaigns matter. And a modern, sophisticated American campaign relies heavily on political consultants and seasoned operatives. Consultants help define the race, develop strategy and tactics, conduct candidate and opposition research, explore the mood of the public through qualitative and quantitative survey research, use both old media and new online communication tools to persuade voters, and employ complex technologies to mobilize voters. At all levels of the electoral arena, modern campaigns cannot hope to be effective without the guiding disciplines of professional consultants.

This thoroughly updated edition of Dennis W. Johnson's classic text, originally titled *No Place for Amateurs*, highlights the growing importance of social media, targeting and analytics, Super PACs and dark money in a post-*Citizens United* world.

Dennis W. Johnson is professor emeritus and former associate dean of the George Washington University Graduate School of Political Management.

Political Consultants and American Elections

Hired to Fight, Hired to Win

Third Edition

Dennis W. Johnson

Routledge
Taylor & Francis Group

NEW YORK AND LONDON

First published 2016
by Routledge
711 Third Avenue, New York, NY 10017

and by Routledge
2 Park Square, Milton Park, Abingdon, Oxon, OX14 4RN

Routledge is an imprint of the Taylor & Francis Group, an informa business

© 2016 Taylor & Francis

Library of Congress Cataloging in Publication Data
A catalog record for this book has been requested

ISBN: 978-1-138-78635-6 (hbk)
ISBN: 978-1-138-78636-3 (pbk)
ISBN: 978-1-315-73187-2 (ebk)

Typeset in Garamond
by FiSH Books, London

Printed and bound in the United States of America by Edwards Brothers Malloy on
sustainably sourced paper.

To Pat, with all my love

Contents

Tables

Preface to the Third Edition

Much has changed and much has remained constant in the world of campaigns, elections, and professional political consulting since the previous edition of this book, written in 2007. Two presidential elections, the most expensive in history, were conducted, and, particularly in the two Obama presidential campaigns, we saw the formidable application of technology and digital communication. For many years, campaigns had been experimenting with the tools of microtargeting, sophisticated algorithms, and online communication. But, in 2008, we experienced a breakthrough. The Obama Online Operation, so-called "Triple-O," a staff of about thirty rewrote history by integrating online technology and presidential campaigning. The McCain forces were close behind in applying and integrating technology, but always seemed a step or two behind Obama. The 2012 presidential race saw even greater deployment of technology, with the Obama team spending well over $100 million to seek out, identify, and persuade voters, and get them to the polls.

In the past decade, there have been enormous changes in online communication. When the last edition of this book was being prepared, the iPhone was just being launched as the new revolutionary device, the "smart phone." In 2007, MySpace was still an important social media site. Facebook had 20 million users in April 2007; by March 2013, it had 1.1 billion. Twitter had not been invented yet, neither had Pinterest; Reddit was still in its infancy. Few people had ever heard of an avatar and the idea of smart phone "apps" was still a year away. Just as our lives have become more and more plugged in, so too have our political campaigns, and their attempts to convince and mobilize voters.

Another very important change in campaigns and elections has been the explosion of money coupled with the emergence of "Super PACs" (political action committees), 527 groups and social welfare organizations employing independent expenditures on behalf of candidates, or (more often) against candidates. The 2008 presidential election cost about $1.6 billion; that was nearly twice the cost of the 2004 presidential election, and triple the cost of the 2000 election. The 2012 presidential contest cost even more, with over $2 billion raised and spent by the candidates, political parties and outside groups. But what was different in 2012 was the extent of money coming from super wealthy individuals. In an unsuccessful effort to beat Obama, the Koch brothers, Charles and David, and the committees they created, spent over $400 million, while casino billionaire Sheldon Adelson spent over $150 million.

The biggest impetus for such spending came from a U.S. Supreme Court decision in early 2010 that struck down federal bans on corporate money in campaigns. Now corporations, wealthy individuals, and labor unions could spend as much as they wanted, without having their names or the amounts of their campaign contributions disclosed, and often hiding behind innocuous-sounding organizational names. News organizations quickly dubbed this new hidden money as "dark money." Now, it seemed, the gates were wide open for targeted and lavish spending to try to support or defeat candidates for office, all hiding under the label of independent expenditures. The campaign finance reforms enacted in 2002 have now been almost completely eviscerated and it has become a wild west of spending in presidential and congressional campaigns.

The public mood has soured; the voters' trust in elected officials, from members of Congress to the president, has sunk alarmingly. During the second term of George W. Bush, the public became exasperated. There seemed to be renewed hope, however, with the historic election of Barack Obama, but inaction, gridlock, and intense partisan sniping have eroded Americans' trust and confidence in all forms of government. One result was the emergence of the Tea Party movement, which has displayed a visceral distaste for all things Obama, and which has brought a near civil war within the Republican Party. The country seems more and more divided, politically and culturally, and the public discourse gets more raw and unpleasant.

With these new political and campaign realities has come a change in the title of this book. The original title, *No Place for Amateurs*, reflected a different era. So much has happened in the past fifteen years: increases in citizen engagement, partisan activism, microtargeting and campaign technology, and investments of money into campaigns, that a change in title was necessary.

Consultants are often vilified, blamed for the negative and cynical tone of campaigns, and seen as unwanted filters between candidates and potential voters. The mid-term elections of 2010, which saw the ascendance of Tea Party winners, were particularly nasty, with vicious, personal attacks against candidates and boat-loads of money spent to convince voters and get them out to the polls. The 2014 mid-terms, with control of the U. S. Senate at stake, were equally as vicious, with record-setting amounts of money poured into them by outsiders. And without missing a beat, we begin preparing for the 2016 presidential election. America truly is the land of elections and the land of political consultants.

I would like to thank the students, faculty, and other readers from around the world who have shared their comments, criticisms, and encouragement. I particularly thank my students and colleagues at the Graduate School of Political Management, George Washington University. Thanks to my editor Michael Kerns and the fine production team at Routledge, and, as always, to my dear wife Pat for her unflagging support.

Dennis W. Johnson
Chatham, Massachusetts

Introduction:

Canvassing the Political Landscape

The United States is the land of elections. We hold more elections, more frequently, than any other modern society.[1] Altogether, there are approximately 513,200 popularly elected officials in the United States, and over a million elections are held in every four-year cycle.[2]

The United States is also the land of political consultants. There are about seven thousand political consultants who play an increasingly important role in the conduct of national, state, and local elections.[3] Professional consultants are found in virtually every campaign for president, senator, representative, big-city mayor, and governor, and in many state legislative and other elected offices. Altogether, about fifty thousand campaigns a year are managed or assisted by professional political consultants.

American elections come in many shapes and sizes, from headline-grabbing, billion-dollar presidential campaigns to low-profile local contests in which voters are often unaware of the contest until they see the candidates on the election-day ballot.

Campaigns

Campaigns can be placed into one of several categories, based on the size of the electorate, the relative importance of the office being pursued, and the degree of involvement of professional campaign consultants.

Statewide Elections: This category includes races for U.S. senator, governor, attorney general, lieutenant governor, and other statewide-elected officials. These elections generally attract considerable attention and are usually expensive, competitive, and issue-oriented. This is particularly true in statewide contests in the mega-states of California, Texas, New York, and

1

Florida, with their multiple media markets, complex and varied political cultures, and heavy reliance on television advertising. In statewide contests, especially for the Senate or governorship, candidates rely heavily on the skills and services of professional consultants.

Presidential Primaries and General Elections: While the presidency (along with the vice presidency) is our only national office, campaign strategists focus on key statewide contests. During the year or so before the primaries, presidential hopefuls seek out organizational help and early money. Then come the key early primaries, in which candidates rely on grassroots mobilization, telemarketing, and old-fashioned shoe leather to woo party loyalists. Later, during the general election, the mathematics of the electoral college requires careful deployment of campaign resources. Campaign commercials and voter mobilization are concentrated on key media markets and states while giving national audiences glimpses of the campaign through televised debates. These campaigns are thoroughly profession-alized, usually relying on the best campaign consultants in both parties.

Statewide Initiatives and Referenda: During the past decade, there have been a record number of initiative and referendum contests held throughout the states. This form of direct democracy is big business and is becoming an increasingly lucrative market for political consultants. Some of the most expensive campaigns in the 1990s and early 2000s were ballot initiatives, several with budgets well exceeding $40 million. Especially in the California market, some ballot initiatives surpass Senate and guberna-torial races in the amount of campaign funds spent. Big budgets attract media consultants, pollsters, general strategists, and a growing number of specialists in initiative and referendum campaigns.

Major Elections Below the Statewide Level: Elections in this category include mayoral races in large cities, congressional district races, and elections in major urban counties. Serious candidates in most of these elections employ professional campaign consultants. Some of these elections involve far larger electorates and bigger campaign budgets than do statewide elections. For example, the mayoral election in New York City, with an electorate drawn from 7.3 million people and the most expensive media market in the country, easily surpasses most statewide elections in size and budget. However, most elections in this category are congressional contests in districts that are roughly equal in population—about 690,000 residents. Mayoral races and urban countywide races in this category are those in which the electorate is over 500,000 in population.

Medium-Sized Elections Below the Statewide Level: This category includes mayoral and city council elections in cities with a population of about two hundred and fifty thousand, state legislative races, and other campaigns. These elections are being transformed most rapidly from amateur to professional. While many medium-sized elections still have low budgets and little media attention, others are becoming more competitive, more expensive, and based on professionally driven strategies.

Small Elections: This category, with by far the largest number of elections, includes town campaigns, rural county campaigns, and races far down the ballot in big cities. Some of the techniques of professionalized campaigning might filter down, but consultants are rarely used. These races are too low budget, the stakes are too small, and they are below the radar screen of professional consultants. These campaigns essentially count on name recognition of candidates and face-to-face meetings with voters and have low-budget advertising through posters, yard signs, and last-minute advertisements in local newspapers.

Professionals and Citizen Engagement: Throughout this book, I refer to amateur and professional campaign workers. First, a few words about the difference between the two. Amateurs often have personal interests in the candidate, the office, and the issues. They might have worked for the candidate or party in the past; they may have a personal stake in the election, or may be looking for employment if their candidate wins. They can usually be relied upon to help other candidates in upcoming elections, but are almost always limited to their city, county, or state. Amateur campaigners are often strongly motivated by issues of public policy and receive little or no compensation for their efforts. Election work is not their principal source of income nor is it their full-time profession.

Amateur status carries no normative baggage. An amateur campaign can be filled with dedicated, intelligent, hard-working volunteers who know the dynamics of state or local politics and who can develop an effective campaign message and can implement a winning strategy. Many amateurs have a high degree of political sophistication and proven electoral skills.[4] But amateur campaigns also can be understaffed; the organization may be unable to rely on volunteers and friends to perform all the campaign duties, unable to run an efficient, strategically smart race, and simply outgunned when facing an opponent's professionally driven campaign.

In contrast, professional political consultants have some level of detachment from the candidate and the campaign. The professionals might admire their candidates, agree on issues, and work very hard to help them win. But the professional is at least one or two emotional levels removed from the intensity and personal involvement found in most amateur campaigners. In many cases, consultants will personally disagree with the policies of the candidates or have less than the highest regard for them as individuals. Yet, in the end, these factors are secondary. The job of the professional consultant is to get the candidate elected to office; quite simply, that is what the professional is paid to do.

Many professional consulting firms juggle more than one campaign at a time. Some of the most successful pollsters, media firms, phone banks, and fundraising firms may have ten to forty campaigns in progress throughout the country at various stages in the election cycle. Further, professional consultants are permanent fixtures on the election landscape. Candidates will come and go, but consultants will be there to guide them and their successors through the election process.

Many thousands of other political activists are involved in campaigns, year in, year out. They work for the national, state, and local political parties, labor unions, businesses and trade associations, and ideological and special-interest groups intimately involved in election activities. They are indeed political professionals, who are usually the unseen lubricant for a successful election: the get-out-the-vote specialists, the membership organizers, the petition signers, the fundraisers, and volunteer coordinators. Their work is integral to electoral success and is discussed especially in relationship to opposition research, fundraising, get-out-the-vote, and phone banks.

Presidential contests bring out a whole new level of political activism and enthusiasm, and the 2008 and 2012 elections saw extraordinary increases in citizen involvement. Many thousands of political activists and volunteers were used by the national political parties, labor and business groups, and 527 and other organizations. Thousands, perhaps millions, more political activists now get their information and motivation through email and political blogs.[5] Their potential as a political force was shown in the 2008 Obama campaign and in the re-election campaign in 2012.

The increase in citizen activity is a good sign. The high stakes of presidential elections, with their razor-thin margins in 2000 and 2004, brought out thousands of loyalists willing to participate in the most basic of campaigning activities. It would be a healthy sign indeed if that enthusiasm were carried over to less exciting, less glamorous elections, such as congressional or mayoral races. But, for many citizens, campaigning is a mere spectator sport. Too many are disenchanted with politics, feeling isolated from public life, uninterested in issues, and, therefore, unlikely to help out in campaigning, or even to vote. Perhaps electronic activism will provide the spark for civic engagement, but that certainly remains to be seen.

Modern, sophisticated campaigns cannot hope to be effective without the guiding disciplines of professional consultants. But citizens cannot simply become spectators; there is much that they can do to recover their place in elections and democratic choice.

Notes

1 Seymour Martin Lipset, *American Exceptionalism: A Double-Edged Sword* (New York: W.W. Norton, 1996), 43.

2 U.S. Bureau of the Census figures cited in "Over Half Million Elected Officials in U.S.," *Campaigns and Elections*, May 1996, 54. This figure includes primaries and runoff elections; many of the elected contests are for one- or two-year terms. Not included in these figures are the many initiatives and referenda, bond issues, constitutional amendments, and other ballot issues found at the state and local level.

3 Ron Faucheux, "Consultants on Trial," *Campaigns and Elections*, October/November 1996, 5. Walter DeVries estimated that 12,000 individuals made all or most of their incomes as professional consultants. "American Campaign Consulting: Trends and Concerns," *PS: Political Science and Politics,* March 1989, 21.

4 See James Q. Wilson, *The Amateur Democrat: Club Politics in Three Cities* (Chicago, Ill.: University of Chicago Press, 1962). Wilson's focus was on the amateur office seeker, but it has relevance here for looking at those who assist candidates running for office. The typology of professionals and amateurs is explored in Frank J. Sorauf and Paul Allen Beck, *Party Politics in America,* 6th ed. (Glenview, Ill: Scott, Foresman and Company), 120.

5 Peter W. Wielhouwer, "Grassroots Mobilization," in *The Electoral Challenge: Theory Meets Practice,* ed. Stephen C. Craig (Washington, D.C.: CQ Press, 2006), 163; Mark Leon Goldberg, "Ashes of ACT," *American Prospect,* March 2006, 17.

PART

I

PROFESSIONAL

CAMPAIGNING:

NEW

REALITIES,

NEW

CHALLENGES

1

Political Consultants and Professionally Driven Campaigns

There is nothing political consultants love more than celebrating their own genius.

—Barack Obama in a 2013 video tribute to
David Axelrod and David Plouffe[1]

I want to thank my superb campaign team ... I want to thank the architect, Karl Rove.

—George W. Bush's 2004 reelection victory speech[2]

I don't want to read about you in the press. I'm sick and tired of consultants getting famous at my expense. Any story that comes out during the campaign undermines my candidacy.

—Bill Clinton to his 1996 reelection consultants
Dick Morris and Doug Schoen[3]

For years, David Axelrod, a Chicago-based political consultant, was known in Democratic circles as the operative who understood big city politics and could help African American candidates win mayoral elections. Axelrod, known by friend and foe as "Axe," had helped Dennis Archer (Detroit), Michael R. White (Cleveland), Anthony Williams (Washington, D.C.), Lee Brown (Houston), and John F. Street (Philadelphia). Axelrod also helped John Edwards in his 2004 presidential bid, Deval Patrick running for Massachusetts governor, and Eliot Spitzer in the New York gubernatorial contest. By 2008, David Axelrod and his media Chicago-based firm, AKPD Media and Message, had worked in over one hundred and fifty state, local and national races. When Democratic candidates started vying for the 2008 party nomination, Axelrod could count five as former clients: Tom Vilsack (former Iowa governor), John Edwards (former U.S. senator from North Carolina), and three current U.S. senators, Hillary Clinton (New York), Chris Dodd (Connecticut), and Barack Obama (Illinois). Axelrod took a chance on the youngest and least experienced, the senator from Illinois. In 2002, Illinois state senator Barack Obama sought out Axelrod, seeking his assistance in a run for the U.S. Senate seat. Axelrod advised Obama to wait, possibly run for mayor of Chicago later; but Obama was in a hurry. "My involvement was a leap of faith," Axelrod later told an Obama biographer.[4]

Obama was also assisted by Axelrod's business partner, David Plouffe, who earlier in his career had helped Iowa senator Tom Harkin run for the Democratic presidential nomination in 1992. In 2003–2004, Plouffe was senior adviser to Missouri congressman Dick Gephardt's presidential nomination bid. For Obama, Plouffe took on the most important and visible job of his career, the senior strategist and campaign manager of the 2008 campaign. Plouffe worked behind the scenes; he was remarkably low-keyed and hardly known to the public. Few even knew how to pronounce his last name (hint: Pluff). Plouffe, Axelrod, and the team of consultants, advisers, and staffers, ran one of the most remarkable and efficient presidential campaigns ever, first defeating Hillary Clinton in the long, drawn-out primaries, and then defeating John McCain in the general election.

When Obama became president, Axelrod joined the White House as senior strategist, assuming a role similar to that filled by Karl Rove during the George W. Bush administration. After Axelrod left the White House in early 2011 to prepare for the Obama re-election drive, he was succeeded by Plouffe as senior adviser.

A third member of the Obama team was Jim Messina, who worked for Senator Max Baucus of Montana, also worked as chief of staff for New York representative Carolyn McCarthy and then Senator Kent Conrad of North Dakota. During the 2008 election, Messina was deputy to David Plouffe, and when Obama won, he headed up Organizing for Action, the Obama grassroots advocacy program. Messina was tapped by Obama to lead the re-election campaign in 2012.

A *New York Times* reporter described Axelrod as "lumbering, sardonic, and self-deprecating"[5]—a far cry from the attack-dog frenetics of James Carville or the good-ol'-boy-with-a-hand-grenade-in-his-back-pocket persona of Lee Atwater. Nevertheless, Axelrod made the rounds of television talk shows and Sunday press show appearances, in defense of the president and his policies. David Plouffe remained relatively invisible, despite writing a best selling memoir of the 2008 election, *The Audacity to Win.*[6] Jim Messina, while also appearing on many news outlets, like Plouffe, is still relatively unknown to the general public.

Political consultants are supposed to operate offstage, letting their clients, usually candidates seeking election, take center stage. After he helped Bill Clinton win the presidency in 1992, James Carville, who became an instant celebrity and media presence, decided not to work in the White House, but concentrated on international clients, giving speeches and writing books, and becoming one of Clinton's staunchest defenders during his battles with Congress and the special prosecutor's office. Dick Morris, who had aided Bill Clinton during his 1980s gubernatorial campaigns, secretly worked for Clinton's reelection, then during the spring of 1996 became a media target, leading to Clinton's complaint that Morris and pollster Douglas Schoen were grabbing too much attention. Morris grabbed too much attention, as it turned out. In September 1996, *Time* magazine dubbed consultant Dick Morris as "the most influential private citizen in America."[7] Just days before the 1996 Democratic National Convention, a smiling, confident Bill Clinton was featured on the cover of *Time,* and pasted on Clinton's shoulder was a cutout photo of Morris. *Time* was sending its readers a backhanded pictorial message: here is the most powerful man in the world, who fought his way back from political oblivion, and perched on his shoulder is the reason why. Suddenly the once-secretive, behind-the-scenes consultant was a household name and a political celebrity. But just a few days later, on the eve of Clinton's acceptance speech at the Democratic convention, word came out that Morris had been involved with a prostitute and that he shared sensitive White House information with her. Morris abruptly left the campaign, one step ahead of being fired. Morris, an early and ardent defender of both Bill and Hillary Clinton, later turned against both, in a series of books, through frequent appearances on conservative cable television shows, and through his own website and online communication.

Another major political consultant, who had labored behind the scenes, but became increasingly visible and controversial during the Bush II years and into the Obama years was Karl Rove. In the early 1990s, when George W. Bush first thought about running for governor, Karl Rove already was known as the Texas Republican Party's fiercest and most successful political consultant. Few Texans had ever heard of Rove, but those in power and those seeking power knew him well. Years earlier, Rove was the "boy genius" of the Republican Party, tapped by the senior George Bush to head the national College Republicans. Once settled in Texas in 1977, Rove became a political consultant. That year, Republicans held just one of the thirty statewide offices; by the time he left in 2000 to become senior adviser to the new president, George W. Bush, Republicans held all twenty-nine statewide offices and dominated both houses of the state legislature by substantial majorities.

Many of those Republicans who won statewide office were clients of the influential consulting firm of Karl Rove and Company. His company specialized in the new field of direct mail: identifying likely voters, dividing them into hundreds of subgroups, crafting messages specifically appealing to their concerns, and sending millions of pieces of mail asking for donations and their vote. But Rove did more than simply churn out direct mail pieces. He foresaw the fundamental, tectonic shift in Texas politics and knew how to take advantage of new opportunities.

Karl Rove also had a reputation for rough, "no holds barred" politics. That reputation went all the way back to 1973, during the Watergate era, when *The Washington Post* reported that young Karl Rove was teaching "dirty tricks" to college Republicans.[8] In Texas, both Republican and Democratic opponents accused him of fighting dirty, and going for the opponent's jugular in ways never seen before, even in rough-hewn Texas politics.

In the Bush administration, Karl Rove sat at the pinnacle of American power as senior political adviser to the president. He's been on countless magazine covers, the subject of a PBS *Frontline* documentary, hailed by loyalists, and grudgingly acknowledged by critics as the most important political operative in the country. Years ago, he was the brilliant, aggressive political consultant who hand-picked the neophyte George W. Bush out of a crowd of potential candidates for the Texas governorship and master-minded an upset victory over the popular incumbent governor Ann Richards. Rove became well known today because of George W. Bush, and Bush reached the Oval Office thanks in large part to Karl Rove. In the current era of unlimited and unreported money, the aptly called "dark money," Rove has reappeared as co-founder and major adviser to American Crossroads, Crossroads GPS (Grassroots Policy Strategies). Of all the major political consultants during the past thirty years, Rove remains controversial within his own party, feared by his opponents, and a major force in American politics.

For years, Americans had been unwittingly exposed to campaign posturing and manipulation engineered by political consultants. In the 1990s, they grew curious about the manipulators. Suddenly, political consultants were hot properties. Movies, documentaries, and books gave us a glimpse of consultants at work. A film documentary, *The War Room,* made media stars of James Carville and George Stephanopoulos in Bill Clinton's 1992 presidential campaign headquarters. Reporter Joe Klein's best-selling *roman à clef, Primary Colors*, detailed with unnerving accuracy the seamy side of the presidential quest by an ambitious young Southern governor and his avaricious campaign team. Later John Travolta starred as the silver-haired, young presidential candidate in the inevitable movie version.[9] *Vote for Me,* a PBS documentary, showed hard-charging New York media consultant Hank Sheinkopf patiently coaching his candidate, an Alabama Supreme Court judge, on the fine points of camera angles and voice projection. Another film documentary, *The Perfect Candidate,* chronicled the highly charged campaign of conservative lightening rod Oliver North and his consultant Mark Goodin as they battled and lost to the uninspiring, wooden Charles Robb in the 1994 Virginia Senate race.

In the movie *Wag the Dog*, the president's spin doctor (Robert De Niro) and a high-powered Hollywood mythmaker (Dustin Hoffman) conjured up a wartime incident in Albania to cover up the president's sexual indiscretions with a twelve-year-old girl. The long-running television drama, *The West Wing*, featured earnest, energetic White House aides scheming with political consultants.[10] During the 2008 presidential contest, Republican vice-presidential choice Sarah Palin drew immediate press attention, and soon the backroom drama of the campaign was portrayed in the HBO movie *Game Change*, starring Julianne Moore (Sara Palin), Woody Harrelson (Republican consultant Steve Schmidt), and Ed Harris (John McCain).[11]

Bookshelves were filling up with insider accounts by political consultants. Well-traveled, controversial Republican consultant Ed Rollins skewered many of his campaign rivals and former clients in a book entitled

Bare Knuckles and Back Rooms.[12] On the dust jacket was the middle-aged, balding Rollins, poised with his boxing gloves, ready to take on the rough and tumble of politics. Ray Strother's memoir settled some political scores and told how a "redneck" helped invent the business of political consulting. Lee Atwater was the subject of a biography appropriately entitled *Bad Boy.* Carville and his Republican-operative wife, Mary Matalin, teamed up on the lecture circuit, hawked credit cards and aspirin in television commercials, and wrote a best-selling memoir, *All's Fair: Love, War, and Running for President.*[13]

Carville, Stephanopoulos, and Paul Begala reappeared during the Lewinsky scandal and the impeachment hearings. Begala and Carville later teamed up to write several best-selling books urging Democrats to defeat Bush and his policies, and to contribute their collective wisdom to "shout" television through CNN's *Crossfire.*[14] Stephanopoulos, meanwhile, singed by the president's betrayal, distanced himself from the White House, and publicly criticized Clinton's behavior in his memoir, *All Too Human.*[15] He then went on to become a chief Washington correspondent for ABC television. Dick Morris, too, resurfaced on talk shows, wrote political columns, advised Clinton on how to deflect criticism during the Lewinsky scandal, and later turned on both Bill and Hillary.[16]

Karl Rove wrote his memoirs, *Courage and Consequence,* so have Democratic media consultant Robert Shrum, David Axelrod, and Democratic pollster Stanley Greenberg, and several other political consultants. All have their stories to tell, their sides of issues to defend, and their own perspectives on politics and high-stakes elections.[17]

Despite the notoriety and self-promotion of Rove, Morris, Carville, and others, the celebrity consultant is the exception, not the rule. Most political consultants toil in the background, content to ply their craft in anonymity. Even at the presidential campaign level, consultants generally labor in obscurity. Few Americans recognize the names of influential consultants like Matthew Rhoades and Russ Schriefer (Mitt Romney, 2012), Steve Schmidt and Rick Davis (John McCain, 2008), Tad Devine and Bob Shrum (John Kerry, 2004), Mark McKinnon and Matthew Dowd (George W. Bush, 2004), or Donna Brazile and Carter Eskew (Al Gore, 2000).

Political consultants, both controversial and anonymous, have become essential players in the increasingly technological, fast-paced, often brutal world of modern elections. Through it all, they have changed the face of modern American politics.

Political Consultants at Work

In earlier decades, campaigns were financed and run by local or state political parties. Campaigns were fueled by local party activists and volunteers, by family, friends, and close political supporters. By the early 1960s, presidential campaigns and statewide campaigns for governor and senator began seeking out media and polling firms to help deliver their messages to voters. During the next two decades, there emerged both a new industry (political management) and a new professional (the campaign consultant). By the 1980s, every serious presidential candidate, nearly every statewide candidate, and a large number of congressional candidates were using the services of professional political consultants.[18]

The 1990s witnessed yet another transformation. Candidates for office below the statewide level were beginning to seek the advice of professional political consultants. For many candidates, the dividing line was the $50,000 campaign: those who could not raise that kind of money had to rely solely on volunteer services, and those above this threshold usually sought professional assistance.[19] In some local political jurisdictions, record amounts of campaign funds were being raised to pay for campaign services, and races for medium-city mayor, county sheriff, or local judge took on the techniques and tactics once seen only in statewide, professionally managed contests. Professional consulting services, such as phone banks, telemarketing, and direct mail, were supplanting the efforts once provided by volunteers and party loyalists. This multibillion-dollar industry is now directed by professional consultants who make the key decisions, determine strategy, develop campaign communications, and carry out campaign tactics for their clients.

Now, another transformation is occurring. Individual citizens and groups, empowered by email, the Internet, blogging, text messaging, and other forms of online communication, are adding their voices to campaigns and elections. As the title of a recent book argues, politically active citizens are "crashing the gate" of the traditional political dynamics of candidates and consultants.[20] As can be seen in Chapters 6 and 10, these new voices present both opportunities and challenges to political consultants and the business of professional politics.

Many campaign consultants have politics in their blood. They volunteer for candidates and causes while they are in college, work for their political parties in their state capital or in Washington, work for a member of

Congress, or toil away at a variety of statewide and local campaigns before striking out on their own. Over 95 percent of political consultants are white and 81 percent of the principals in campaign firms are men. Particularly since the mid-1990s, aspiring political consultants have sought out graduate-level, skills-based training from the University of Florida's Political Campaigning Program, American University's Campaign Management Institute, the George Washington University Graduate School of Political Management, and several other smaller programs.[21]

The influence of political consultants goes well beyond getting candidates elected to office. They play an increased role in ballot measures by helping clients determine ballot strategy, framing issues, and even providing the campaign foot soldiers who gather signatures for ballot petitions. Consultants use marketing and mobilization skills to orchestrate pressure on legislators. Political telemarketers link angered constituents directly with the telephones of members of Congress. Overnight, they can guarantee five thousand constituent telephone calls patched directly to a legislator's office. Political consultants are also finding lucrative markets internationally, serving presidential and other candidates throughout the world.

In the commercial world, a business that generates less than $50 million is considered a small enterprise. By that measure, virtually every political consulting firm is a small business. Most of the estimated three thousand firms that specialize in campaigns and elections have ten or fewer staffers and generate just several hundred thousand dollars in revenue annually. Only a few media firms generate millions of dollars in revenue; most of this money, however, passes through the consultants' hands to pay television advertising costs.

Leading polling firms, such as the Tarrance Group or Public Opinion Strategies, may have forty to eighty employees; most are support staff working the telephones and part of the back office operations. Quite a few firms are cottage enterprises—one- or two-person boutiques, often in specialty markets, such as event planning, opposition research, fundraising, or media buying. Some political consulting firms operate out of the basement of the principal's home, with no more than telephone lines, computers, fax machines, and online access. For example, even after he became famous as Clinton's principal political adviser, James Carville and his assistants worked out of the "bat cave," a basement studio apartment on Capitol Hill that served as Carville's home and nerve center for his wide-ranging political operations.

Firms that rely solely on campaign cycles are exposed to the roller coaster of cash flow: many lean months, with very little money coming in from clients, countered by a few fat months when the bulk of the revenue pours in. In addition to the on-off flow of cash, the firms must deal with the logistical difficulties of juggling many candidates during the crucial last weeks of the campaign cycle and the enormous time pressures of a busy campaign season. Some consulting firms have around-the-clock operations during critical weeks of the campaign. These political emergency rooms are geared to handle any last-minute crisis. During long stretches when there are few campaign opportunities, professionals and support staff may have to be let go until the cycle picks up again.

One of the most difficult but necessary tasks is to even out the steep curves in the election cycle so that money and resources flow more regularly. Consultants have developed several strategies for this: convince candidates to hire consultants earlier in the cycle, stretch out the amount of time they stay with campaigns, and seek out off year races, especially down the electoral ladder, such as mayoral races, general assembly, and other local contests, many of which in past years would not have sought professional assistance. Consultants are becoming more involved in the growing business of initiatives, referenda, and issues management. Many of these campaigns are tied to the same election cycle as candidate campaigns, but others are tied to local, state, or congressional issue cycles. Political consulting firms also pursue clients from the corporate and trade association world, issue advocacy, and international clients. By spreading out business, consulting firms are able to stay competitive, smooth out the peaks and valleys of the election cycle, and keep their heads above water.

In the 1980s, firms began to shift away from heavy reliance on candidate campaigns. For example, Matt Reese, one of the founders of the political consulting business, who had worked for more than four hundred Democratic candidates, changed direction after the 1982 elections to concentrate on corporate and trade association clients. Republican consultant Eddie Mahe shifted his business from 100 percent candidate-based in 1980 to about 15 percent candidate-based in the early 1990s, picking up corporate and other clients. In the mid-1970s, Walter Clinton's pioneering political telemarketing firm, the Clinton Group, gained 90 percent of its work from candidates, but has since moved away from reliance on candidates to issue advocacy and corporate work. Many successful consulting firms have followed this pattern and now have much of their business coming from noncandidate campaigns.[22]

As corporations have discovered the value of grassroots lobbying and issues management, consultants who specialize in direct mail and political telemarketing have shifted focus to legislative and issues work. Corporate and trade association organizations took special notice of the successful political consultant-orchestrated grassroots campaign run against President Clinton's 1993–1994 healthcare proposal. For political consultants, such work is often far more lucrative, more reliable, and less stress inducing than working for candidates in competitive election cycles. Some of the most successful political consulting firms have less than half of their revenue coming from candidate campaigns.[23]

Winning is Not Enough

Politics, like sports, is a zero-sum game—someone wins, someone loses. In business, success can be measured by increases in market share or profitability to shareholders, but in political consulting it is determined by winning or losing. However, winning is not enough. Perception and expectation play important roles as well. A consultant's reputation can be hurt when a client was expected to win by a wide margin but just barely manages a victory. Though consultants sometimes tout their winning streaks, when the streak is ten easy wins with little or no real competition, it loses its luster. The consulting firm that takes on the tough fight, steers the dark horse to victory, or puts up a much better fight than expected, will build its reputation.

For the professional political consultant, losing is part of the game. Campaign consultants can be "hot" for two or three election cycles and then suffer crippling losses. Even the most successful consultants have suffered major defeats. James Carville, for example, began his late-blooming career with a series of bitter losses and then became famous within the small fraternity of political consultants by winning several key gubernatorial races. His reputation grew when he helped Harris Wofford overwhelm a seemingly invincible Richard Thornburg in the Pennsylvania 1989 special election for U.S. Senate. Carville became a celebrity during the 1992 Clinton presidential campaign, but subsequently went on to lose a string of campaigns. Then he decided to concentrate on the international political market with clients throughout Europe, the Middle East, and Latin America.

There is not a great deal of stability for political consulting firms. The best are sometimes toppled by their own mistakes, by the tides of politics, or by the lackluster performances of their own clients. Consultants working for marginal candidates may not get paid on time or paid the full amount for services rendered or even paid at all. Some consultants simply lack the business skills or patience to keep their companies afloat. Busy firms have gone bankrupt and firms have folded because partners were impatient with internal business details.[24]

It is relatively easy to break into the political consulting business, and, in every campaign cycle, scores of new firms are created. Following each election cycle, there is a substantial turnover at the national parties, and ambitious (and often soon-to-be-unemployed) campaign operatives join established consulting firms or decide to begin their own business in polling, research, fundraising, and other special services. Often junior partners, chafing at their subordinate status in established consulting firms, set up their own operations. Since the 1980s, the increasing number of consulting firms has led to greater competition and, in many cases, stagnation in prices charged for professional services.

Some of the best-known consulting firms have had acrimonious disputes among partners, with the firms splitting and dividing up their client base. Looking at Democratic polling firms alone, Washington-based political analyst Stuart Rothenberg observed that "change is so endemic because most firms are merely collections of individuals who stay together for convenience. When disagreements about personality, money, or the direction of the firm crop up, there are few institutional loyalties to keep the firm together."[25]

What Consultants bring to Campaigns

Candidates, not consultants, win or lose elections. In 2012, voters chose Barack Obama, not campaign manager Jim Messina; they rejected Mitt Romney, not pollster Neil Newhouse. Candidates alone face the voters and ultimately bear the responsibility for the tone and expression of their campaign. Sometimes reputations are diminished and images tarnished by the campaign itself. For example, George H. W. Bush will be remembered for permitting a down-and-dirty campaign that included the infamous "revolving door" and race-tinged Willie Horton commercials in his 1988 presidential campaign. In that same year, Michael Dukakis will be remembered for his ride in a military vehicle, hunkered down in an oversized battle helmet, looking goofy. Mitt Romney will be remembered for his inartful candid characterization of "47 percent" of Americans as "dependent on the government, who believe they are victims" during the 2012 presidential campaign.

While candidates are ultimately responsible for their campaigns, there is no way they can compete, let alone win, without professional help. Professional consultants bring experience, direction, and discipline to the campaign. Few enterprises are as unpredictable, vulnerable, and chaotic as a modern campaign. So much can go wrong. The candidate might go "off message," in which case the campaign loses focus; internal party feuds might threaten the success of the entire campaign; fundraising might fall short of expectations, choking the life out of the entire enterprise. All the while, the opponent's campaign is raising more money, attacking with a sharp and clear message, redefining the race in its own terms, grabbing media attention, and efficiently mobilizing its resources. Campaign professionals are needed to bring order out of chaos, maintain message and strategy discipline, and keep the campaign focused. Republican consultant Lee Atwater was fond of saying that he knew that the message of his campaign was hitting home when he would go to a local Wal-Mart and ask shoppers what they thought of the contest and they would simply parrot the message he had developed.

In the months before the 2004 Democratic primary, the Howard Dean campaign engaged in a unique experiment: let the message and direction of the campaign flow from the bottom up, rather from the top down. It was indeed a unique idea, but in the end, a flawed one. To manage the chaos, the competing interests, and messages, the Dean campaign needed, above all, structure and discipline. When it lost these elements, it lost its momentum and ability to win.

Professionals also take campaign burdens off the candidate. Campaigns are exhausting, placing extraordinary physical and emotional demands upon the candidate. The campaign staff, and especially the campaign manager, absorb as much of the stress of the campaign as possible. A campaign manager may serve as official campaign optimist, psychologist, and handholder for the candidate or, often, the candidate's spouse. The manager will make the tough personnel and tactical choices when the campaign starts going badly, and be the unofficial heavy (or whipping boy) when needed.

Consultants, particularly those in niche or vendor markets, provide legal, tax, and accounting services for the increasingly complex financial disclosure reporting requirements. They provide expertise in buying television time and placing radio and television commercials. Consulting firms capture and analyze television commercials aired by opponents and other races, and offer both quantitative and qualitative analysis from survey research, focus group, and dial-group findings. Increasingly campaigns depend on specialists who also can provide a technological edge. Consultants provide online retrieval systems and websites, computer-assisted telephone technology, voter and demographic databases, and geo-mapping and sophisticated microtargeting techniques so that a campaign can know, block-by-block and house-by-house, who is likely to vote and for whom they would cast a ballot. Strategists are able to use predictive technologies, traditional statistical techniques, such as regression analysis, and new artificial intelligence technologies, such as neural nets and genetic algorithms to target potential voters.[26]

Above all, consultants bring experience from other campaigns. Every campaign has its unique circumstances, events, and dynamics. But campaigns are also great recycling bins. After a consultant has worked in fifteen or twenty-five races, campaigns begin to fall into predictable patterns: messages and themes, issues, and tactics reappear, taking on slight variations—new twists to old challenges. Veteran consultants can save a candidate from making mistakes, spot opportunities quickly, and take advantage of changing circumstances. As veteran consultant Joseph R. Cerrell put it (tongue in cheek), we need consultants "to have someone handy who has forgotten more about media, mail, fundraising, and strategy than most candidates will ever know."[27]

Growing reliance on professional consultants is costly; the price of admission to elections has risen substantially. The campaign, for many candidates, becomes an exhausting full-time game of chasing dollars. Consultants have seen business grow because of the superheated fundraising activities of the national Democratic and Republican parties, the explosion of new money raised over the Internet, Super PAC spending on independent expenditures, and issue advocacy campaigns.

The best consultants are not afraid of a fight. They know that, in many cases, an election can be won only if they drop the pretense of reasoned, civilized campaigning and take the gloves off. Campaigns engage in rough tactics because they work. Opposition researchers dig deep into personal lives, seeking out misdeeds and character flaws. Pollsters test-market negative material before focus and electronic dial-meter groups. Then the media team cuts slash-and-burn, thirty-second clips, using all the tricks of the trade: unflattering black-and-white photos of the opponent, ominous music and sound effects, and distorted features, salted with authentic-sounding textual material, often taken out of context. The direct mail pieces may get even uglier. The goal is to drive up the opponent's negatives, to paint the opponent in such unflattering ways that enough voters develop only a negative view of that candidate.

Certainly not all campaigns use negative tactics. Candidates are often very reluctant to engage in mudslinging or demagoguery. Voters are turned off by negative campaigns and feel alienated from the democratic process. But campaign consultants see negative campaigning as a tool, not so much a question of political ethics or morality. If the only way to win is to go negative, then negative it is.

Professional consultants bring many weapons to the fight. The campaign's theme and message are communicated through television and radio commercials, through direct-mail pieces, and increasingly through campaign websites, blogging, cell phones, and email. These communications are developed and honed through the use of sophisticated research analyses, especially survey research, focus groups, and dial-meter sessions. Even more fundamental is the campaign's deadliest weapon—candidate and opposition research, which is the subject of Chapter 4.

Notes

1   Video shown at the AAPC annual meeting, Washington, D.C., in honor of Axelrod and Plouffe being inducted into that organization's Hall of Fame, April 6, 2013.
2   *New York Times*, November 4, 2004, 2.
3   Richard Stengel and Eric Pooley "Masters of the Message," *Time,* November 18, 1996, 18.
4   Cited in Robert G. Kaiser, "The Player at Bat," *Washington Post*, May 2, 2008, C1; David Mendell, *Obama: From Promise to Power* (New York: HarperCollins, 2007). On Axelrod's political career, see David Axelrod, *Believer: My Forty Years in Politics* (New York: Penguin, 2015).

5   Ben Wallace-Wells, "A Star Strategist Offers Democrats a New Vision," *New York Times*, March 30, 2007.

6   David Plouffe, *The Audacity to Win: The Inside Story and Lessons of Barack Obama's Historic Victory* (New York: Viking, 2009).

7   *Time*, September 2, 1996.

8   John Saar, "GOP Probes Official as Teacher of 'Tricks'," *Washington Post*, August 10, 1973, A16. On Rove's career, see James Moore and Wayne Slater, *The Architect: Karl Rove and the Master Plan for Absolute Power* (New York: Crown Books, 2006); James Moore and Wayne Slater, *Rove Exposed: How Bush's Brain Fooled America* (New York: Wiley, 2005); and Carl M. Cannon, Lou DuBose, and Jan Reid, *Boy Genius: Karl Rove, the Architect of George W. Bush's Remarkable Political Triumphs* (New York: Public Affairs, 2003).

9   Joe Klein, *Primary Colors* (New York: Random House, 1995). Much of the hype associated with this book centered around the anonymity of the author. A year after its publication, Klein, a *Newsweek* reporter, was uncovered as its author.

10   Hollywood has long had an interest in politics and campaigns. In Frank Capra's *Meet John Doe* (1941), vagrant Gary Cooper played the American everyman in the tale of a crooked politician's presidential bid. In another Capra film, *State of the Union* (1948), Spencer Tracy portrayed a well-meaning businessman who wanted to run for the presidency. Paul Newman was a young lawyer running for office faced with a blackmail scandal in *The Young Philadelphians* (1959). Henry Fonda and Cliff Robertson were presidential candidates who faced off at a national party convention in *The Best Man* (1964). Idealistic Robert Redford followed his consultant's script in a run for the Senate in *The Candidate* (1972). Richard Gere was a hot-shot American consultant plying his trade in Latin American politics in *Power* (1986), and Tim Robbins campaigned as a phony populist in *Bob Roberts* (1992). *Wag the Dog* was based on Larry Beinhart's 1993 novel, *American Hero*. Presidential sexual exploits have become something of a cottage industry for writers of fiction: Charles McCarry's sexually hyperactive president in *Lucky Bastard* (1998) married a leftist ideologue and became a pawn of the KGB; Marilyn Quayle and Nancy Northcott conjured up a philandering president and a left-wing conspiracy in *The Campaign* (1996), and Erik Tarloff told of an extramarital affair between the president and his chief speech writer's girlfriend in *Face Time* (1998). Netflix series *House of Cards* (2013–present), adapted from the BBC series of the same name, portrays the conniving, power hungry Frank Underwood; ABC television's *Scandal* (2012–present) shows the sometimes tawdry, always scandalous, adventures of the president's former media adviser.

11   *Game Change*, directed by Jay Roach, produced by Tom Hanks, Garry Goetzman, Jay Roach and Amy Sayers; HBO Films, March 10, 2012. The movie was based on the book of the same name written by Mark Halperin and John Heilemann.

12   Edward Rollins with Tom DeFrank, *Bare Knuckles and Back Rooms* (New York: Broadway Books, 1996).

13   Mary Matalin and James Carville with Peter Knobler, *All's Fair: Love, War, and Running for President* (New York: Random House, Simon and Schuster, 1994).

Carville also wrote *We're Right, They're Wrong: A Handbook for Spirited Progressives* (New York: Random House, Simon and Schuster, 1996).

14   James Carville, *...And the Horse He Rode in On: The People v. Kenneth Starr* (New York: Simon and Schuster, 1998). Carville and Paul Begala have written several books together.

15   George Stephanopoulos, *All Too Human: A Political Education* (Boston: Little, Brown, 1999).

16   Dick Morris, *The New Prince: Machiavelli Updated for the Twenty-first Century* (New York: Renaissance Books, 1999). Morris has written several other books since this effort.

17   Karl Rove, *Courage and Consequence: My Life as a Conservative in the Fight* (New York: Simon and Schuster Threshold Editions, 2010); Robert Shrum, *No Excuses: Concessions of a Serial Campaigner* (New York: Simon and Schuster, 2007); Axelrod, *Believer*; Stanley Greenberg, *Dispatches from the War Room: In the Trenches with Five Extraordinary Leaders* (New York: Thomas Dunne Books, 2009).

18   Larry Sabato, *The Rise of Political Consultants: New Ways of Winning Elections* (New York: Basic Books, 1981). See also Frank I. Luntz, *Candidates, Consultants, and Elections* (New York: Basil Blackwell, 1988); Karen S. Johnson-Cartee and Gary A. Copeland, *Inside Political Campaigns* (New York: Greenwood, 1997); Robert V. Friedenberg, *Communication Consultants in Political Campaigns: Ballot Box Warriors* (Westport, Conn.: Praeger, 1997); David A. Dulio, *For Better or Worse? How Political Consultants Are Changing Elections in the United States* (Albany: State University of New York Press, 2004); Stephen C. Craig, ed., *The Electoral Challenge: Theory Meets Practice* (Washington, D.C.: CQ Press, 2006); and Dennis W. Johnson, *Campaigning in the Twenty-First Century: A Whole New Ballgame?* (New York: Routledge, 2011).

19   Ron Faucheux and Paul S. Herrnson, "See How They Run: State Legislative Candidates," *Campaigns and Elections*, August 1999, 25.

20   Jerome Armstrong and Markos Moulitsas Zuniga, *Crashing the Gate: Netroots, Grassroots, and the Rise of People-Powered Politics* (White River Junction, Vt.: Chelsea Green, 2006).

21   Dulio, *For Better or Worse?* 45–53; Robin Kolodny, "Electoral Partnerships: Political Consultants and Political Parties," in *Campaign Warriors: Political Consultants in Elections*, ed. James A. Thurber and Candice J. Nelson (Washington, D.C.: Brookings Institution Press, 2000).

22   Michael Clark, "Selling Issues: Political Consultants Are Shifting Their Business to Include Campaigns without Candidates," *Campaigns and Elections*, April/May 1993. See also David L. Rosenbloom, *The Election Men: Professional Campaign Managers and American Democracy* (New York: Quadrangle Books, 1973), 50.

23   For example, Clinton reelection campaign and second-term pollsters Mark Penn and Doug Schoen also have worked for AT&T, Texaco, Chemical Bank, Citibank, Control Data, Eastman Kodak, Honeywell, Major League Baseball, Nynex, Procter and Gamble, Sony, and the Trump Organization. They also have worked for candidates in Latin America, Israel, Greece, Turkey, and the Philippines.

Peter Baker, "White House Isn't Asking Image Advisers to Reveal Assets or Disclose Other Clients," *Washington Post,* May 19, 1997, A8.

24 The partnership of Dick Morris and Richard Dresner, for example, ended in bankruptcy in 1982, even though they had an extraordinary number of clients.

25 Stuart Rothenberg, "Change Is Good: The Consultant Soap Opera," *Roll Call*, March 13, 1995.

26 Hal Malchow, "The Targeting Revolution in Political Direct Contact," *Campaigns and Elections*, June 1997, 36–9. See Chapter 6 for discussion of these new technologies.

27 Joseph R. Cerrell, "Do Political Consultants Harm the Electoral Process?" CQ *Researcher* 6, no. 37 (October 4, 1996): 881.

2

Running for Office:
Not for the Faint of Heart

The modern campaign is a high-tech, high-maintenance, high-anxiety, high-concept monstrosity where response time is instant. The candidate may have never held office. The manager is a professional political consultant who may be juggling three other races. The pollster samples public opinion every night for weeks. The press is frantically looking for dirt on the campaign and his or her every relative, dead or alive. The television budget may be larger than the gross national product of Niger. And if your ads don't slash and burn, you'll lose.

—Former political consultant Ed Rollins[1]

Anybody who says he enjoys campaigning is either a liar or a psychopath.

—Former Representative Barney Frank[2]

Running for office is not for the faint of heart. Especially in high-octane, professionally driven contests, candidates must have stamina, determination, and thick skins. They must endure the cynicism and mistrust of voters; even worse, they must endure voter indifference and disinterest. Candidates expose themselves and their families to the prying eyes of professional researchers digging into every corner of their lives. They must brace themselves against the attacks from their opponents and from well-funded ad campaigns by unknown groups attacking them usually during the last days of the campaign. Rather than spending time meeting voters and talking about issues, candidates are forced to devote most of their time begging for campaign funds. Ed Rollins and Barney Frank are both right: campaigns can be monstrosities, and running for office is certainly no picnic.

The Sour Mood of the Public

Candidates today have to face the harsh realities of public opinion; most voters today don't trust, admire, or respect politicians. Our confidence and trust in government and institutions have steadily deteriorated over the past forty years; we are more suspicious of Washington and entrenched politicians, and public service has lost much of its distinctiveness and attraction. Several studies have tracked this erosion of public trust and confidence. One report, commissioned by the *Washington Post,* the Henry J. Kaiser Family Foundation, and Harvard University,[3] found that America had become a nation of "suspicious strangers" who have lost faith in the federal government and virtually every other national institution.[4] Furthermore, Americans had also lost faith in one another. Only 35 percent of the public in 1995 said they could trust others, down from 54 percent in 1964 surveys, and citizens who distrusted others were suspicious of government and significantly less likely to vote in the last two national elections.[5]

There was an even steeper decline in confidence in the federal government. In 1964, about 76 percent of respondents said that government could be trusted "about always or most of the time" to do the right thing. Trust levels fell to 20 percent in the late 1970s, in large measure due to Watergate, economic dislocations, and the Iran hostage crisis. They rebounded to 40 percent in the 1980s, but then slowly eroded. In 1995, only 25 percent of respondents agreed that the federal government "about always or most of the time" did the right thing.[6]

Adding to this sour mood is a growing dislocation between what people want from the government and what they are willing to pay for it. Robert J. Samuelson described the American mood as in an "almost permanent state of public grumpiness," based on inflated expectations of what the federal government can or should provide and the contradictory expectations that citizens should not be stuck with the bill to pay for such services.[7]

Many Americans, especially in the first half of the 1990s, harbored outright anger toward government, public leaders, and politics. Anger became the political watchword of the mid-1990s and had much to do with the Republican triumphs in the 1994 congressional elections.[8] Many citizens, disturbed by what they saw as posturing, finger pointing, and unfulfilled promises of entrenched legislators, perceived Congress and especially the Democratic leadership as a "public enemy." Leaders from both parties worried about the absence of civility, the decline of intelligent dialogue, and the "rising decibels of hate in political discourse."[9] This pent-up citizen aggravation of the 1990s fed into the hands of conservatives, challengers, and anti-establishment candidates.[10]

In 2006, five years after the September 11 attacks, the public mood was equally sour: disgust with the partisan bickering in Washington, distrust of both Republicans and Democrats, frustration with George W. Bush, and a significant majority of citizens asserting that the country was off track. The distrust was fueled by congressional scandals, the post-Hurricane Katrina sense of wholesale government incompetence, and, above all, the festering war in Iraq, and continued unease over terrorist threats. Added to the public frustration was the ranting of pundits on talk radio and television, newspaper opinion writers, bloggers, and other self-appointed guardians of the truth. As National Public Radio host Tom Ashbrook has written, "Pundits relentlessly pump irate, intemperate, ideological opinion to their audiences. A vulnerable audience becomes colored with this poison."[11]

Immediately after Barack Obama took the oath of office in January 2009, a new movement sprung to life, the Tea Party. It had been long in coming, from the protest movement centering around Ross Perot in the 1990s, to Jesse Ventura and the Reform Party in the late 1990s, through Ron Paul and his libertarian movement, culminating in his run for the presidency in 2008. Upset with Washington politics, distrustful of President Obama, fearful of government taking over more of their lives and curtailing personal freedom, the Tea Party movement began spreading through the ranks of conservative voters, many of whom traditionally aligned with the Republican Party. Their resentment of President Obama was fueled by their distrust of the sweeping Affordable Care Act, which was quickly dubbed "Obamacare". Professional consultants and political operatives got into the act, with the Tea Party Express created in 2009 by Republican Sal Russo in California. The Tea Party Express and others began raising millions of dollars to fight against both Obama policies and moderate Republicans. One of their email fundraising solicitations sent out in February 2013 said, "Help us tell Establishment Republicans that they cannot push the Tea Party aside just because we make them feel uncomfortable when we oppose their tax-and-spend ways by making a donation TODAY!"[12]

In a historic midterm election, Republicans, sparked by Tea Party anger and activism, swept to victory in 2010, winning sixty-three seats in the House of Representatives and six in the Senate. President Obama hit it on the head when he said that Democrats took a "shellacking."[13] Establishment Republicans felt considerable pressure from Tea Party activists, especially after several high-profile losses of their long-serving colleagues in primaries to Tea Party candidates. Even after it seemed that the Tea Party movement had lost some of its steam, in 2014, Republicans were shocked when House majority leader Eric Cantor, a conservative from Virginia, was soundly defeated by a Tea Party-backed rival, college professor David Brat, in a primary. Those same angry voices, fuelled by recording-breaking amounts of outside money, helped propel Republicans in November 2014 to the majority in the U.S. Senate and increase their majority in the House of Representatives.

In today's political climate, anger and resentment abound, and we are becoming more culturally and political polarized. Journalist Bill Bishop, writing in 2008, called it the "Big Sort": where individuals are clustering into homogenized communities, not simply by where they live, but by what they read, who they associate with, what they listen to on television and see on the Internet.[14]

Where are the Voters and Campaign Volunteers?

What could be an even greater problem for candidates is getting voters simply to pay attention. For many citizens, politics and public life have become wholly irrelevant to their lives. For them, politics is boring, politicians lie and cheat, and voting is a waste of time. These disenchanted nonvoters are the toughest challenge to candidates. Writing in 1992, political scientist Ruy Teixeira observed that the decline in voter turnout since 1960 had been "substantial and serious."[15] Despite legislation and court actions to simplify registration and ballot procedures, fewer people now take the time and effort to vote. Lukewarm citizens have many excuses not to participate—apathy and disinterest, irritation and disillusionment, lack of knowledge, and busy lives focused on more important personal and family matters.

For a short time, however, more citizens seemed to be interested in voting. The 1992 presidential election reversed a thirty-two-year trend of declining voter participation. It turned out to be an interesting election: President George Bush was in trouble, and Bill Clinton and Ross Perot made the race engaging. But four years later, there was a palpable disinterest in the presidential contest between Bill Clinton and Bob Dole, perhaps because for many voters it was a foregone conclusion. Even the press was weary and bored. Television networks, sensing voter apathy, spent only half the time covering the 1996 election as they had on the 1992 election. Many voters were not paying attention. Incredibly, just before the vice-presidential debate between Al Gore and Jack Kemp, fully 40 percent of the American public did not know that Jack Kemp was Bob Dole's running mate. On election day, 11.6 million fewer citizens cast their ballots than in the 1992 presidential contest.[16] Voter disinterest was most evident in the youngest voters. Only 30 percent of Americans between eighteen and twenty-four years bothered to vote in the 1996 presidential elections. In the 1998 congressional elections, just 36 percent of the eligible voters of any age cast their ballots, making it the lowest rate of voting since 1942.[17]

Voter turnout edged up slightly in 2000. Then, during the 2004 election, it reached 60.4 percent of voting-age adults, thanks to an intense voter registration and mobilization drive by both political parties and their allies.[18] But turnout can be both fragile and fickle, subject to voter anger, apathy, and disappointment with the performance of political leaders. The 2008 presidential election saw voter turnout of 62.3 percent, but then it dropped in 2012 to 57.5 percent. Looking at it another way, in 2012, voter turnout dropped in every state except two, Iowa and Louisiana, and while 126 million citizens voted, 93 million stayed at home. Barack Obama received 6.85 million fewer votes than he received in 2008, despite the enormous sums spent on get-out-the-vote drives. Turnout during the Republican-only primaries in 2012 was just 15.9 percent of eligible voters. That record low turnout of 1998 did not last long: during the 2014 midterm elections, even fewer eligible voters turned out.[19]

By 2012, thirty states and the District of Columbia permitted early and absentee voting. Some states permitted voting as early as the first week of

September, and one estimate is that some 32.3 million voted early.[20] Early voting changes the dynamics of a campaign. We used to think of an election as a "one day sale:" all attention is focused on election day. But with early voting candidates and their campaigns have to adjust their tactics to reach early voters. In past elections, early and absentee voters tended to be Republicans, but in 2008 and 2012, such voters were more likely to be Democrats.

In recent years, there has been a flurry of state laws trying to restrict who can vote on election day. According to the Brennan Center for Justice at New York University Law School, at least one hundred and eighty bills had been introduced since 2011 in forty-one state legislatures that would have an impact on the right to vote. The bills were designed to require photo identification, proof of citizenship, make voter registration harder, or reduce the early voting and absentee voting opportunities.[21] Why change the law? Some argued that it was to clean up voting rolls, that were replete with wrong addresses, duplicates, even dead people still on the voting books. The Pew Center on the States had found much that needed to be cleaned up: 1.8 million dead people were still on voter rolls, 2.75 million persons were registered in more than one state, and 51 million people were not registered at all.[22] Another reason given for these legislative proposals was to uncover and discourage voter fraud. But was that really a problem? The *New York Times* in an editorial confronted the rash of laws, many coming from Republican-controlled state legislatures, whose principal justification was to stop voter fraud: "Voter identity fraud is all but non-existent, but the assertion that it might exist is used as an excuse to reduce the political rights of minorities, the poor, students, older Americans and other groups that tend to vote Democratic."[23]

During presidential campaigns, the candidates and political parties can usually rely on thousands of volunteers to answers telephones, use social media and email to contact their friends, help round up voters, and work the polling sites on election day. In recent elections, both parties have had extensive field operations. About a decade ago, Republicans appeared to have an upper hand in getting their loyalists to the polls, but Obama's 2008 and 2012 campaigns had superior field operations and ground forces and were better able to get voters out to the polls.

Presidential campaigns can generate considerable excitement and bring out thousands of volunteers. However, it is often a different picture in local, congressional, and even statewide contests. In a way, technology and money have made the campaign volunteer obsolete, but also have shown the potential for energizing and using volunteers.

Up through the 1990s, there seemed to be a dwindling number of people willing to devote their free time to helping candidates, especially at the statewide, congressional, and local levels. Veteran Republican strategist Stuart Spencer once observed that the combination of money and television was leading to the disappearance of volunteers. "Because of the new technology, few campaigns are 'people campaigns' any more. You don't need a bunch of little old ladies stamping envelopes to send out a direct mail piece."[24] Spencer's observation is even more relevant today. Fewer than 5 percent of American adults engage in any kind of political activity other than voting, and few contribute money to political causes.[25] In many ways, campaigns are becoming spectator sports, with fewer volunteers assisting in the campaigns.

But there are exceptions, and with today's online communication it is far easier to energize committed volunteers. Well before the online revolution was the seemingly implausible challenge of college professor Paul Wellstone against incumbent Senator Rudy Boschwitz of Minnesota in 1990. Outspent nearly five to one, Wellstone's campaign used its limited resources on clever, professionally produced commercials that attracted considerable free media attention. But Wellstone also relied on an army of grassroots supporters from labor, feminist, and environmentalist causes for his upset victory over Boschwitz.[26] Six years later, when Wellstone was up for reelection, his campaign was transformed. It became a professionally driven, $6 million juggernaut, and Wellstone was able to fend off Boschwitz in a rematch.[27] Wellstone needed all the money, grassroots support, and help he could get, because the National Republican Senatorial Committee had targeted this 1996 race and had pumped $1.5 million into negative advertising against him. Even more improbable was Jesse Ventura's successful bid to become governor of Minnesota in 1998. Starting with a shoestring budget and little visibility, this charismatic former professional wrestler and radio talk show host was able to tap into voter disenchantment to humiliate his two mainstream rivals, Norman Coleman and Hubert H. Humphrey III. Barnstorming the state, using the Internet to energize volunteers, Ventura was able to bring back a grassroots enthusiasm that Minnesotans had not seen since the early Wellstone days.

As a candidate for the 2004 Democratic presidential nomination, Howard Dean combined electronic communication with old-fashioned personal contact. His campaign created the first presidential candidate blog site, raised millions of dollars online, and used Meetup.com like-minded Dean supporters through house parties, bringing together and energizing a pool of volunteers.

Ned Lamont, who in 2006 defeated Senator Joseph I. Lieberman for the Democratic nomination in Connecticut, also blended old-fashioned techniques with the new. He used the liberal blogging community, particularly through the *Daily Kos*, to advocate his antiwar views and criticize Lieberman's support of Bush's war policies. Early on, Lamont's campaign used a website to attract a thousand volunteers, seeking out supporters in each of Connecticut's one hundred and sixty-nine municipalities. The campaign also used house parties, similar to those of the Howard Dean campaign, and Lamont personally went to hundreds of the gatherings.[28]

David Brat, Tea Party-backed economics professor, stunned the Republican establishment and House majority leader Eric Cantor in 2014. Cantor's campaign did not see defeat coming, even up to election day. The Cantor campaign spent over a million dollars on television advertising trying to show Brat as a "liberal college professor" who did not fit into the conservative suburban Richmond, Virginia, congressional district. But the label of liberal professor was laughable, with Tea Party activists probably laughing the hardest. Cantor's ads backfired, giving Brat more publicity and name recognition than his bargain-basement campaign could afford. Cantor's professional pollster did not pick up the warning signs, and Cantor himself was far too complacent. Brat supporters, fired up and upset, with little money but plenty of energy, pulled off a ten-point upset in the primary.

Each of these illustrations has one thing in common: a discontented electorate just waiting to be galvanized into action. With the online tools of email, blogging, social media, and mobile phones, it becomes vastly easier for the right candidate to connect with supporters and voters.

Anti-Washington, Anti-Incumbent Mood

Years ago, Washington experience somehow became a liability rather than an essential prerequisite for the nation's highest office. In their presidential campaigns, Jimmy Carter, Ronald Reagan, and Bill Clinton all boasted to voters that they were not a part of the "Washington mess." Many Republicans turned to George W. Bush because of his Texas upbringing and experience, and Al Gore, trying to rekindle his faltering primary campaign, moved his headquarters out of Washington and back to his political home base in Tennessee. Just about every candidate running for a seat in Congress vows to bring a fresh, honest voice to Washington. They promise to bring Missouri (or Idaho, Texas, or Midwest) values to Washington, not Washington values to Missouri.

Senators and members of Congress also found themselves vulnerable to charges of "going Washington." Many tried to inoculate themselves by downplaying their Washington experience. In the 1990s, few incumbents created campaign commercials with their smiling faces framed by the U.S. Capitol, and their reelection literature did not brag about Washington connections and power. Once a proud feature on any incumbent's campaign literature, the Capitol dome conveyed new meaning as a symbol of a corrupt, unresponsive big government, with its strings pulled by high-priced lobbyists.[29]

Incumbents quickly learned to dance to a new tune. Years before, many incumbents had shed their party label in reelection commercials and literature; during most of the 1990s they were shedding their incumbency as well. Washington insiders and power brokers transformed themselves into embattled champions of the folks back home, fighting against the federal government's greed and hubris. Incumbents found a winning theme in railing against Washington. In his 2006 Maryland senatorial bid, Republican Michael Steele's television ad has him telling Maryland voters, "I know what you're thinking; I know what you're feeling. Washington has no clue of what's going on in your life." Nick Lampson, who was running for Tom DeLay's old seat in Texas, used a bullhorn to read his deficit spending proposals to supporters. "Since Washington has a hard time hearing [the] message, we thought we'd raise the volume," Lampson said on his television ad. Sheldon Whitehouse, the 2006 Democratic candidate for the Senate from Rhode Island also bashed Washington: "To see what's happening in Washington right now is pretty close to disgraceful. We need to improve the ethical climate in Washington."[30] Many other candidates, particularly Democrats, used the scandal-and-disgrace theme immediately after the late September 2006 episode involving Republican congressman Mark Foley and underage House pages.

Challengers, without fail, contend that incumbents have lost touch with reality, have forgotten the people back home, or have let incumbency go to their heads. In the late 1990s, Jesse Ventura hit this sentiment right on the head. He was not running against Washington, or against an incumbent governor, but against the lowest form of the species, the career politician. In a rap-style radio commercial for his gubernatorial campaign, Ventura's backup singers wailed: "We don't want some suit who tows the party line" and "we demand a leader with a spine." Then Ventura growled, "I don't play that game" and "I'm no career politician," as the backup singers breathlessly chanted, "Jesse, Jesse, Jesse." Ventura defeated two well-established "suits," thanks to the votes of many young, disaffected Minnesotans who, in record numbers, cast ballots for the first time.

This anti-Washington, anti-incumbent mood hurt some candidates and helped others. Challengers with anti-Washington themes encountered receptive audiences and found inspiration from successful insurgent campaigns, particularly from Tea Party-backed candidates in recent elections.

Rand Paul, following in his father's footsteps, entered politics and became U.S. senator from Kentucky in 2011. Paul was backed by the Tea Party, advocates libertarian principles and is a sharp critic of President Obama and Washington politics. His 2012 book, *Government Bullies: How Everyday Americans are being Harassed, Bullied, and Imprisoned by the Feds*, sets the tone for much of Paul's approach to politics.[31] Ted Cruz became another star of the Tea Party in 2012, when he won the Republican primary in Texas by defeating the establishment-backed and well-financed lieutenant governor David Dewhurst, and becoming the junior senator from Texas in 2013. Both Paul and Cruz, with their sharp anti-Washington rhetoric, are presidential aspirants in 2016.

Political Party Transformation

State and local political parties in America were at the peak of their influence and structure during the latter part of the nineteenth century.[32] In the earlier decades of the twentieth century, political parties were the main agents for elections, providing the funds and all important workers; parties were also the training ground for candidates. Yet, by the 1960s, parties had lost much of their impact and were no longer the main focus of candidate elections.[33] Campaign finance reform, the proliferation of political action committees, the creation of the political consulting industry, and the rise of the candidate-centered campaign, all were important factors in the declining importance of political parties. Television, too, became a dominant force in

Talk radio also became an important agent for political communication. After the Reagan administration rescinded the Federal Communications Commission fairness clause for radio broadcasts, talk radio shows mushroomed. In 1983, only fifty-three radio stations had news/talk formats; today, there are more than one thousand such formats, with the total number of stations remaining relatively constant at nine thousand four hundred during this time. Talk radio has hit a popular chord and is especially effective with conservative audiences.

Conservative political talk radio has become the great feeding trough of citizens' anger, distrust, and ridicule. Howard Kurtz observed that talk shows have become a "powerful vehicle that trumpets the most extreme and polarizing views, that panders to sensationalism, that spreads innuendo and misinformation with stunning efficiency."[41] Talk radio has also become a useful weapon for candidates, especially those with an outsider image or appeal. For example, two-time Republican presidential candidate Patrick Buchanan found talk radio to be a convenient rallying point for disgruntled voters in the New Hampshire primary in February 1996. He appeared on many local conservative talk radio shows, made his case to voters, answered calls from true believers, and urged his followers to show up on election day. For Buchanan, talk radio was an ideal election tool; the medium was "free," the audience was deeply sympathetic, and he could personally make his point directly to his listeners. He spoke, they listened and came out to vote. In the early and mid-1990s, conservative talk radio hosts throughout the country claimed credit for energizing voters and helping to elect conservatives to federal and local office.

Cable television and talk radio have spawned new stars on the political horizon. Larry King, a longtime, little-known radio disc jockey, became a fixture in national communications when Ross Perot announced his 1992 presidential ambitions on King's television show. King regularly hosts political personalities, show business stars, and presidential hopefuls. Lobbing softball questions to his guests, King has become a favorite with ambitious politicians seeking free media coverage. Rush Limbaugh, with an equally modest background, broke onto the national scene in 1988, and has been able to parlay bombast, humor, and bluff into a loyal following of some twenty million daily listeners by the late 1990s, blasting away on radio and television at liberals (and, especially, Hillary Clinton), and calling for the impeachment of Bill Clinton long before the Lewinsky episode. Limbaugh's show was carried on more than six hundred and fifty stations, and while his audience—97 percent white, 60 percent male and middle aged—made up only 10 percent of the population, it has the highest level of voter registration.[42]

New York radio personality Don Imus, who has called Clinton a "redneck bozo" and a "lying weasel," was named one of the twenty-five most influential Americans in 1996 by *Time* magazine, and has claimed that all he wants from guests on his radio show is to "goad them into saying something that ruins their life." Clinton and other politicians nevertheless put up with Imus' abuses because his morning show is aired in ninety-five markets and is heard by approximately ten million listeners throughout the nation.[43] As former senator Bill Bradley candidly put it, "The number of people who come up to me in New Jersey and say 'I heard you on Imus' is fifty to one hundred times the number who say, 'I saw you on *Face the Nation*'."[44]

In 2006, the top twenty-five talk radio hosts were overwhelmingly conservative in their political viewpoints. Rush Limbaugh led the list with 13.5 million listeners, followed by Sean Hannity (12.5 million), Michael Savage (8.3 million), Dr. Laura Schlessinger (8 million), and Laura Ingraham (5 million). Air America Radio, the self-styled progressive alternative to conservative talk radio, found its best-known host, Al Franken (soon to become U.S. senator from Minnesota), in twenty-fifth place with 1.5 million listeners. Altogether, about 17 percent of the American adult population listen to talk radio.[45]

Traditional radio is listened to by 94 percent of persons twelve years of age or older.[46] By 2005, however, the face of radio had changed. Listeners had many more options: satellite radio, Internet-only stations, podcasts, MP3s, smart phone and tablet music apps were making radio more and more portable and accessible. Newspapers continue losing readership and advertising revenue and, for sound economic reasons and simple survival, have added online versions. Younger readers, especially, turn to the Internet for their news rather than rely on newspapers, magazines, or even television.

Yet, even with a twenty-four-hour blur of communications, it is sometimes next to impossible for a candidate for office to receive news coverage. Presidents, impeachment, and scandals will always have their day on television, but not so the candidate running for Congress, or even for governor. For many candidates, it is impossible to get any free media— even ten seconds in a news clip on local television.

The New Media

Thanks to the Internet, even marginal candidates have an inexpensive, efficient way of communicating with voters. Candidate websites and other forms of online communications may prove to be the most important, transforming factors in politics and campaigning. Candidates and campaigns have rapidly adapted to online communication. In 1994, hardly any campaigns had websites, but by 1998 nearly 70 percent of all federal, state, and local campaigns had them.[47] Campaign websites were particularly attractive in these early years because web users were better educated, more likely to vote, and more interested in politics than the average adult. One 1996 online survey found that 90 percent of web users were registered to vote and that 63 percent had participated in their most recent local, state, or national election. Both figures were much higher than the United States general population, in which slightly over 60 percent of the adult population were registered to vote and approximately 42 percent had voted in the 1994 elections. By 1998, with Internet usage becoming more commonplace, the audience profile began to look more like that of the average voter.[48]

By 2004, the Internet had become an essential part of American politics and campaigns. As online expert Michael Cornfield notes, the role of the Internet in contemporary politics is multifaceted: "Part deliberative town square, part raucous debating society, part research library, part instant news source, and part political comedy club."[49] Social media, blogging, Twitter feeds, smart phone and tablet apps, and other communication tools became essential to any serious political campaign, ideological organization, or nonpartisan watchdog groups interested in politics, campaign finances, ethics, and election news. (A list of several of the best campaign-related websites is found in the Appendix and further discussion of online communications is found in Chapter 6.)

Rapid-Fire Communications

Candidates now have to be prepared for "real-time" campaigning, the rapid-fire communications of charges and countercharges leveled between candidates. This has been one of the most significant changes in campaign communications. In earlier years, an attack might have simply gone unanswered, or weeks would go by before a response. That has changed. Today in presidential and in many gubernatorial and congressional races, response is nearly instantaneous, even anticipated in advance.

A pioneer in rapid response techniques was Democratic media consultant Frank Greer. Working for Douglas Wilder against Republican Marshall Coleman for the 1989 Virginia governor's race, Greer prepared generic response ads in advance of an actual attack by the Coleman campaign. Film was shot and voiceovers, music, and graphics were prepared in advance. Only last-minute details of the charge and the response were needed to fill in the blanks. A Coleman attack ad would appear on television at 9:00 p.m. and Wilder media consultants, thanks to their advanced preparation, had their counterattack ads ready for airing the next morning.

Since then, response time has gotten even shorter, and campaigns have been using all the tools of online communication and technology to create response ads and get them before the public as soon as possible. The effective rapid-response campaign has done the research in advance, anticipated media and opponent questions, and prepared responses, and prepared radio, television spots, Twitter feeds, Internet advertisements, and social media responses to fight back and counter charges.

Rapid-response commercials were dubbed "crash ads" or "crash spots" during the 2000 campaign. Thanks to new digital cameras, the George W. Bush campaign was able to tape (or digitize) their candidate at 11:30 a.m. on a Tuesday morning in New Hampshire, cut the footage down to thirty seconds, email the proposed script and a computer-generated Quick-Time video to the Texas campaign headquarters for approval, and meet the Manchester, New Hampshire, television station's 3:00 p.m. deadline for the next day's commercials. In pre-digital days, the campaign would have needed a cameraman and a sound man, the editing would have taken far longer, and video tapes would have to be sent to the television station by overnight courier.[50]

Campaigns that cannot keep up are campaigns that will not win. In today's communications war, there is no time to rest. All-news radio, expanded television news, Internet services, and social media sites now extend political coverage to any time, day and night. An attack made against a candidate at noon might rebound through many news outlet sources and be rebutted, counter charged, and rebutted again before the 11:00 p.m. evening news. Campaigns can become electronic shouting matches. If lucky, a candidate will receive 15 seconds on the evening news to counter a charge, sometimes even less. Campaign communication has to be able to turn on a dime, the candidate has to bombard listeners with clever phrases and quick rejoinders in ten-second sound bites, and hope that voters are paying attention. Lost in this bumper-car game of real-time rapid response are thoughtful, articulate responses with substance and depth.

Outside Voices

Candidates have to contend with more than their opponents; now they have to worry about third parties, sometimes known and other times not known, that are trying to influence the outcome of the election. Some of the most important sources of outside influence have been the state or national parties, which offer funds, organizational support, and party advertising. But, in recent years, other voices have been added to campaigns. Outside organizations interject their own campaign messages, using independent expenditures and issues advocacy advertising as their vehicles. Because of these outside interests, local congressional contests have become nationalized as battlegrounds between national pro-choice and anti-abortion organizations, term limit advocates, and labor or pro-business forces. These outside groups, and others, bombard the airwaves with television commercials trying to persuade voters. The League of Conservation Voters targeted the "dirty dozen," its list of the members of Congress with the worst environmental records; seven of them were defeated in 1996. As Paul Taylor wrote during the 1996 presidential campaign, candidates "now share the election megaphone with a cacophony of other voices."[51]

But that cacophony is nothing compared with the outside voices of today. During the 2004 presidential election, outside interests were heavily involved. The best-known group, Swift Boat Veterans for Truth, hammered away at John Kerry's war record in Vietnam. Outside voices were relatively quiet during the 2008 presidential election, primarily because both candidates, John McCain and Barack Obama, discouraged outsiders to become involved.[52] But it was a far different story in 2012. Conservative activists and billionaires Charles and David Koch, through their network of political action committees, Super PACs, and non-profit organizations spent at least $407 million in television advertising, grassroots activities, and get-out-the-vote drives to try to defeat Barack Obama. They recruited like-minded rich conservatives, but their names and the amounts they contributed have not been made public.[53] Of all the political ads run by Republicans in the 2012 presidential election, just over one-third were run by the Romney campaign; the remainder were financed and aired by outside organizations. By contrast, the Obama campaign aired about two-thirds of all the Democratic presidential ads, while outside groups aired the rest. The outside ads for Republicans came mostly from Restore Our Future (Romney PAC), American Crossroads and Crossroads GPS (Karl Rove), Americans for Prosperity (Koch brothers), and the National Rifle Association. Democratic outside groups included Priorities USA Action, Service Employees International Union (SEIU), and the American Federation of State, County and Municipal Employees (AFSCME).[54]

Chasing Campaign Dollars

The modern campaign is mostly about raising money, especially in its early stages. In presidential campaigns, this is called the "invisible primary," the year or so before the Iowa caucus and New Hampshire primary when candidates are busily raising money, flying from one part of the country to another for fundraising events, and using direct mail, the Internet, and telephone solicitation to gain campaign dollars.[55]

Candidates for statewide office especially rely on early money and early political support. Early contributors vote with dollars, indicating how political insiders see the election shaping. The media pays attention, writing stories about the fundraising abilities of candidates, proclaiming frontrunners and also-rans depending on how well they are raising campaign dollars.

The cost of campaigns have risen steadily. From 1990 through 1996, there were fifteen Senate races that cost more than $10 million each; the $1 million House campaign, once highly unusual, became commonplace. The elections of 1996 were by far the most expensive in American history, only to be replaced by those of 2000, then 2004, which have been supplanted by 2008 and 2012 elections. Altogether, the presidential candidates and their allies in 2012 raised and spent more than $2 billion. Winning candidates for the House of Representatives routinely spend more than $1 million, and it is not unusual to see $20 or $30 million spent on U.S. Senate or gubernatorial contests.[56] Some local legislative races that once might have cost $35,000 now are eight to ten times more expensive. In recent cycles, nearly as much has been spent in California ballot issue contests as has been spent on presidential elections. The pressure on candidates and campaigns to raise money is relentless and often crowds out other important campaign activities. During the final weeks of the campaign, while candidates should be delivering speeches and attending rallies, they may find themselves attending private fundraisers, trying to eke out another $150,000 to pay for the last week of television commercials.

Campaign dollars and professionalized campaigns go hand in hand. When news accounts report that a campaign has $2 million in the bank, this tells only a fraction of the story. The $2 million war chest means that the campaign can afford the services of pollsters, media consultants, opposition researchers, direct mail, and professional fundraisers, and can blanket the television market with hundreds of commercials.

Stepping into the Mud Field

Individuals seeking elective office frequently have to pay a high personal price. Campaigning is not a sport for the timid or for those whose egos bruise easily. More attention is paid to the personal lives of candidates than ever before; campaigns probe deep into public and private records of opponents, searching for misdeeds, financial irregularities—any ammunition to use against the candidate.

Negative campaigning has increased sharply over the past two decades and has become a key ingredient in many campaign arsenals.[57] Hard hitting, factual information might be unpleasant but it helps inform the public. In this sense, "negative" campaigning is an important and often potent weapon. The public can benefit from robust debate on policy positions and information about candidate voting records and an incumbent who hasn't been doing the job (or a challenger who isn't up to the job).[58] The real concern is the ugly nature of some campaign attacks. Too often, campaigns get vicious, even when the facts are correct. Charges are blown out of proportion, taken out of context, and become irrelevant to the campaign. Sometimes, the charges are beyond the political statute of limitations—they drag up ancient information that clearly doesn't matter or is so personal that it should be out of bounds.

There are several long lasting consequences of this vicious streak in campaigns: good potential candidates are driven away, voters become disgusted with campaigns and candidates, the business of political consulting is given a black eye, and elections and democratic choice are denigrated in the process. Professional researchers, who comb through personal records and electronic databases, provide much of the raw ammunition for vicious campaigning, and campaign media consultants are more than willing to use that data.

Candidates for public office, whether they are challengers or veteran incumbents, face many tough obstacles. Given the uncertainty, the loss of privacy, and the enormous physical and emotional drain on candidates, who would want to run for public office? Even more importantly, how many good, honorable people are dissuaded from running because it just isn't worth it?

Notes

1   Ed Rollins with Tom DeFrank, *Bare Knuckles and Back Rooms* (New York: Broadway Books, 1996), 339–40.

2   From the film documentary *Vote for Me* (1996).

3   *Washington Post,* Kaiser Family Foundation, and Harvard University, *General Social Survey and American National Election Studies,* 1996. For analysis and background, see Richard Morin and Dan Balz, "Americans Losing Trust in Each Other and Institutions," *Washington Post,* January 28, 1996, A1, and other articles in the series. Data from National Election Study, from 1964 through 1992, have been widely used to demonstrate the declines in levels of trust. See also *Why People Don't Trust Government,* ed. Joseph S. Nye Jr., Philip D. Zelikow, and David C. King (Cambridge, Mass.: Harvard University Press, 1997); Andrew Kohut, ed., *Deconstructing Distrust: How Americans View Government* (Washington, D.C.: Pew Research Center for the People and the Press, 1997); and Peter D. Hart and Robert M. Teeter, "Findings from a Research Project about Attitudes toward Government," conducted for the Council for Excellence in Government (unpublished, 1995).

4   Morin and Balz, "Americans Losing Trust." In writing about the changing norms and values of American society, Uslaner observed that "people trust each other less in a multiplicity of ways. Americans are unhappy with themselves," they are increasingly dissatisfied with the nation's lack of honesty and standards of behavior, and their voices are becoming increasingly shrill. Eric M. Uslaner, *The Decline of Comity in Congress* (Ann Arbor, M.I.: University of Michigan Press, 1994), 84–5. See also "Civility in the House of Representatives," Report No. 10 (Annenberg Public Policy Center, University of Pennsylvania, 1997).

5   Morin and Balz, "Americans Losing Trust," A6. Teixeira argues that feelings of political cynicism have "no significant independent effect" on an individual's

likelihood of voting. See Ruy A. Teixeira, *The Disappearing American Voter* (Washington, D.C.: Brookings Institution, 1992), 32.

6   *Washington Post*/Kaiser/Harvard survey. The specific wording of the questions is as follows: "Would you say that most people can be trusted or that you can't be too careful in dealing with people?" and "How much of the time do you trust the government in Washington to do the right thing?" See also Robert Samuelson, *The Good Life and Its Discontents: The American Dream in the Age of Entitlement 1945–1995* (New York: Times Books, 1996).

7   Samuelson, *The Good Life and Its Discontents*, 4.

8   Susan J. Tolchin, *The Angry American* (Boulder, Colo.: Westview, 1996), 19.

9   John R. Hibbing and Elizabeth Theiss-Morse, *Congress as Public Enemy: Public Attitudes toward American Political Institutions* (New York: Cambridge University Press, 1995), 148; and Tolchin, *The Angry American*, 3. But see Jack Citrin, "The Angry White Male Is a Straw Man," *Public Affairs Report* 37 (January 1996): 1.

10   Richard Morin in an article accompanying David S. Broder, "Cure for Nation's Cynicism Eludes Its Leaders," *Washington Post*, February 4, 1996, A1.

11   Tom Ashbrook, "Journalism Mirrors the Public Mood," *Nieman Reports*, Winter 2004, 48.

12   Dan Morain, "Fracture Within GOP Adds to Tea Party Coffers," *Sacramento Bee*, February 13, 2013.

13   William Branigan, "Obama Reflects on 'Shellacking' in Midterm Elections," *Washington Post*, November 3, 2010.

14   Bill Bishop, *The Big Sort: Why the Clustering of Like-Minded Americans is Tearing America Apart* (New York: Mariner, 2008).

15   Teixeira, *The Disappearing American Voter*, 57.

16   David Cay Johnston, "Voting, America's Not Keen On. Coffee Is Another Matter," *New York Times*, November 10, 1996, E2. Johnston notes that more people (an estimated 95 million) watched O. J. Simpson take his freeway ride in the white Bronco than cast ballots in the 1996 general elections (92.8 million).

17   Mark Strama, "Overcoming Cynicism: Youth Participation and Electoral Politics," *National Civic Review*, Spring 1998, and " '98 Voter Turnout Rate Was Lowest in 56 Years," *Washington Post*, February 10, 1999, A14, citing election analysis by Curtis Gans.

18   David E. Campbell, "Voter Turnout and Vote Choice," in *Guide to Political Campaigns in America*, ed. Paul S. Herrnson (Washington, D.C.: CQ Press, 2005), ch. 8.

19   Bipartisan Policy Center, *2012 Voter Turnout* (Washington, D.C., November 8, 2012), http://bipartisanpolicy.org/library/report/2012-voter-turnout (accessed February 14, 2015). Center for the Study of the American Electorate, American University, "Nation, Primary Turnout Hits New Record Low in States," Curtis Gans, director, October 10, 2012. On the 2014 election, see Charlotte Alter, "Voter Turnout in Midterm Election Hit 72-Year Low, *Time*, November 10, 2014, http://time.com/3576090/midterm-elections-turnout-world-war-two/

(accessed February 28, 2015). The 2014 turnout figures were based on research conducted by Professor Michael McDonald, University of Florida.

20 Michael McDonald, "2012 Early Voting Statistics," U.S. Elections Project, George Mason University, November 6, 2012.

21 "Election 2012: Voting Laws Roundup," Brennan Center for Justice, New York University School of Law, October 11, 2012, www.brennancenter.org/content/resource/2012_summary_of_voting_law_changes (accessed February 14, 2015).

22 Pew Center on the States, "Inaccurate, Costly, and Inefficient: Evidence that America's Voter Registration System Needs an Upgrade," February 2012, www.pewtrusts.org/en/research-and-analysis/reports/2012/02/14/inaccurate-costly-and-inefficient-evidence-that-americas-voter-registration-system-needs-an-upgrade (accessed February 14, 2015).

23 Editorial, "Voter Harassment, Circa 2012," *New York Times*, September 21, 2012.

24 Quoted in Frank I. Luntz, *Candidates, Consultants, and Campaigns* (New York: Basil Blackwell, 1988), 32.

25 Richard Harwood, "All-Pro Politics," *Washington Post*, March 23, 1996, A15.

26 Dennis J. McGrath and Dane Smith, *Professor Wellstone Goes to Washington: The Inside Story of a Grassroots U.S. Senate Campaign* (Minneapolis, M.N.: University of Minnesota Press, 1995).

27 Eric Pianin, "In Wellstone-Boschwitz Rematch, Attacks Seem to Have Backfired," *Washington Post*, October 22, 1996, A14.

28 Shailagh Murray, "Lamont Relied on Net Roots—And Grass Roots," *Washington Post,* August 9, 2006, A5.

29 Robin Toner, "The 1994 Campaign: Image of Capitol Maligned by Outsiders and Insiders," *New York Times*, October 16, 1994, 1.

30 Paul Fahri, "Candidates Get to Washington by Distancing Themselves," *Washington Post,* October 12, 2006, C1.

31 Rand Paul, *Government Bullies: How Everyday Americans are being Harassed, Bullied, and Imprisoned by the Feds* (New York: Center Street, 2012). There were a number of charges that Paul had lifted materials from materials written by the Cato Institute, Heritage Foundation, *Forbes* magazine, and other sources. Andrew Kaczynski, "More Instances of Plagiarism in Rand Paul's Book," *BuzzFeed News*, November 7, 2013, www.buzzfeed.com/andrewkaczynski/more-instances-of-plagiarism-in-rand-pauls-book-lets-duel#3qu8ef3 (accessed February 14, 2015).

32 Frank J. Sorauf and Paul Allen Beck, *Party Politics in America*, 6th ed. (Glenview, Ill.: Scott, Foresman, 1988), 98.

33 Paul S. Herrnson, *Party Campaigning in the 1980s* (Cambridge, Mass.: Harvard University Press, 1988); and Paul Allen Beck, *Party Politics in America*, 8th ed. (New York: Longman, 1997).

34 James A. Reichley, *The Life of the Parties: A History of American Political Parties* (New York: Free Press, 1992), 8. See, in particular, Thomas E. Patterson, *Out of Order* (New York: Knopf, 1993), on the role of the media in presidential campaigns.

35 See Herrnson, *Party Campaigning in the 1980s*, 5; and Beck, *Party Politics in America*, 167, on signs of the national party's comeback.

36 See Doris Graber, *Mass Media and American Politics* (Washington, D.C.: CQ Press, 1996); Stephen Ansolabehere, Roy Behr, and Shanto Iyengar, *The Media Game: American Politics in the Television Age* (New York: MacMillan, 1993); Richard Joslyn, *Mass Media and Elections* (New York: Random House, 1984); Montague Kern, *30-Second Politics: Political Advertising in the Eighties* (New York: Praeger, 1989); Dean Alger, *The Media and Politics* (Englewood Cliffs, N.J.: Prentice Hall, 1989); and F. Christopher Arterton, *Media Politics: The News Strategies of Presidential Campaigns* (Toronto: Lexington, 1984).

37 As Ansolabehere et al. put it: "The troubles in the world of network television can be summarized in two words: cable television." *The Media Game,* 26.

38 Pew Research Center for the People and the Press, "The C-SPAN Audience: After 25 Years," March 2, 2004, www.people-press.org/2004/03/02/the-c-span-audience (accessed February 14, 2015).

39 Project for Excellence in Journalism, "The State of the News Media 2004," Pew Research Center, March 19, 2004, www.stateofthenewsmedia.org/2004 (accessed February 14, 2015).

40 Merrill Knox, "Fox , No. 1 for 12 Straight Years, Sheds Viewers Too," *TVNewser,* January 2, 2014, www.mediabistro.com/tvnewser/2013-ratings-fox-news-1-for-12-straight-years-sheds-viewers-too_b208937

41 Howard Kurtz, *Hot Air: All Talk, All the Time* (New York: Times Books, 1996), 19.

42 Study conducted by Times Mirror Center for the People and the Press, reported in Timothy Egan, "Triumph Leaves No Targets for Conservative Talk Shows," *New York Times*, January 1, 1995, A1.

43 Howard Kurtz, *"Imus-Be-an-Idiot," Washington Post*, March 31, 1996, C5. Yet, Maureen Dowd, of the *New York Times,* observes that Imus "is the best political interviewer. He's read everything, and he gets to the heart of everything." Quoted in "Time's 25 Most Influential Americans," *Time*, April 21, 1997, 21.

44 Kurtz, "Imus-Be-an-Idiot."

45 "Top Talk Radio Audiences," *Talkers Magazine*, Spring 2006 (www. talkers. com); Pew Research Center for People and the Press, "New Audiences Increasingly Politicized: Online News Audience Larger, More Diverse," (June 2004).

46 Project for Excellence in Journalism, "State of the News Media 2006."

47 Ron Faucheux, "How Campaigns Are Using the Internet," *Campaigns and Elections,* September 1998, 22–4.

48 Georgia Institute of Technology, Graphics, Visualization, and Usability Center, "World Wide Web Survey, Sixth Semi-Annual Survey," December 1996, www.cc.gatech.edu/gvu/user_surveys/survey-10-1996 (accessed February 14, 2015); and Pew Research Center for the People and the Press, "The Internet News Audience Goes Ordinary," Andrew Kohut, director, January 14, 1999.

49 Lee Rainie, John Horrigan, and Michael Cornfield, "The Internet and Campaign 2004: A Look Back at the Campaigners," March 6, 2005, www.pewinternet.org/2005/03/06/the-internet-and-campaign-2004 (accessed February 14, 2015).

50   Howard Kurtz, "Bush Team Relying on Quick Impact of 'Crash Ads,'" *Washington Post*, January 22, 2000, A9.

51   Deborah Beck, Paul Taylor, Jeffrey Stanger, and Douglas Rivlin, "Issue Advocacy Advertising during the 1996 Campaign," University of Pennsylvania, Annenberg Public Policy Center, Report No. 17, September 16, 1997, 3.

52   Stephen K. Medvic, "Outside Voices: Super PACs, Parties, and Other Non-Candidate Actors," in *Campaigning for President 2008: Strategy and Tactics*, ed. Dennis W. Johnson (New York: Routledge, 2009), 151.

53   Daniel Fisher, "Inside the Koch Empire: How the Brothers Plan to Reshape America," *Forbes*, December 5, 2012; Kenneth P. Vogel, "Koch World 2014," *Politico*, January 24, 2014.

54   John C. Tedesco and Scott W. Dunn, "Political Advertising in the 2012 U.S. Presidential Election," in *The 2012 Presidential Campaign: A Communication Perspective*, ed. Robert E. Denton, Jr. (Lanham, Md.: Rowman & Littlefield, 2014), 78 and Evan Tracey, "Political Advertising: When More Meant Less," in *Campaigning for President 2012*, ed. Johnson, 92–106.

55   Arthur T. Hadley, *The Invisible Primary* (Englewood Cliffs, N.J.: Prentice Hall, 1976); Emmett H. Buell Jr., "The Invisible Primary," in *In Pursuit of the White House: How We Choose our Presidential Nominees*, ed. William G. Nayler (Chatham, N.J.: Chatham House, 1996). See also David Himes, "Strategy and Tactics for Campaign Fund-Raising," in *Campaigns and Elections: American Style*, ed. James A. Thurber and Candice J. Nelson (Boulder, Colo.: Westview, 1995), 62ff.

56   Anthony Corrado, "The Money Race: A New Era of Unlimited Funding? In *Campaigning for President 2012*, ed. Johnson, 59.

57   See Michael C. Pfau and Henry C. Kenski, *Attack Politics: Strategy and Defense* (New York: Praeger, 1990); Stephen Ansolabehere and Shanto Iyengar, *Going Negative: How Political Advertisements Shrink and Polarize the Electorate* (New York: Free Press, 1995); Karen S. Johnson-Cartee and Gary A. Copeland, *Negative Political Advertising: Coming of Age* (Hillsdale, N.J.: Lawrence Erlbaum Associates, 1991); and Victor Kamber, *Poison Politics: Are Negative Campaigns Destroying Democracy?* (New York: Plenum, 1997). See also Richard R. Lau, Lee Sigelman, Caroline Heldman, and Paul Babbitt, "The Effects of Negative Political Advertisements: A Meta-Analytic Assessment," *American Political Science Review* 93 (4) (December 1999): 851–75; Richard R. Lau and Gerald M. Pomper, "Effectiveness of Negative Campaigning in U.S. Senate Elections," *American Journal of Political Science* 46, no. 1 (January 2002): 47–66.

58   On this point, see William G. Mayer, "In Defense of Negative Campaigning," *Political Science Quarterly* 111 (1996): 440; also John G. Geer, *In Defense of Negativity: Attack Ads in Presidential Campaigns* (Chicago, Ill.: University of Chicago Press, 2006).

3

Case Study: Challenging an Incumbent U.S. Senator: The Realities of a Tough, Hard-Fought, Professional Campaign

Competitive U.S. Senate races provide good examples of the use of modern campaign techniques and the role played by political consultants. While Senate campaigns vary widely,[1] there are many common features.

In this hypothetical campaign, Barbara Allyn and Senator Robert Porter are fictitious, but they represent a composite of candidates in several recent Senate campaign cycles. Many of the details and circumstances surrounding this race are left purposively vague. We do not know, for example, what state this race is in, who the president is, or what election cycle we are in. We do know that Allyn is a Democrat and Porter is a Republican. And we know that this is a well-executed campaign with sufficient time and resources to employ the most sophisticated techniques and talent available.[2]

Our focus is on Barbara Allyn, who is challenging a one-term senator, Robert Porter. Allyn has been minority leader in the state General Assembly for six years and is a tested, attractive force in the party. She may face early rivals; still, she is considered to have the best chance of capturing her party's nomination.

The Context of the Campaign

Every campaign starts with a list of "givens," realities that face both candidates, and "all strategy, tactics, message resources, and decisions must originate from this foundation."[3] Some of these givens, however, present more of a challenge than others. Following are several key elements facing Allyn and her campaign.

Off-Year Election: There is no presidential or gubernatorial election held during this election cycle; the senate contest is the biggest race in the state. Thus, no other major race will dominate the news and set the agenda. It should be easier to purchase advertising time during the last crucial weeks of the campaign and, finally, statewide funding sources will not be siphoned off to the gubernatorial and presidential contests.

An Expensive State to Run In: The most effective way to reach voters in this state is through television advertising. The state has six media markets, two of which are relatively expensive. One of those costly media markets serves three states; consequently, many of the television advertisements aired during the last weeks of the campaign will be wasted on viewers who cannot vote in the state. During the last two competitive statewide contests, the gubernatorial election two years ago and the other senate seat four years ago, each of the major candidates spent between $10 million and $12 million, with the greatest amount of money spent on television advertisements.

Challenger Facing an Incumbent: Members of the House of Representatives running for reelection historically have a much better chance of winning than do members of the Senate, despite the recent challenges that incumbent Republicans have faced from Tea Party candidates.[4] One study of senate elections concluded that the main reason many senate incumbents are defeated is that they attract strong challengers who are able to spend large amounts on their campaigns.[5] Allyn is an attractive, strong candidate, and she will have a sizeable campaign war chest. But money alone won't buy elections. There are plenty of examples of well-financed senate challengers who have come up short. The Allyn campaign is not worried about raising sufficient funds; rather, it is worried about how skillfully Porter will be able to use his power of incumbency to influence this race.

Statewide Electorate is Very Competitive: The state has been a fairly even political battleground: Democratic and Republican parties are relatively equally matched. Barack Obama won the state twice, but so did George W. Bush. The governor and one senator are Democrats, and the other senator, Porter, is a Republican. Neither side should expect an electoral advantage or disadvantage in this race.

Female Office Seeker: Only once before, twenty-six years ago, has a woman been elected to a major office in this state, and never to the Senate. The "year of the woman" that seemed to carry so much appeal in 1992 is now ancient political history and has little resonance in this year's state politics. Polling will later tell Allyn's campaign that she receives little advantage from female voters and a slight disadvantage among male voters.

Defending an Unpopular President: Allyn might possibly be dragged down by the president, who is of her own party. He has lost popularity in recent years, and, frankly, voters are tired of him and his unfulfilled policies. She will have to distance herself from him and ultimately make painful political choices when inevitably asked to defend the president's record on a variety of issues.

The Challenger

Barbara Allyn is quick-witted and personable, people like her, she appears trustworthy and looks good on television. Representative Allyn is an attractive candidate who is married to a successful executive, and they have two telegenic grade-school children. At forty-three, she is a refreshing contrast to the incumbent who is twenty-five years her senior.

Allyn is a veteran campaigner who has run for office four times previously. She is tireless, willing to put up with the numbingly long days and nights on the road, and she does not panic or fluster easily. She can absorb criticism with the best of public officeholders and is an excellent speaker, very knowledgeable about state issues and policies. She should be a formidable television debater and, as minority leader in the state General Assembly, she has ready access to political support and funds.

Even though she has run for office four times previously, Allyn is still relatively unknown to the state's voters. Her previous elections were all in a district with a total population of 115,000 in a state of eight million. Her political base is located away from urban population centers. She is well known to the capital crowd and party insiders, but registers only 10 percent name recognition from the general population. Until now, Allyn has never assiduously courted the free media; she is still a novice when it comes to social media. While everyone knows her in the General Assembly, hardly anyone at the local shopping center would recognize her.

The Incumbent

Allyn's opponent has used the advantages of incumbency very effectively. Senator Porter, who won his seat five years ago by only 3 percent, has since used his incumbency to strengthen his hold on the office. While fairly bland and colorless, his name recognition is 55 percent, thanks to an aggressive use of free media, especially for two high-profile events: he enjoyed almost six weeks of widespread media exposure as he fought for flood relief benefits for the western half of the state, and he appeared on the *Oprah Winfrey Show* with a ten-year-old girl, a constituent, who badly needed hospital care, but had been stymied by federal regulations. That television appearance was five years ago, but people still remember it. Senator Porter's legislative record is considered mediocre at best, but people like him, and his approval rating has topped 60 percent.

Further, Porter has systematically courted reelection campaign funds. He has been especially effective in raising political action committee money, and after five years in office has been able to wipe his original campaign debt clean and now has over $3 million in the bank. Another sobering thought for Barbara Allyn: the interest accruing every month in the Senator's campaign account is more than she has ever had to raise in any of her previous campaigns. Senator Porter has already begun assembling his reelection campaign team—veteran, topnotch political consultants and a seasoned network of local party workers who helped during his first campaign. He can also count on millions coming from several conservative Super PACs which are determined to get him reelected.

The one immutable factor is time. Election day will come soon enough, as what has to be done in the meantime is formidable. Every campaign goes through several phases, from the quiet early moments when the decision to run is made, through the relentless months of fundraising, to the intense, noisy, and public days at the end of the election. This is what the Allyn campaign faces.

Phase One: The Decision to Run

Beginning eighteen months before election day, several key aspects of the campaign are set in motion.

Establishing Support and Getting Advice from the Core Group: This phase involves serious discussion with family, close political allies, and a few influential political insiders and financial supporters. While her decision to run is not firmly set, anyone who is plugged into state politics knows that Allyn is seriously thinking about it. The rumors fly among the politically well-connected within days of the first discussions; indeed, rumors have been circulating for months. "Who will take on Porter?" is a favorite topic in the corridors of the General Assembly and in the watering holes of lobbyists and journalists.

Gathering Political and Financial Support: Barbara Allyn and her close associates are seeking insider political and financial support. This is the crucial "elite" campaign—to determine who among the state's money givers and political influentials are willing to assist. An exploratory committee, Friends of Barbara Allyn, is established and seeking early sponsorship. The committee establishes a website. While purchasing the domain name, www.friendsofbarbara.com, the committee also purchases three other sites, including www.allynforsenate.com. (What the campaign doesn't know is that pranksters and provocateurs have bought up several other domain names, have established anti-Allyn websites, Twitter accounts, and other weapons to use against her.)

In phase one, fundraising is the crucial activity, and much of it must be handled by the candidate herself. Some early backers are eager to contribute—that is the easy part; but then comes the much harder sell, to potential contributors who are sitting on the fence, waiting to see which way the political winds will blow, not ready to commit themselves and their money too soon. At this stage of fundraising and gathering support, Allyn must be involved in one-to-one conversations. Her finance chairman is a lawyer–lobbyist with extensive contacts in politics and fundraising. He has laid the groundwork for her fundraising calls, has put together the extensive lists of prospectives, and has introduced Allyn to financial backers at dinners, quiet meetings, and over the telephone. Well connected and experienced as a fundraiser, he is still considered an amateur, just as nearly all the supporters and volunteers for Allyn's early campaign have been.

Signing Up Key Political Consultants: This is also the time when Allyn chooses her general campaign consultant and polling and media specialists. Allyn has worked with both Washington- and state capital-based consultants before: a Washington-based polling firm, a state-based phone bank service, a regionally based media consultant, and a state-based fundraiser have been used in recent years by her party's House caucus. She has used two of the consultants for her own reelection campaigns and they have a track record with the state party as well.

It is important to have a solid political consulting team signed up early;

this is part of the insider game of the election. With a general consultant, pollster, and media consultant on board, she now looks like a serious candidate. Political action committees, the national party, and the media are quickly concluding that this campaign is indeed going places.

Phase one is the longest part of the campaign and it requires considerable on-on-one persuasion and planning. The campaign headquarters is the Allyn's basement home office, which is equipped with three landlines, half a dozen smart phones, two borrowed computers, and a couple of iPads.

Several others have been mentioned as potential challengers, including the former lieutenant governor, a wealthy businessman with no political experience, and a colleague in the General Assembly. Two of them have already formed exploration committees, and the third, the wealthy businessman, has already talked with several media consultants. Above all, Allyn wants to avoid a primary fight. She is convinced she would prevail, but the primary would drain resources away from her main objective, a clear shot at the incumbent. Much of her effort in this phase is to convince political insiders and funding sources of her viability. Scaring off potential rivals from her own party is part of that strategy.

The most important news coming out of this phase of the campaign is the newspaper and television stories indicating how much potential candidates have managed to raise in campaign funds. These stories come out just days after the Federal Election Commission (FEC) quarterly financial reporting deadlines. There is a big push to deposit as many dollars and to hold off on as much spending as possible, so that the FEC report can show a healthy amount of cash on hand. Allyn is increasingly seen as a serious candidate because of her fundraising abilities. The early money—the "smart money"—is coming her way.

The other important news, unmentioned in the media, is the private, insider speculation that Barbara Allyn has all but locked up the most important party supporters, has signed up twenty of the party's most influential money people, and has endorsement commitments from a majority of the party's county and city chairs. This is reinforced by the news that the governor's senior political aide is working behind the scenes for Allyn. This sends a strong, clear message to the political leaders throughout the state to get behind the Allyn campaign.

The public and private assessments of Barbara Allyn are so strong that the other potential challengers are backing away and probably will not press for a primary fight. One of the biggest battles, thus, has already been won: Barbara Allyn has used her organizational skill, friends, and political muscle to fend off potential rivals for the party's nomination.

Phase Two: Preannouncement

Ten months before election day, this is one of the busiest and most crucial stages in the campaign. On the recommendation of the general consultant, a campaign manager has been chosen. Toward the end of this phase, the press secretary will be selected and a skeletal staff assembled, many of who are volunteers. Now with a paid staff of three (campaign manager, press secretary, and fundraising assistant) and six to eight volunteers and part-timers, the campaign has moved out of the Allyn basement office to a vacant storefront in a strip mall—low rent, rather shabby facilities, but serviceable nonetheless.

More Fundraising: The most important campaign activity in phase two is raising funds. Nearly all of Allyn's time is spent trying to raise money—through small events and, especially, through individual telephone calls to potential donors. This is a difficult, time-consuming, but absolutely essential task that can only be accomplished by the candidate. Day after day, Allyn tackles the list of potential contributors, all of who have to be contacted personally, with a campaign worker nagging her to make the calls. This is tough, humiliating work; in many cases, she has to nearly beg for funds and support.

The challenge of raising money becomes much more daunting when the candidate is a long shot or is running against an incumbent. If money cannot be raised, there is no chance the campaign will succeed against Porter. Barbara Allyn knows that the fundraising task is formidable. Her finance team has set a very high goal of raising $1.5 million by announcement day, only five months away. To reach that goal, nearly $75,000 has to be raised each week. By contrast, Allyn's first race for the General Assembly eight years ago cost a total of $32,000.

The task becomes even more difficult because Senator Porter has been raising money for at least three and a half years and thus far has salted away over $3 million. Very few political action committees are willing to hedge their bets and give Allyn campaign funds, since they have supported Senator Porter in the past and the senator's campaign will aggressively court them again.

Undaunted, the Allyn's finance committee puts together its fundraising goals and strategy. The overall budget will be $11.5 million, an ambitious figure, but certainly not unprecedented in this state. The campaign probably cannot match the funds that Senator Porter will gather, but the general consultant is convinced that Allyn can run a competitive race even while spending $1.5 million or $2 million less than Porter. However, there is a further complication. Many of the individual, reliable campaign contributors are close to being tapped out. They were hit hard just eighteen months ago in the very expensive governor's race and the presidential election. Allyn could not start fundraising while the governor's race was going on; consequently, she is off to a slow start.

Twenty-five percent of the contributions will have to come from political action committees, another 60 percent from individual donors, and Allyn is counting on the state and national parties to help with the remaining 15 percent. Allyn has only about $25,000 left from her last race for the General Assembly. She cannot directly use that money for this election, but following the advice of several party leaders, she has used that money to buy computers, mobile phones, and other equipment, which she will then "lend" to her Senate campaign. Money is trickling in over her campaign websites, but averaging only a few hundred dollars a week.

Barbara Allyn has a special reserve, but no one is comfortable talking about it. She could spend nearly $1 million of her own family money, although this would be an enormous burden on her family's financial wellbeing and could possibly place strains on her marriage. Her campaign team is also banking on several key progressive Super PACs and labor unions to mount and sponsor independent ads against Senator Porter. No one talks openly about these, but behind the scenes several possibilities are being considered.

Researching the Record: During this period, the professionals have begun to do their work. The research consultant is one of the first professionals hired, on the recommendation of the media and polling advisers. The researcher has worked for approximately a dozen strong Senate challengers in the past three election cycles and has a quick understanding of the job ahead—combing through the public records of both Allyn and Senator Porter. The researcher will compile a coherent, strategically defined record on Allyn's career: her state legislative service and her work in the previous governor's Task Force on Education Reform; her financial disclosure statements, tax records, and other financial matters; her husband's corporate and wide-ranging business dealings; potential problems with the family; and myriad other issues. At the same time, research has been started on Senator Porter's record. This is a fairly daunting task because, in addition to his five years as senator, he has also served eight years as a congressman and four years as lieutenant governor. The research consultant charges $5,000 per month to do a complete search of both candidates and will continue throughout the remainder of the campaign.

Focus Group Research: The polling firm will conduct preliminary focus group research to determine the general mood of the electorate and its knowledge of Barbara Allyn. The basic focus group script is written, relying heavily on the campaign research already completed. The campaign will conduct at least two focus groups in the four largest media markets. The participants, eight to twelve individuals in each focus group, were carefully chosen to represent the undecided, but persuadable, voters who will ultimately determine the outcome of this race. There is an extraordinary amount of anticipation in the campaign about the focus groups. The candidate, and many on the campaign staff, want to attend the focus groups. This is the first statewide test of Allyn's strengths and weaknesses. Being as diplomatic as possible, the pollster convinces the candidate that she should not be present, and that only the media consultant, general consultant, campaign manager, and the research consultant should observe the focus group proceedings.

All eight focus group sessions are completed in a two-week time period at a total cost of $58,000; the polling firm prepares the narrative analysis and the findings are given to the campaign. The focus group research conclusions are generally optimistic, but also indicate an uphill struggle. Hardly any participants could identify Barbara Allyn, but when they were read a description of her and saw several video news clippings, they were enthusiastic; they were more positive when she was identified with certain salient issues: tax cuts, getting tough on crime, and education reform.

Benchmark Survey: Using information gathered from candidate and opposition research and findings from the focus group analysis, the polling firm prepares its questions and strategy for the benchmark poll. The results of this lengthy first survey tell the campaign that most voters in the state are fairly content with their lives and feel that the direction the country is taking is more positive than two years ago. While this is good news in a general sense, these findings trouble Allyn's pollster, as good news tends to favor the incumbent, not the challenger. More troubling are the poll data showing that Senator Porter, while his support is soft, has 55 to 60 percent name recognition and a 60 percent approval rating. Allyn has a long way to go. Her name recognition still hovers around 20 percent, but her negative ratings are less than 10 percent and her positive approval rating is above 40 percent; the rest of the voters simply don't know enough about her. This statewide survey, using a sample size of 1,730, cost the campaign $27,000.

Candidate research, focus groups, and polling information form the blueprint for launching the campaign. This information is used alongside updated analysis of state voting patterns, demographic trends, and other tools to target where the probable voters are and how they can be persuaded to vote. All of this information and the realities of the campaign context form the building blocks of this campaign. It's now up to Allyn's senior strategists and consultants to develop the message, strategy, and tactics for the unfolding campaign.[6]

Phase Three: Announcement Day

Two weeks before announcement day, Barbara Allyn resigns her position as minority leader to devote herself to campaigning full-time. She could have kept drawing a state salary throughout the campaign, but had declared very publicly several months ago that she considered it unethical for her to receive a taxpayer salary while running for a different office.

By announcement day, eight months before election day, several things are already in place. The campaign staff is geared up, particularly the campaign press office; the press packets and information on the campaign are prepared. The skeleton campaign staff of three months ago has now swollen to between ten and fifteen campaign workers, a volunteer coordinator, and a network of twenty-five to thirty volunteers. A professional speechwriter has been hired to craft the stump speech—the basic message that will be given throughout the campaign—and the media consultants have put together a ten-minute candidate biography.

The announcement day is planned with close to military precision. The campaign staff forms an advance team to be in place at each of the stops on announcement day. The announcement day stops are planned for each of the principal media markets, with press packets tailored for each market. The overarching goal on announcement day is to have the candidate appear on all local television stations, every radio outlet, and all newspapers. Every news outlet can download her announcement speech and biography, plus a press kit. Barbara Allyn will be interviewed live on morning news shows in the two largest media markets and, if time permits, in the other markets as well. The campaign's official website, two months in preparation, is now ready for unveiling during the announcement and the press and public can download both audio and video podcasts of Barbara Allyn. She has established her own YouTube site and already has fifteen videos posted on it. The old Friends of Barbara Allyn website will stay in use and will link to the new official site.

Announcement day is an exercise in planning and coordination; endorsements are gathered and key groups are assembled at the televised events. Announcement sites are selected to provide maximum television interest; every site and all the staging—including the list of invited guests—are carefully chosen and vetted with local political allies. The strategy is to use children at every event to emphasize the recently developed campaign theme—protecting our kids' future. Campaign expenses are beginning to mount; staff salaries and office expenditures are running at $55,000 per month. Announcement day expenses alone, the most being for the rented helicopter that shuttles Allyn to the different media markets, will cost another $60,000.

Phase Four: Shoring up Political Support

One of the critical activities in this phase, seven months before the election, is to secure the candidate's base of support. If this base is not secure, the election is surely lost. At this stage, every group of supporters wants to meet with Allyn; no one wants to be excluded. This becomes a scheduling headache of the first order. The candidate must maximize her time, meeting with the right people at the right times, and must avoid wasting time and resources. Allyn, in her earlier enthusiasm, had wanted to declare publicly that she would visit every county and every city in her sweep across the state. Cooler heads prevailed; she will visit only those places and groups that will yield maximum political potential. Like the media plan, her schedule must have direction, strategy, and rationale.

As in every other phase, fundraising overshadows everything else. Allyn is raising far more than ever before in her career, but it is not enough. A fundraising consultant is brought in to help put together events targeted at individual donors of $2,000 and at political action committees. It is painfully clear that the usual reliable sources of funds will not be enough, that the campaign will have to go beyond the state to look for funds. During this phase, twenty-seven fundraisers have been planned in-state, and others are planned in New York City, Los Angeles, Miami Beach, and Washington. Allyn, of course, will have to attend every one, taking precious time away from home-state campaigning. These fundraisers are time consuming but necessary facts of life for the Allyn campaign, and the money anticipated from local events will hardly close the fundraising gap.

The campaign has also been tapping the state party's list of supporters. Still, this will not be enough, so the campaign has hired a direct mail fundraising firm to assist in broadening the fundraising base. Using lists from the national party, several nonprofit organizations, and others, the campaign has added a whole new layer of direct mail possibilities. Direct mail solicitation is very expensive, a $220,000 up-front proposition, and much of the early money spent on direct mail will not yield cash resources until later in the campaign. Money has never come into an Allyn campaign as fast or as much as in this race thus far, but the task of raising funds is daunting, and expenses are rapidly eating away at campaign contributions.

The campaign website, www.allynforsenate.com, encourages supporters to contribute, and gives a secure link so they can deposit funds into the campaign. The online contributions are coming in at a steady clip, but the average contribution is fairly small, less than $50. So far, only about $47,150 has trickled into the campaign from online solicitation.

Phase Five: Long Summer

The summer season, with six months before the election, has been a discouraging one for the Allyn campaign. Fundraising has slowed and there has been hardly any media attention given to the race. Even worse, there seems to be little interest among the public. Allyn attends rallies, barbecues, Memorial Day and Fourth of July parades, and other events throughout the summer, but she gets the nagging sense that few people really care about the election, and is getting frustrated that all her efforts are for naught. Though a savvy and experienced campaigner, Allyn has never been involved in a statewide race before, and never in one that has lasted as long as this.

A late May poll in the state's largest newspaper contains some worrisome numbers: Allyn's name recognition inched up, but only to 28 percent. Her own pollster reassures her that voters simply have not focused their attention on this race and will not do so until after Labor Day. Privately, the consultants are quite concerned. They have seen this pattern too many times before—a candidate who, despite pouring her heart and soul (and millions of dollars), into the campaign, does not seem to connect with the voters. The consultants and the campaign press secretary begin mapping out a free media drive for the rest of the campaign. The goal is to get Barbara Allyn on as many morning, noon, and evening newscasts as possible, to use every opportunity to be on friendly talk radio programs, and to use every photo opportunity possible to boost her name recognition and positive numbers. A number of political blog sites are generating interest in this race. In July, Allyn's campaign gets an unanticipated, though minor, free media boost. Her campaign website is chosen as one of the ten best political sites in a university study.

Commercials: The campaign learns from inside sources in one of the television network affiliates that the Porter campaign plans a major media buy during the third week of June. The timing is somewhat unorthodox; this is very early in the campaign and voters are not at all focused on the race. Allyn's consultants speculate that Porter's own polling numbers show his support to be growing soft, and his campaign wants to air some positive biographical spots to bolster his standing. Or, perhaps, Porter wants to flex his campaign muscle and tempt Allyn to run costly television advertising to counter his. The Allyn campaign holds firm and does not run television spots, but the Allyn pollster does a quick survey of six hundred registered voters. The Porter television ads, which aired throughout the state, cost an estimated $420,000. The Allyn poll results show, however, that there was only a slight positive bump for Porter in name recognition and approval.

The Allyn media team has prepared six separate commercials of its own, including a three-minute soft biographical commercial introducing Allyn to state voters. All six commercials were test-marketed by four separate focus groups, which measured, ranked, and criticized the efforts. Allyn's biographical commercial had a heavy emphasis on her family's roots in the state, her values, and her role as a modern mother concerned about her kids and community. Allyn reminded her media consultant of Senator Elizabeth

Warren's progressive "we're all in this together" image; it worked for Warren, it might work here. Allyn very much wanted to keep her children out of the glare of publicity, and especially out of television commercials, but her media consultant persuaded her to show her kids in the television ads because the children had the highest positive rating of all visual images shown to the focus groups. In response to the focus groups' comments, Allyn changed her hairstyle, stopped wearing three of her favorite pantsuits, stopped using the words *progressive* and *Democrat,* and sharpened her critical comments against her opponent.

Because of the focus group reactions, five of the six commercials were reworked and were readied for the next phase of the campaign. On a gamble, the media consultant and pollster convinced Allyn to add more humor, self-deprecation, and an "I'm not from Washington" punch to her commercials. Knowing that they will probably never outspend Porter, the Allyn campaign needed catchy ads that would generate large amounts of free publicity. They planned to do some irreverent ads like the ones Joni Ernst did in the 2014 Iowa senate race: Ernst, who worked on a farm and had castrated hogs, said she was going to Washington to make the politicians "squeal."[7]

The focus groups also were shown the Porter commercial; it brought only a lukewarm response, much as the consultants had guessed. Porter had spent over $400,000 and gotten very little in return.

Telephoning for Dollars: The campaign absolutely must raise more money so that the television media blitz can be launched in early September. Despite personal appeals from Allyn, the scores of fundraisers she has attended, and the seven very expensive direct mail appeals for funds, the campaign must reach out to other voters and hit those who have already contributed funds. The campaign brings in a telemarketing firm that specializes in political fundraising. Thirty thousand telephone calls will be made during the final weeks of August and early September to solicit campaign funds. The direct mail appeal was marginally successful; the telemarketing, though more expensive, should yield a better return of contributors.

Phase Six: Ten Weeks Out

Television and Radio Advertisements: The Allyn campaign has held off until ten weeks before election day to begin its paid media. This will be the most expensive portion of the campaign, with nearly $2 million devoted to television and radio advertising during these last ten weeks. Weeks ago, the media consultant's senior ad buyer reserved time on television and. radio outlets in the six media markets. Network television shows will get the bulk of the advertising dollars, followed by a few selected cable shows, then radio. The strategy is to advertise on television shows that especially appeal to women, general audiences in the morning, the local noontime news, and popular night-time broadcasts. This is a high-cost strategy, especially for the popular network television shows, which charge very high prices for both local and national advertising. The radio budget is devoted to "drive time," the important morning and late-afternoon shows that attract large commuter audiences. The media buyer tries to get her on drive-time shows with a general audience, but also specifically targets African American females.

The media buyer is having difficulty getting the choicest advertising spots—a sure sign that Porter and unknown Super PACs have gotten there first and are planning an even greater airwave assault. On the advice of the media consultant, a specialty firm is hired to monitor the opposition's ads during this crucial time of the campaign.

Outside Attacks: Six weeks before the election, the local television stations in all six media markets are saturated with thirty-second television ads highly critical of Allyn. Barbara Allyn is seen in a very unflattering black-and-white photo spliced into a montage of toxic waste spills, sick children, and poisoned wildfowl. Rapidly scrolling across the screen are twelve environmental votes in the General Assembly that Allyn had missed during her six years of service. In bold red letters beside each vote is the word "absent," pulsating on the screen. In a voice-over dripping in sarcasm, the narrator snaps, "She says she loves kids and trees, but when it came time to stand up and vote, where was she? Barbara Allyn—all talk, no action. Barbara Allyn—if she can't show up for work, does she deserve a promotion? (Paid for by the Committee to Protect Our Kids' Future, J. Otis Burkewood, treasurer.)"

This ad is mean-spirited, unfair, and underhanded. It is also perfectly legal. Allyn is one of eight Senate and thirty-two congressional candidates being attacked by the so-called Committee to Protect Our Kids' Future. This is the opening shot of what will be an $18 million media buy orchestrated to hit throughout the week. The Committee to Protect Our Kids' Future, a 527 group, is funded mostly by a consortium of the fifteen largest waste disposal companies in the country. The Porter campaign publicly disavows any prior knowledge of the ads and, at a news conference, Senator Porter decries outsiders trying to influence the campaign. These attack ads continue for the next two weeks.

At the same time, a mysterious new website appears: www.TheReal-BarbaraAllyn.com. The home page, with boldface type, "The Real Barbara Allyn," features a cartoon caricature of Allyn looking like a frazzled, loud-mouthed screamer. The five pages of the website show Allyn making blatantly false and outrageous statements: "Make me your Senator or I'll scratch your beady little eyes out." "Porter is an idiot and anyone who votes for him is an idiot; come to think of it, my husband is an idiot." "Liberal? You want liberal? Hell, you ain't seen nothin' yet, baby. Send me up to Washington, and I'll beat the crap outta those Tea Party crazies." Click on each of the statements and out comes the audio of a screaming Barbara Allyn. This website claims that it was produced by "a bunch of regular voters who are fed up with the Barbara Allyns of this world." No other identification is given. A check of the domain registration proves elusive— this rogue website was registered under a fictitious name and a phony telephone number. The site gathers considerable media attention, shows up on YouTube, then after three weeks it disappears as mysteriously at it emerged.

Subsequently, a blog pops up called "Fed Up with Barb." More than 200 "citizens" write scurrilous comments about her. "American Patriot" complained that Allyn was "liberal scum," "Mom & 4Kids" objected to Allyn's "spending like a drunken sailor," "FedUpSallyAnn" wrote that Allyn would cripple the American family. All pretty nasty and all written overnight by some unknown group of probably three or four people. There's a Twitter account, #crazyBarbara, that pounds away at Allyn's character and her record. All of it is vicious, nearly all of it is taken out of context or out and out lies.

The Opposition: Porter's first ads were run in June and were soft biographical pieces. Since then, no ads have run—until now. Starting in early September and continuing through the third week of October, Porter saturates the major television stations with wicked combinations of negative-positive ads. The biting thirty-second ads attack Allyn's record, then rattle off Porter's accomplishments. The commercials are deftly done; there are no direct attacks on Allyn's character, nothing to offend women voters. Porter is taking the offensive, and the ads are carefully timed and spaced apart to have the maximum impact. The ads are hitting hard and directly at three weaknesses that Allyn's own consultants had spotted long ago: Allyn's voting absences during her General Assembly days, her refusal to support the death penalty, and an episode six years ago in the General Assembly in which four legislators were forced to resign because of bribery charges (Allyn was not involved, but was now being accused of not doing enough to punish the legislators involved). Porter's pollsters are reading the same numbers and focus group impressions as Allyn's pollsters, and coming up with the same vulnerabilities.

The Allyn senior strategists try hard to avoid playing defensive advertising. Porter has set the pace and has delivered the first blows. The Allyn media consultant decides to scrap three of the commercials already made and shoot new ads to counter the most damaging charges made by Porter. The new commercials are quickly produced from old video footage—the commercials are not tested through focus groups, as political instinct and creativity take over and the media team quickly puts the counterattack ads on the air. During the first two weeks following the Porter attack ads, the Allyn campaign's media plans are caught off stride. However, by the first of October, the Allyn media is back on its basic message.

Candidate Debates: Barbara Allyn is good on her feet; she wants to debate Porter throughout the state. The Porter campaign wants no debates at all, or as few as possible seen by as small an audience as possible. Why give Allyn free television exposure? Porter is wooden, phlegmatic, and not good with the give-and-take of the debate format. With the state League of Women Voters as the intermediary, the two campaigns decide, after much maneuvering, to have one debate, broadcast statewide on a Friday night and rebroadcast on public television the next Sunday afternoon. Porter has won the tactical battle. Few people will watch on a Friday evening (scheduled opposite an important football game of the state's flagship university), and fewer still will watch public television on Sunday. Besides, the public television viewers are already solidly in Allyn's camp. As long as Porter makes no egregious errors, there will be no damage to his campaign, and really no advantage to Allyn's. Both candidates are well prepared (Allyn's campaign even hires a debate coach), there are no "silver bullets," no knockout punches thrown. Both campaigns have party officials, other elected leaders, and consultants ready at the end of the debate to tout to the press the overwhelming victory of their side. The evening television news programs devote twenty seconds to the entire debate, with Allyn and Porter getting in the predicted sound bites and the television reporters uniformly intoning that "Allyn and Porter go head to head in their one and only debate." Later tracking polls show that the debates had negligible impact on voters.

Phase Seven: The Final Push and Election Day

Two weeks before the election is the period of highest intensity and anxiety in the campaign. Every media outlet is hit each day through orchestrated last-minute paid television and radio spots and through as many free media sources as possible. Allyn will be going around the state nonstop, to rallies, media events, and other campaign appearances.

Get-Out-The-Vote Drive: Money from 527 groups comes to the rescue. Over one million dollars in labor and some corporate contributions have poured into the state party to operate telephone banks and help in the get-out-the-vote drive. These funds technically do not go to Allyn's Senate campaign (although there is little else of importance going on election-wise in the state this year) and, thus, are not hard money. The funds go to the state's coordinated campaign activities. The national party is also supporting a get-out-the-vote drive, thanks to a last-minute injection of funds. The same telemarketing firm that has been soliciting for fundraising is doing the get-out-the-vote telephone calls. About 200,000 calls have been made by the firm, which is supplemented by party loyalists making last-minute phone calls and volunteering to man the polls and drive targeted voters to the polls if necessary. This good news is muted by the almost certain knowledge that funds are pouring into the Porter campaign from outside sources at an even faster rate.

Tracking Polls: The final two weeks of tracking poll results are coming in and are analyzed daily at the early-morning conference call between the pollster, campaign manager, and media consultant. The tracking results indicate that Allyn is closing to within four percentage points of Senator Porter statewide, with significant gains in two of the strongest media markets. Porter's media barrage is not having the negative impact the Allyn campaign had feared, and the Allyn message seems to be catching hold. Voters are now more focused on this race and they like what they see in Barbara Allyn.

Last-Minute Personal Funds: This is an excruciating time for Allyn personally. She has made the decision to put up $500,000 of family money for the final media buys. The campaign has fallen short of its fundraising goals and has run out of money for the final days. The television stations insist on up-front payments. If Allyn wins, there is a very strong chance that she can recoup the loan made to her campaign. If she loses, it will be very hard for her to gather enough funds from outside sources to repay her loan. She makes the gutsy move to put up her own money.

Last-Minute Media Barrage: During this last phase, enough airtime has been reserved for the final push of Allyn commercials. The ads are all positive, encouraging citizens to vote for Allyn; they are the most creative, catchiest spots in the Allyn campaign. The trouble, however, is that the Porter campaign has put out another barrage of ads that slam Allyn, while praising Porter. Allyn will spend approximately $750,000 on last-minute airtime; the Allyn campaign estimates that Porter will spend at least $250,000 more than that.

Push-Polling Attack: The Allyn campaign learns over the last weekend before election day that someone, presumably with the Porter campaign, is making thousands of telephone calls to probable voters under the guise of conducting a poll. Unknown to Allyn, but known to the Porter campaign, a major telemarketing firm has been hired, paid for by a 527 group, Committee for American Family Values, which is composed primarily of major corporate interests. This is a classic push-poll operation. Under the guise of a legitimate poll, the telemarketing firm, hired by the Committee for American Family Values, asks potential voters pointed and misleading questions about Allyn. Two examples: "Barbara Allyn missed more committee votes than practically any legislator. Doesn't that make you wonder about how hard she'll work for us?" "Would you still vote for Allyn if you knew that she supports Obamacare and other liberal programs that increase your taxes?"

Anti Abortion Attack: Allyn is also attacked during the last Sunday before the election by an orchestrated effort in fundamentalist and other right-wing churches. With messages from the pulpit and with leaflets on cars parked in church parking lots, churchgoers are urged not to vote for her. Allyn's campaign anticipated this, as it had happened in several statewide races before. Allyn forces have done their work to get thousands of African American voters to the polls, through the same vehicles, and also through a network of powerful African American preachers and their churches, congregations, and radio listeners. She has counted on organized labor to assist her, but her state has a very weak labor movement, and her campaign does not expect much assistance from this usually reliable but rather weak ally. National labor support has supplied a good deal of support, but local labor is unwilling and frankly unable to supply the manpower for canvassing and get-out-the-vote assistance.

Coming up Short

On election day, exit polls conducted by the wire services and early Internet reporting confirm what had been disturbing the campaign manager's sleep for weeks: not enough money, not enough clout at the end, clobbered by the resources of the incumbent and his supporters. Allyn loses to Senator Porter by 2.3 percentage points. Later FEC figures would show that Porter spent over $10.5 million, with an extraordinary push at the end of the campaign. Allyn's campaign spent just $7.8 million and is now about $500,000 in debt, not counting the personal loan of $500,000. As much as that half-million dollar debt hurts, what pains Allyn more is the gnawing question of whether spending another half-million of her own funds at the end would have closed that gap and helped achieved victory. A series of debt-retirement fundraisers are planned for late November and early December to try to capture some of the $200,000 that Allyn owes to campaign creditors. But it's really tough to get donors to give to defeated candidates.

The campaign headquarters closes three weeks after the defeat; none of the staff remaining during those three weeks is paid—all cash had been spent to pay for pressing campaign items. Allyn has a poignant telephone conference call with her lead consultants. They commiserate, share a laugh about Porter's stuffiness, and talk around but never really get to the heart of why she lost. They also talk about her political future. Allyn is thinking about the governor's office, which will be vacant in two years. Right now, she will not even discuss this with her husband, but she knows she has a good chance to grab the nomination.

By early December, the campaign manager has lined up a Senate race in Kentucky; the pollster and media adviser are in Aruba for the presidential contest and the warm weather. Senator Porter's reelection committee is planning the next year's fundraising events, with the goal of having $2 million cash on hand by the end of the first year of his new Senate term.

Lessons in the Aftermath

Money, Above All: Allyn was outspent by Senator Porter and his Super PAC allies (Table 3.1). Altogether, the Allyn campaign and the pro-Allyn Super PACs spent about $10.1 million, while the Porter campaign and the pro-Porter (and anti-Allyn) Super PACs spent about $17.6 million. Her campaign consultants knew it would be difficult to outspend an aggressive incumbent, but they felt that $7 million would be sufficient to run a respectable race. Allyn ran a far more efficient race. She spent less on direct mail expenditures and far less on campaign overhead than Porter. Allyn had a greater percentage of her funds devoted directly to campaigning, and each vote cost $2.44 less than the votes gathered by Porter. But efficiency counts for little. Allyn was outspent, her opponent poured on a last minute barrage of television commercials and an effective get-out-the-vote drive, and she lost in a relatively close race.

Not counted in these totals were the approximately $6.42 million spent by 527 groups and Super PACs and another $3 million (though we don't know for sure) spent by groups that did not have to report to the FEC. Nearly 75 percent of that $9.42 million was targeted to help Porter or to attack Allyn.

Challengers Face an Extraordinary Uphill Battle: While Senate challengers have a much better record of defeating an incumbent senator than House challengers have, it still is an uphill fight. Porter was relying on his name recognition, his assiduous use of the free media, and his campaign's long range organizational and fundraising efforts. Porter was also banking on the general mood of the state's voters. Times were relatively good, the

TABLE 3.1 BREAKDOWN OF EXPENSES AND VOTE EFFICIENCY

	Rep. Allyn	*Sen. Porter*
Total amount spent on campaign ($)	7,804,214	10,546,321
Overhead ($)	1,200,830	1,714,242
Fundraising ($)	1,006,810	1,310,050
Spent directly on persuading voters ($)	5,102,490	7,023,000
Votes received (*n*)	926,398	970,747
Total spent per vote ($)	8.42	10.86
Estimated Spending by Super PACS ($)	2,310,000	7,114,000

economy was in good shape, there was no compelling reason to kick the incumbent out of office. Despite all the commercials, direct mail appeals, telephone calls, and local news coverage, most voters barely paid attention to the race. Turnout was extremely light, despite Herculean efforts by both sides to get people out to vote. Many voters were unfocused, unsure of Allyn, and in the end content to reelect a relatively safe, nonthreatening incumbent.

While Barbara Allyn used some of the best consulting talent in her party, her opponent was able to match her in talent. In many ways, this contest featured the best strategic and creative minds in both parties going up against each other in a tough, aggressive race. Allyn's communications were sharp, clever, and memorable, but Porter's were equally up to the task. Porter had the advantage of more funds to spend on commercials, plus the help of an advertising blitz from an outside advocacy group.

Notes

1   Alan I. Abramowitz and Jeffrey A. Segal, *Senate Elections* (Ann Arbor, M.I.: University of Michigan Press, 1992), ix. See also Gary C. Jacobson and Raymond Wolfinger, "Information and Voting in California Senate Elections," *Legislative Studies Quarterly* 14 (1989): 509–29, on the Alan Cranston-Ed Zschau 1986 California Senate race. For a description of a quirky, refreshing campaign that relied on both a grassroots effort and modern advertising, see Dennis J. McGrath and Dane Smith, *Professor Wellstone Goes to Washington: The Inside Story of a Grassroots U.S. Senate Campaign* (Minneapolis, Minn.: University of Minnesota, 1995).

2   See Dorothy Davidson Nesbitt, *Videostyle in Senate Campaigns* (Knoxville: University of Tennessee Press, 1988), for an examination of three hypothetical Senate races with the focus on message development; and Richard F. Fenno, Jr., *Senators on the Campaign Trail: The Politics of Representation* (Norman: University of Oklahoma Press, 1998). See also ed. James A. Thurber and Candice J. Nelson, eds., *Campaigns and Elections: American Style* (Boulder, Colo.: Westview, 1995); and Daniel M. Shea, *Campaign Craft: The Strategies, Tactics, and Art of Political Management* (Westport, Conn.: Praeger, 1996).

3   Shea, *Campaign Craft*, 27. See also William R. Sweeney, "The Principles of Planning," in *Campaigns and Elections: American Style*; Barbara G. Salmore and Stephen A. Salmore, *Candidates, Parties, and Campaigns* (Washington, D.C.: Congressional Quarterly Press, 1989); and Linda L. Fowler, *Candidates, Congress, and the American Democracy* (Ann Arbor, M.I.: University of Michigan Press, 1993), especially the summary of research on House races, 100–2.

4   See John A. Ferejohn, "On the Decline in Competition in Congressional Elect-
     ions," *American Political Science Review* 71 (1977): 166–76; Fowler, *Candidates,
     Congress, and the American Democracy*; and Paul S. Herrnson, *Congressional Elections:
     Campaigning at Home and in Washington*, 2nd ed. (Washington, D.C.: CQ Press,
     1998).
5   Abramowitz and Segal, *Senate Elections*, 115.
6   See Denise Baer, "Contemporary Strategy and Agenda Setting," in Thurber and
     Nelson, eds., *Campaigns and Elections*; and Shea, *Campaign Craft*, ch. 2.
7   Joni Ernst commercial, available on *YouTube* at www.youtube.com/watch?
     v=p9Y24MFOfFU (accessed February 15, 2015).

PART

WEAPONS

OF

MODERN

CAMPAIGNING

4

Political Research: Digging up the Dirt

If you've got two people doing research, have your best one researching your candidate and the other researching your opponent.

—James Carville[1]

Campaign researchers will never be celebrities, going on talk shows and identified by the public at large. They prefer to do their work quietly, behind the scenes, digging through piles of documents and online databases. Despite their sometimes nefarious reputation, political researchers often provide valuable information to campaigns. Research comes in two related forms: candidate (or incumbent) research and opposition research. Candidate research is both an offensive and defensive weapon; it builds the case that the incumbent has established a solid record of achievement, it spots weaknesses in the incumbent's record, and it devises strategies to protect that record. Opposition researchers go on the attack; they seek out and exploit the weaknesses of the opponent.

At its best, political research gives shape and focus to complex events, sharpens the distinctions between candidates, builds its case with solid evidence, and helps develop critical but fair conclusions. At its worst, political research crosses the line of decency and fairness, is used ruthlessly for character assassination, and becomes the indispensable weapon in "gotcha" campaigning.

Political research is critical to modern campaigning. With increased emphasis on negative advertising, campaigns must respond quickly and decisively. They can do so only if they have their facts assembled and rebuttal themes crafted. That is where politics research is key. No serious campaign can do without it. During the height of the 1988 presidential campaign, chief Republican strategist Lee Atwater remarked that "the only group I was very interested in having report to me directly was opposition research."[2]

In the 2012 presidential campaign, political research was used to sharply and critically define both the records and character of Mitt Romney and Barack Obama. At its most sophisticated, political research is a campaign specialty dominated by professionals, working either for their political parties or as private consultants, who are adept at ferreting out information and using it to maximum political advantage. In recent years, professional campaign researchers have been joined by private investigators, former police officers, ex-CIA and FBI agents who have honed their skills in the rough-and-tumble worlds of corporate espionage, national security, and criminal investigations.[3]

The Nature of Political Research

Political research, especially candidate and opposition research, bears little resemblance to academic social science research. The latter follows well-understood norms and disciplines. In academic research, great care is taken in developing research questions, proposing suitable explanations, defining concepts, and testing hypotheses.[4] Data are chosen and used with caution, verification often depends on rigorous quantitative analysis using well-developed statistical and other instruments, findings are usually couched in circumscribed language, and definitions and words are chosen with precision. Academic research is usually presented as tentative, part of a much larger universe of knowledge yet to be discovered; the work of other researchers is acknowledged and given due recognition.

These are not the norms and standards of political research. James Carville, a brilliant student of applied political strategy, had little patience with social science research, and his attitudes typified those of many of his colleagues. He understood the importance of survey research and focus group analysis, but otherwise had little appreciation for the disciplines and processes of social science research. When I was first introduced to Carville and was being considered for a position as research director for a Senate campaign, he brushed me off: "I don't need any goddamned professor on this campaign. Trouble is, they can't get off the can and make a decision. To them, everything is gray. I want black and white. I want to nail our opponent. I want to rip his head off. I want answers and I want them now."[5]

Campaign research is unequivocally applied research. The goal is to build the best possible case for a candidate, or, if it is opposition research, to find the most damaging information to be used against an opponent. There is no time or place for hypothesis testing or theory building. Tangential research and information gathered after the election is over are of no value.

There is a premium on accuracy of information. Political researchers are extraordinarily careful to get the facts correct—the right vote on an amendment, the exact quote from a newspaper article, or the precise amount of money reported on a financial disclosure statement. Inaccurate information can quickly taint an entire research operation. When the opposition campaign or the press discovers errors of fact, the entire research operation can be swiftly rendered useless. Critics often charge that a campaign's facts are wrong. Usually, however, the facts are not wrong. Often the real problem is not in the accuracy of the research, but in its interpretation and questionable use in the campaign. Political research does not seek to weigh sides and present a balance; it seeks to build a case and, in doing so, often pushes well beyond the norms of objectivity.

In a hotly contested 2002 U.S. Senate race in Georgia, challenger Saxby Chambliss launched a bitter and controversial ad against incumbent senator Max Cleland. Cleland, a decorated former Army officer and Vietnam veteran, lost both legs and his right arm when a grenade exploded. He later served as secretary of the U.S. Veterans Administration before becoming a U.S. senator. The Chambliss campaign ran this ad, which featured photos of Osama bin Laden and Saddam Hussein:

[Voice-over]: As America faces terrorists and extremists, Max Cleland runs television ads claiming he has the courage to lead.

He says he supports President Bush at every opportunity, but that's not the truth.

Since July, Max Cleland voted against President Bush's vital homeland security *efforts* 11 times.

But the record proves, Max Cleland is just misleading.[6]

One of the television ads morphed the faces of Cleland and Saddam Hussein. The Chambliss campaign ad made it appear that Cleland had voted against the Homeland Security bill itself, when, in fact, Cleland voted against several secondary provisions in the bill, particularly to protect civil service employees at the new department. Republican senators Chuck Hagel of Nebraska and John McCain of Arizona, both decorated veterans, protested loudly against this attempt to smear Cleland's reputation. In the end, Chambliss defeated Cleland, and many commentators pointed to the negative, distorted television ads as a significant reason for the outcome.[7]

Representative David R. Price (Democrat, North Carolina) introduced legislation that amended the Bipartisan Campaign Reform Act to include a "stand by your ad" provision. Starting in 2008, all federal candidates have to acknowledge that they "approve this message" in each of their ads. This meant that incumbent senator Elizabeth Dole was responsible for this very dubious ad in the closely watched North Carolina senate race between Dole and challenger Kay Hagan. Here are some excerpts:

Elizabeth Dole: I'm Elizabeth Dole and I approve this message.

Narrator: A leader of the Godless Americans PAC recently held a secret fund-raiser in Kay Hagan's honor.

Ellen Johnson, executive director of the Godless Americans PAC, but not identified as such in the commercial: There is no God to rely on.

Johnson: There was no Jesus.

[The ad then shows Bill O'Reilly of the television show "The O'Reilly Factor" asking the Godless Americans PAC director, David Silverman the following]:

O'Reilly: Taking "under God" out of the Pledge of Allegiance, you're down with that?

Silverman [Unidentified]: We're down with that.

O'Reilly: "In God We Trust"—are you going to whip that off the money?

Silverman [Unidentified]: Yeah, we would.

Narrator: Godless Americans and Kay Hagan. She hid from cameras. Took Godless money. What did Hagan promise in return?

[The ad then shows an image of Hagan, with a female voice-over declaring: "There is no God!"]

The problem was that Hagan, who once was a Sunday school teacher at her Presbyterian church, never said "There is no God," and the fundraiser was not hosted by the Godless PAC (although it was one of the forty-two co-hosts). But that did not matter; the Dole campaign put the scurrilous ad on the airwaves. This may have been a sign of the desperation of the Dole campaign, because Senator Dole lost by over eight percentage points.

There is no evidence that the "stand by your ad" provision has constrained any candidate. But at least candidates now have to "own" the attack ads that their media consultants have produced.

In the first of these two examples, political researcher dug up the eleven votes Cleland cast, then media consultants took that information and smeared the senator with untruths and innuendo. In the second, researchers discovered a highly dubious link with a controversial political action committee, and the media team tried to weave together a guilt-by-association charge that Hagan was somehow "godless." As these examples suggest, in political research, information is often highly selective, the rules of causation and correlation are thrown out the window, and conclusions are presented in the starkest of terms. The research conclusions become all the more damaging in the hands of the media consultant who mixes in even more hyperbole through distorted images, imaginative music and sound effects, and voice-overs laced with sarcasm.

Candidate or Incumbent Research

Analysis of the campaign's own candidate is the most important research of all. It is tempting to concentrate only on the opponent, leaving candidate research as an afterthought. But the campaign that neglects its own candidate runs the great risk of not being able to defend against an attack and of not taking full advantage of the candidate's record of legislative and constituency achievements.

When the candidate is an incumbent officeholder, there is usually a built-in advantage for conducting research. U.S. senators or members of Congress are permitted by House and Senate ethics rules to use their own staffs to conduct research on their own records. Compiling such research is supposed to be done only for official, noncampaign purposes, such as the preparation of reports and newsletters. But, throughout Capitol Hill, it is widely acknowledged that congressional staffers, whose salaries are paid by taxpayers, are also conducting vital, but not necessarily lawful, campaign research. Congressional and Senate offices can be assisted by the resources of other legislative services, such as the Senate Computer Center or the Congressional Research Service of the Library of Congress, which compile and produce extremely helpful information on the legislators' achievements and voting records. The staffs for governors, big city mayors, and, to some degree, state legislators have similar built-in advantages of access to public information and professional staff support.

However, incumbents are turning more to professionals to conduct their candidate research. Three reasons stand out. First, as the glare of public disclosure increases, incumbents do not want to be accused of using staffers to conduct campaign research while on the taxpayers' payroll.[8] A professional consultant on the campaign payroll demonstrates that the campaign, not the taxpayers, is paying for candidate research. Second, staffers cannot objectively assess the successes and failures of their boss's record; in doing so, they are being asked to judge their own work. A professional researcher can coldly and objectively assess the performance of the incumbent—and, by extension, the staff. The third reason is more subtle, but just as important. Legislative staffers think primarily in terms of process and issues, not politics. What may look so very crucial in the hothouse of the legislative arena, in a committee markup, or in an amendment may have absolutely no bearing in the campaign battle. Seasoned professional researchers bring experience from many campaigns; they instinctively sense what research is politically salient and what parts of a candidate's career are simply irrelevant: to the campaign fight ahead.

At the heart of the entire reelection campaign is the central question: why should this politician be returned to office?[9] Incumbent research must provide answers to some very simple but extraordinarily important questions: What did the incumbent promise to do, and were those promises kept? Does the incumbent work hard? How has the incumbent helped people like me and others in our state? All in all, why does this elected official deserve to go back to Washington?

The incumbent is highly vulnerable because everything in the public record is fair game for analysis, criticism, and distortion. For the challenger, conducting opposition research is easier—find the three or four critical weaknesses, test them in focus groups and through polling, and then bear down on them throughout the campaign.

The incumbent needs to be on the firmest ground when saying to voters, "When I ran for office five years ago, I promised to do four things when I got to Washington. And thanks to your help, we've won each of those fights." Promises come in a variety of forms. Candidates may assure voters that they will always come back home on the weekends, never miss a vote, be honest, or make sure the state gets a larger share of federal funds. Many times the promises made during the hectic days of running for office do not materialize. When that realization sets in, the campaign must be prepared to defend a vulnerable record.

In 1986, North Dakota senator Kent Conrad promised voters that if the federal budget deficit were not reduced by 80 percent during his first term in office, he would not seek reelection in 1992. The budget deficit did not go down and, true to his word, Conrad announced that he would not run again.[10] As circumstances had it, Conrad's senior Senate colleague Quentin Burdick died five months later, leaving a vacancy. Conrad did not run for his old seat, but ran for and won the vacant Burdick seat. Conrad had the courage to keep his word, and the North Dakota voters had the unforeseen chance to reaffirm their faith in Conrad as their senator. Since 2000, several members of Congress quietly reneged on their promise not to seek reelection.

During the 1988 presidential campaign, Michael Dukakis was attacked for not upholding promises he made as governor of Massachusetts in this Bush television ad:

Voice-over: Michael Dukakis promised not to raise taxes. But, as governor, he imposed the largest tax increase in Massachusetts's history. He promised jobs, but since 1984 Massachusetts lost ninety thousand blue-collar jobs. He promised less spending, but spent at a greater rate per capita than any other governor in America. And now he wants to do for America what he's done for Massachusetts. America can't afford that risk.[11]

The best known and most damaging unkept campaign promise cost George H. W. Bush dearly. When he proclaimed, "Read my lips, no new taxes," at the 1988 Republican National Convention, Bush received extraordinary media coverage and accolades from the party faithful. This pledge was central to the Bush 1988 campaign message, but he was left with the daunting task of living up to it during his presidency. When he broke the pledge in 1990, voters remembered and were unforgiving in 1992.[12]

Promises made and kept are more than a mere catalog of accomplishments. They reflect on character and leadership, and when promises are highly visible and not kept, as in the Bush case, they can become politically fatal.[13] Every incumbent running for reelection must know what has been promised and have credible explanations for the promises not kept.

A campaign must also have a clear understanding of the incumbent's accomplishments from many angles. The research reports listing those accomplishments must be arranged in a variety of formats: (a) by key constituency groups, such as suburbanites, women, the elderly, and veterans; (b) by year in office, to ward off charges that the incumbent has not really done anything except during election year; (c) by media market, city, and county; (d) by issues and subject areas; and (d) by the names of individuals who were assisted. The accomplishments may be categorized as legislation introduced (or blocked), grants and financial assistance secured, important votes cast, favorable ratings to be used on interest group scorecards, supporting or standing up to the administration, and so on. For the campaign and professional research team, it is time to take credit and translate accomplishments into easily understood and politically compelling themes.

A thorough accomplishments file would have ready answers to hundreds of campaign-relevant questions. The range of questions can be bewildering, but the research must be done and answers readily accessible:

• What are the ten most important things you have accomplished each year in office?
• How many times have you visited each of the state's counties and cities, and what federal grants have you been able to obtain for them?

- Why did you vote for Obamacare?
- Why did you vote against increasing the minimum wage, but at the same time vote for a pay raise for members of Congress? Why aren't you willing to return your pay increase to the treasury?
- Why did you receive only a 55 percent approval rating on the League of Conservation Voters' most recent environmental scorecard?
- In what specific ways have you stood up to (or supported) the president's agenda?

The most effective accomplishments are those issues that connect with people's concerns and their lives.'[14] When portrayed as personal vignettes, they can become very compelling:

- Senator A forced the EPA to close eight toxic waste dumps. Now our communities are healthier and our children are much safer.
- Twelve hundred new jobs have come to our community thanks to Senator A's tough action in Washington.

Connecting with voters is the paramount task of the campaign. When a senator spends weeks in negotiation over the complicated provisions of a trade agreement, those efforts begin to connect only when voters understand that the senator is fighting for jobs and good wages. Taking a stand against a technical amendment on a budget rescission makes sense only when voters understand that their children's generation will be better off because of this action. If voters cannot understand the relationship to their lives and communities, any legislative or policy accomplishment, no matter how important, will be ineffective.

But a campaign has to make sure that accomplishments can be justified and believed. During the 2000 presidential campaign, Vice President Al Gore was mocked for his claim of having created the Internet. The campaign ad shows a kitchen with the television set broadcasting a speech by Al Gore.

> *Female voice*: There's Al Gore, reinventing himself on television again. Like I'm not going to notice? Who's he going to be today? The Al Gore who raises campaign money at a Buddhist temple? Or the one who now promises campaign finance reform. Really. Al Gore, claiming credit for things he didn't even do.

Al Gore [on TV]: I took the initiative, in creating the Internet.

Female voice: Yeah, and I invented the remote control, too. Another round of this and I'll sell my television.

For each accomplishment, the research team often prepares two sets of documents. The first, and most important, is written in clear, simple prose, and is available for reprinting at rallies, in persuasion literature, press releases, on the campaign website, and in other campaign advertising. The second set, kept by the campaign and available to the press when necessary, is the fully documented version, giving complete citation to amendments introduced, federal officials called, dollars awarded for a local project, newspaper clippings, and video files. The second version is crucial because of increased scrutiny of a candidate's record by the media and the opposition campaign. The documented second set is not required by law or regulation; it is just smart campaign practice to have it available.

Candidate research must prepare for the inevitable challenge from the opposition. The themes are predictable, as general lines of attack appear in campaign after campaign, and they concern ageless values—the incumbent has lost touch with the people back home, does not work hard, does not stand on principle and changes his mind to please different people, has used the office for personal gain, will say just about anything to get reelected, and, as the sum of all these charges, the incumbent does not deserve to be reelected. The thoroughly prepared candidate research team has to anticipate these charges, prepare rebuttals, check the opponent's record to see if a similar charge can be leveled directly back at the opponent, and take steps to inoculate the campaign against the charge.

Many voters have little interest in politics and only a marginal understanding of policy and legislative issues, and barely know anything about the candidates beyond their names. Television, their primary source of news, generally ignores campaigns or covers them only superficially. Under these conditions, campaign advertising takes center stage, given a relatively free hand in defining the race and the opponent, and often it turns nasty and venal.

The 2006 race for the U.S. Senate in Ohio is an example. In a tough race, incumbent Republican Senator Mike DeWine went directly after challenger Sherrod Brown. DeWine's campaign isolated several votes cast by Brown in the House of Representatives to portray him as "out of touch" with Ohio values.

Mike DeWine: I'm Mike DeWine, and I approve this message.

Announcer [voice-over]: Where does Sherrod Brown stand on protecting America's homeland?

He voted against strengthening criminal laws for terrorist attacks.

He voted against the Patriot Act, which gives law enforcement the tools to fight terrorism.

Brown even voted against the death penalty for terrorists who kill passengers on trains and subways.

Sherrod Brown. Weakening America's security. Out of touch with Ohio values.

The thirty-second ad, of course, does not do justice to Brown's long, complex legislative career. But it is not designed to do so. Just three votes are cited and they are accompanied by vivid pictures of terrorist attacks in an attempt to reinforce the urgency of DeWine's attack.[15]

When people change their minds, it is often a sign of intellectual growth and maturity, but not in politics. When candidates change sides, their opponents quickly see a sign of political weakness or, worse, crass opportunism. For example, Georgia governor Zell Miller, for sixteen years the lieutenant governor and several more years a state legislator, was tagged with the deadly sobriquet "Zigzag Zell" because of the variety of views he had held on several subjects over his long career. Republicans pulled out the "flip-flop" charge against John Kerry in 2004. A funny and devastating ad showed Kerry windsurfing, tacking one way and then the next. The commercial charged that Kerry did the same with his policy stands. He supported, then opposed the Iraq war, the $87 billion for American troops, education reform, and increased Medicare premiums. "Kerry could not make up his mind," the ad seemed to say. To protect against such attacks, candidate research must know every time there has been a change in policy or voting record, and have a clear explanation of why changes were made.

The reputations of officeholders can be quickly tarnished and careers dented by questionable personal financial gain. Every candidate for federal and most state offices must file detailed financial records. In some campaigns, the candidates voluntarily release their income tax returns. Beyond tax returns and financial disclosure statements, there are many public record databases containing critical financial information on taxes paid, tax liens, bankruptcy proceedings, probate settlements, company and stockholder information, and more. Individual contributors and political action committees that financially support the candidate are required to report their gifts to the FEC or file appropriate financial disclosure forms with their state board of elections. Tough questions can come from research into financial records:

- How much money did the candidate give to charity last year?
- Why did the candidate, when sitting on the board of directors of Local Industries, vote to give the chairman a million dollar bonus, while the company laid off five hundred workers in our state?
- How much money did the candidate receive from groups funded by the Koch brothers?

The research team needs to know every aspect of the candidate's financial filings and what might cause embarrassment or inflict political damage. The campaign research team must be able to rebut every possible charge of financial impropriety.

Voters have to show up for work, and so should legislators. When an officeholder does not attend meetings or fails to cast votes, the opposition is handed an easy target. These votes or meetings substitute for the symbolically larger character issue of showing up for work. For example, in a 1998 Washington state congressional race, eventual winner Brian Baird's campaign created a special website, www.missedvotes.com, which listed, by category, the four hundred votes missed by his opponent, state legislator Don Benton. The website had a smiling, cartoon figure of Benton skipping out the Senate door while colleagues watch in dismay, saying, "I don't miss any of the important votes." The website asked, "If most employees skipped work one-fifth of the time, never showing up for work on Monday, would they expect to keep their job? But that's just what Don Benton did last year ... and now he's asking you for a promotion!"

Another version of the inevitable attack commercial looks like this one in the 2006 Pennsylvania Senate race, when incumbent senator Rick Santorum went after his challenger, state treasurer Robert Casey:

Rick Santorum [voice-over]: I'm Rick Santorum, and I approve this message.

Announcer: Bobby Casey loves running for office. Showing up to do the job—that's a different story.

As auditor general, Casey skipped so much work running for governor, he never completed over eight hundred audits, and lost anyhow.

So, he announced for treasurer, where he has skipped work almost half the time campaigning for the Senate.

Bobby Casey. Before running for a new job, shouldn't he show up for the one we already pay him for?

[Text on screen: Paid for by Santorum, 2006].[16]

Members of Congress running for governor or senator are especially vulnerable to the problem of missing votes. They often have to miss scores of votes in Washington while back home campaigning for higher office; and opponents are eager to tell voters every time a vote is missed. Missed votes become even worse when linked with perceived personal financial gain, such as collecting an honoraria fee[17] or attending a political fundraiser. Whenever a legislator misses votes, campaign researchers have to know which were missed and the political fallout involved in missing them, and be able to explain why the candidate was absent.

Officeholders could be vulnerable because of their abuses of taxpayer trust; for example, spending too much money on franked mail, having office staff who are also on the campaign payroll, unwarranted trips by office staffers, lobbyist-sponsored trips for the legislator and spouse, even listing the wrong kinds of magazine subscriptions on an official office account.[18] All of this information is in the public record and much of it can be obtained through electronic databases. The candidate research team must know all facets of the use of the candidate's office and be able to build the case against any charges of misuse of taxpayer funds or voter trust.

Senators and members of Congress cast between three hundred and five hundred roll call votes each year, and these votes are prime evidence of a legislator's policy preferences and ideology. But not all votes are of equal importance. Most votes simply do not matter in a reelection campaign; they are either too technical, tedious, or politically irrelevant. Only when votes mean something to voters back home do they become politically salient. Of the two thousand roll call votes a senator has amassed over a six-year term, perhaps three hundred are truly relevant to the campaign. Further, the politically savvy legislator will have the good sense to know what constituents will tolerate or demand, and will vote accordingly.

But there will always be votes that the legislator will cast with trepidation, knowing that at election time they will have to be defended. Such as:

- Votes that have strong ideological or political repercussions, such as military aid to Israel, gay rights issues, or anything to do with gun control).
- Votes that are of special interest to powerful organizations or constituencies (environmental votes, social security cost-of-living adjustments, Obamacare, raising the debt ceiling).
- Votes that touch on the legislator's perceived personal gain (votes on pay raises).
- A vote for or against sending more American troops into Middle East hotspots.

On these tough votes, legislators rely more on their instincts, on cues they might receive from party leaders, and from the tug of constituent groups than on the advice of consultants. Political consultants generally come in after the fact. The votes have been cast, and now the consultants have to help the candidate explain them or ride out the storm during the campaign.

What often matters more than individual roll call votes are the themes that developed from a set of votes. Voting themes, however, can work both for and against an incumbent:

- *Accomplishment*: Every time special interests have tried to strip away funding for children's health care, Congressman A has voted to prevent them.

- *Attack*: When you add up every spending bill Congressman A has voted for these past four years, it turns out he's one of the biggest spenders in Washington.
- *Accomplishment*: When you add up his votes on tough tax-and-spend issues, you can see why the Defenders of Free Enterprise Committee gave Congressman A its perfect 100 percent approval award.
- *Attack*: Congressman A just blows with the wind when it comes to tax cuts. He voted to cut excise taxes twice last year, then this year voted to increase excise taxes. He said he'd never vote to raise taxes. Why's he lying to us?

Opposition Research

Campaign research usually gets its unsavory reputation because of the tactics and mindset of opposition research. Incumbents and challengers alike will use it as an offensive weapon, but it seems particularly useful for challengers and candidates in tight races. Veteran Republican consultant Terry Cooper stated that opposition research is an increasingly important tool in the campaign of a challenger or lesser-known candidate running for an open seat. Such research is valuable because of voter inertia—the "tendency of the vast majority of the electorate to reelect the incumbent or vote for the better-known candidate unless someone gives them a good reason to do otherwise."[19]

A candidate often has to face intense scrutiny of his public and, increasingly, personal life. Candidates with past public experience, such as a member of the city council or of the state general assembly, should expect that their entire public career will be thoroughly analyzed, and the candidate will be held accountable even for things that were beyond his or her immediate control. For example, an eight-year incumbent of a medium-sized city council might have to explain his consistent pattern of not showing up for subcommittee meetings, but also for the failure of the city to stop the increase of crime or to put its fiscal house in order.

Candidates with no public record are by no means immune from scrutiny. A successful businesswoman turned candidate might have to explain why her children go to an expensive private school, why her company was cited for environmental violations, or, as a member of the board of directors of another company, why she voted to punish union activists.

One of the worst things candidates can do is lie or exaggerate about their careers and achievements. More than one candidate for office has lost an election solely on the basis of disclosures of inflated resumes, such as a padded Iraq war record or a university degree that was never earned. Lies or exaggerations go to the heart of character and integrity and nothing will doom a candidate quicker than being caught lying about personal matters. Opposition research often begins with a thorough examination of the opponent's campaign literature and resume.

At what point in a candidate's career does political research begin? A first-term U.S. senator might conclude, with certain logic, that research on his career would begin with the day he became senator or certainly no earlier than the Senate campaign. But an exhaustive and complete research record would also cover the six years the senator served in the House of Representatives, his four years as lieutenant governor, and the four years he served as district attorney. Opposition researchers might even be interested in the senator's military service record or college days.

The lesson from the 1992 presidential campaign should be clear. Despite a lengthy record as governor of Arkansas, the Bush opposition researchers were far more interested in Clinton's draft records and his months spent in England when he was a young graduate student. During the 1988 presidential campaign, Republican researchers combed through twenty-five years of Boston newspaper clippings to find ammunition against Michael Dukakis, going back to 1949 Brookline city council minutes, where they found a letter sent by Dukakis and several college classmates protesting against U.S. future involvement in Korea.[20] In 2004, researchers honed in on John Kerry's Vietnam record and George Bush's national guard service. In 2008 and even 2012, groups opposed to Barack Obama were reaching as far back as you can go, aggressively going after his birth certificate.

Candidates have to worry about skeletons in their closets. Baby-boomer candidates have to figure out how to respond to charges of using marijuana and other drugs, or explain why they did not serve in Vietnam. Thanks to the Clinton sex scandals, marital infidelity became a skeleton lurking in many candidates' closets. Former vice president Dan Quayle stated that adultery would be "the question" for any candidate in the 2000 presidential contest, and assured anyone listening that he could "pass" that test. Lamar Alexander, Steve Forbes, and George W. Bush all issued statements proclaiming their faithfulness. In Utah, the attorney general sent affidavits to each of the senators and House members requesting that they voluntarily sign an oath proclaiming their marital fidelity. All five legislators refused to sign, but then publicly declared that they have been faithful in their marriages.[21] Some interest groups demand that candidates sign a pledge that they will not raise taxes or support term limits or that they believe in the right to carry guns. The Reverend Lou Sheldon, head of the Traditional Values Coalition, stated that he personally planned to ask all Republican 2000 presidential candidates if they have committed adultery. Opposition researchers, never shy when looking into personal indiscretions, will shed any qualms they might have in searching personal family history and divorce records if marital infidelity becomes fair game in campaigns. They might not be as blatant as porn-ography publisher Larry Flynt, who offered million-dollar bounties to help "out" marital hypocrites during the Clinton impeachment proceedings, but the temptation will be to leave no stone unturned in their efforts.

After September 11, 2001, issues of marital infidelity and moral weakness seemed out of touch with the concerns and mood of the country. But with the growing lobbying scandals in 2006, researchers and investigators returned to familiar grounds of searching out corruption, personal greed, and abuse of office.

The Technology of Research

Few aspects of campaigns and elections have changed as profoundly as the technology of research. Just twenty-five years ago, research was confined almost exclusively to paper and microfiche records—old newspaper clippings, voting records, FEC reports, state and federal financial reporting forms, and a wide variety of public documents. Much of the research work ended up in index cards and three-ring binders, cross-referenced and color-coded.

Many of these basic sources continue to be extremely valuable. Even in the sophisticated days of online resources and the Internet, I found myself in rural Alabama on a steamy August afternoon looking through handwritten records at a county courthouse for a candidate running for Congress. Another client, running for governor in another state, asked me to dig up a potentially embarrassing comment he had made about John F. Kennedy to a small-town newspaper reporter thirty-five years earlier. Many such records, especially pre-computer-age files, never make it onto Google, Lexis-Nexis, or other comprehensive online services, and must still be searched by hand.

The information revolution came first through computerized voting and issues database files. Online services came next, with *The Hotline* as one of the first, a service that political junkies in particular could not resist. *Hotline* material is generated daily, summarizing news accounts about politics from some 250 news sources. The explosion of Internet services, particularly websites, has revolutionized political research. Websites that collect the massive amount of public record information are now at researchers' fingertips. For primary research materials—the backbone of solid political research—online services are indispensable. There is an extraordinary range of public and commercial sources available to political researchers. Candidates for office should now expect that online public record sources will be routinely checked to learn about their business interests, tax records, possible civil and criminal lawsuits, felony and misdemeanor criminal filings, driving records, property records, money owed, probate settlements, and bankruptcy proceedings.

Credit bureau information is particularly tantalizing to a political researcher. The Fair Credit Report Act does not permit the merely curious to search the extensive credit files found in the major credit card bureaus.[22] There must be a legitimate business relationship: an auto dealer, for example, checking on the creditworthiness of a potential buyer. But because there is so much detailed financial information available, campaigns are sometimes tempted to ask a friendly business to make the credit check and hand the material over to the campaign. This is both illegal and risky. A credit check leaves footprints because the name of the business will be reported when a credit check is requested.[23]

Information gleaned from the public record may yield embarrassing items, particularly for candidates whose public posturing is contrasted with private action:

- A wealthy businessman who is running as the defender of the "little guy," but has a long record of suing his own employees for the most petty of reasons.
- A member of Congress who portrays herself as being tough on drugs, but has a string of citations for driving while under the influence of alcohol.
- A candidate who rails against excessive taxes, but fails to pay real estate taxes owed on vacation property.

Researchers (and the general public, for that matter) have to be careful in choosing Internet sites. The Internet is a wide-open communications tool, and the rules of journalistic fair play and ethics no longer apply. Parody and rogue websites and political blogs mushroom during campaigns—they look like campaign sites, and their Internet names are close to sounding legitimate, but, in fact, they are set up by individuals and groups that either want to profit from the campaign or want to make fun of it. Website speculators grabbed the names of possible 2000 presidential candidates. By early 1999, there were at least thirty-seven fake George W. Bush websites, twenty Al Gore fake sites, and another twenty addresses using variations of Steve Forbes' name.[24] Some websites, Twitter feeds, and bloggers have no qualms about posting rumor and speculation, information that legitimate news organizations would never print without substantiation and verification. Mainstream newspapers, such as the *Washington Post*, the *New York Times*, and the *Wall Street Journal*, maintain reputations for accurate reporting; so, too, do their websites. The great majority of political websites are accurate and reliable. But the bewildering array of websites ranges from those that are highly reliable, nonpartisan, and scrupulously fair in their reporting, to those that are highly partisan or filled with inaccurate information, character assassination, and rumor mongering. Many websites and blogs perform valuable civic service, while many others practice guerilla warfare.

There is also an increased awareness of the need to maintain video archives. Traditionally, the printed word was the authoritative source for political research. Now the powerful image on television or over the Internet is even more important. Campaigns find indispensable properly archived of audiotapes and videotapes of nightly news programs, public events, campaign commercials, and campaign events, all categorized by key words, dates, events, and issues.

Technology has increased the pace of campaigns and the need for reliable, complete research that is available instantaneously. In earlier decades, campaigns had the luxury of waiting a week or several days to rebut charges made by an opponent. Today, there is no time for a leisurely response. The communications technology of smart phones, satellite feeds, video conferencing, online databases, email, podcasts, Twitter feeds, and websites require that campaigns be able to respond almost immediately when challenged.

Rapid response comes at a high price, however. Research must be completed, packaged, and available for use very early in the election cycle.

Sophisticated campaigns recognize this and often make candidate and opposition research one of the first commitments of the campaign.

Using Political Research

The best-prepared research team should have every conceivable aspect of its candidate's public and private careers known, analyzed, and explained. The research team should know its opponent's record—both strengths and weaknesses—better than the opponent does. It should be able immediately to refute and punch holes in the arguments made at the opponent's news conferences. The research should be deadly accurate, thoroughly checked, never questioned. The research should also be imaginative, creating potent campaign attack themes from disparate bits of information.

Thousands of hours can be spent on candidate and opposition research in any major campaign. A campaign might have three to five fulltime researchers plus a professional research consulting firm, all combing through the records of the incumbent and challengers. While vast amounts may be collected and analyzed, probably 95 percent of all research material is never used. The agonizing problem for the research staff, however, is not knowing which 5 percent will be crucial to the campaign.

Candidate and opposition research becomes valuable at several stages throughout the campaign. First, campaign research gives the campaign a basic framework of the strengths and weaknesses of the candidate and the opponents. Research can point the candidate to actions that need to be taken: issue areas that have to be addressed or concrete action that needs to be taken, such as offering a high-visibility amendment.

Next, research findings are used in the preparation of focus group scripts and survey questions. Research might show that an opponent has taken positions on eight or ten issues that differ from those of the incumbent, or that an incumbent has a potentially damaging, checkered personal life. These findings may then be tested in focus groups and later in polls to determine their saliency with voters.

Research findings are important for message development. By pinpointing achievements of an incumbent or by highlighting the weaknesses and omissions of the opponent, researchers can help the campaign team develop powerful campaign themes and messages.

Research is also helpful in the preparation of direct mail and political action committee literature, checking sources, developing themes, and providing relevant quotations, newspaper headlines, votes, and other sources to give the literature further weight and credibility.

Research is key for the fact checking of media advertising. To have the utmost in credibility, a campaign advertisement—especially an attack ad—must be grounded solidly in fact. Especially since 1988, news sources have started independently investigating the claims made in television and radio advertising. To increase credibility and visibility, campaigns often preview commercials with journalists. Part of the preview might be a ten- to twenty-page analysis of every single aspect of the advertisement. For example, an attack on a legislator's voting record on a certain issue will include the actual votes, the bills, the newspaper clippings on the stories, and the probable impact on the voters of the state.

Another important use of research, especially later in the campaign, is in debate preparation. Here, issues and analyses are boiled down to their essences. The research team will have prepared the debate fact book containing the anticipated twenty or thirty most difficult questions, the best responses (in fifteen-, thirty-, and sixty-second sound bite answers), the probable attack lines and positions of the opponent, and the records of the candidate and opponent.

Finally, research is vital in the day-to-day charge and countercharge of the campaign. As the rapid-response scenario indicates, an attack must be countered within a matter of hours or minutes, arguments and facts assembled and ready to do battle at a moment's notice.

The Limits and Boundaries of Research

Bare-knuckle, nasty research flourishes at nearly every level of professionally run campaigns. Private investigator Michael Hershman has seen it all: "I've had plenty of people say to me, 'Hey, I want as much dirt as you can get. Is the guy cheating on his wife? Is he doing drugs? Does he gamble? Does he like little boys?' The whole gamut. They want a no-holds-barred investigation."[25] Hershman won't go down this road, but others will.

Why would professional researchers and campaign consultants descend into the gutter of personal vilification? Professional campaign strategists are highly pragmatic; if a tactic works, use it, if it is ineffective, scrap it. Negative campaign research will continue as a weapon of choice simply because it works. Yet there are limits; it cannot reach out farther than the public will tolerate or believe. Unfortunately, the cynical and suspecting public will tolerate just about anything. Many in the public presume that all politicians are crooks and all politicians lie, and many more have no interest in politics or are woefully unfamiliar with basic issues. This leaves campaigns with a clean canvas on which to paint their own picture and their own version of reality. Campaigns and candidates desperate to win are willing to push tolerance and credibility to their limits. Research now probes further into personal and private relationships, delving into areas once considered off limits.

Throughout American history, presidential campaigns have been full of mudslinging and personal invective.[26] Character attacks were particularly vicious in the days before television. Opponents tried to smear Thomas Jefferson, accusing him of being a deist and of having a sexual liaison with his slave Sally Hemmings; Lincoln was portrayed as an illiterate backwoods baboon; Grover Cleveland was criticized for having an illegitimate child; Theodore Roosevelt was accused of being a drug addict; and Warren G. Harding was chastised for fathering an illegitimate child and having a mistress in the White House.

The new medium of television initially may actually have forced campaigns to clean up their acts. Television came into the American home in the early 1950s, but it did not intrude.[27] It came in gently and it fostered a sense of middle-class normalcy and wholesomeness. The rough edges of society were not exposed, television comics practiced self-censorship, and, in sit-coms, dad worked, mom took care of the kids, and they slept in separate beds. Not anymore. Today's television comics routinely offer up "the politician is an idiot" jokes. Campaign commercials think nothing of besmirching a candidate's reputation; amateur videos posted online are part of the Wild West of political commentary, where just about anything goes.

Presidential elections in the 1950s through the mid-1960s generally were relatively free of personal or character-related attacks.[28] There were whispers of Kennedy's womanizing and rumblings about Johnson's wheeler-dealer financial dealings, but few blatant personal attacks on the candidates. However, Watergate, the Vietnam War, and Chappaquiddick changed everything.[29] The public lost confidence in Washington and its elected leaders, the press became much more vigilant, suspicious, and aggressive, and campaigns started taking off the gloves. Political research provided the ammunition.

In the 1976 election, the Ford campaign hired a freelance researcher to check into allegations of extramarital affairs by Jimmy Carter.[30] Revelations of Gary Hart's long-suspected extramarital dalliances broke through to the public in 1984—through Hart's own doing as well as through the reporting of the *Miami Herald.* The pointed and inflammatory political ads that shocked many voters in the 1988 presidential campaign had their roots in earlier senatorial, gubernatorial, and congressional races in the 1980s, in which sharp-elbowed research and media campaigns had stretched the tolerance level of voters.

During the 1980s and early 1990s, the Republican party developed superior campaign research capabilities. Hungry for victory and goaded on by their second-party status, Republican leaders raised and invested enormous sums of money in all facets of party development. Especially over the past twenty years, Republicans have devoted more money, talent, and resources to candidate and opposition research than have Democrats, who have been playing a difficult game of catch-up.

In 1988, the Republican opposition research team, with over a hundred staffers and volunteers, worked around the clock in three shifts with a budget of $1.2 million to examine the life and career of Michael Dukakis.[31] Republicans mounted an even more sophisticated $6 million opposition research effort in 1992 against Bill Clinton'[32] As the *Newsweek* election reporting team observed, Lee Atwater, during his brief leadership of the Republican National Committee (RNC), built the RNC headquarters into a "state-of-the-art (opposition research) war machine."[33] The RNC opposition research's data storage and retrieval technology "was perhaps the flashiest in American politics."[34] The object of the research was much less Bill Clinton, governor of Arkansas, than Bill Clinton, flawed public servant. The Republican research team went directly for Clinton's alleged extramarital affairs and his draft record.

At the same time, the Clinton campaign paid private investigator Jack Palladino more than $100,000 in 1992 to probe into allegations and rumors of Clinton's womanizing. Some two dozen women were targets of Palladino's damage-control inquiries.[35]

The Republican opposition research efforts in 1992 demonstrate both the possibilities and limitations of political research. The Bush–Quayle research team dispatched operatives to Little Rock, where it collected thirty file drawers of state papers, bought microfilms of the Little Rock and Pine Bluff newspapers for the past twenty years, and subscribed to every daily and weekly newspaper. Friendly academics obtained hundreds of hours of Clinton from C-SPAN on the pretext that they needed the videotapes for scholarly research.[36]

However, the extensive probing into Clinton's personal life and character had only limited value to the Bush–Quayle campaign. First, if Bill Clinton was vulnerable, so was George Bush. The Bush–Quayle opposition research team had amassed large files on Clinton's "waffles, straddles, ducks, dodges, and fibs." But Clinton gained immunity from charges of waffling because if voters remembered anything at all about George Bush, it was his "read my lips" pronouncement and his subsequent reneging. "Clinton is a pathological liar," a Bush–Quayle staffer said. "Unfortunately, George Bush is the only politician in America who can immunize him against that tag."[37]

Second, voters simply did not believe that the worst charges could be true. Both Bush and Clinton campaigns believed that one of the most damaging indictments against Clinton was a successful lawsuit charging that the state of Arkansas was criminally negligent in treating poor and abused children under its care. Years had elapsed before Governor Clinton did anything to clean up this problem, and it would have been easy to charge him with inept leadership. But when this issue was tested before focus groups, participants essentially dismissed the charge "as a fairy tale; it sounded too horrible to be true."[38]

Finally, voters were not particularly interested in Clinton's character flaws. The Bush campaign was desperate to find a silver bullet—that explosive charge that would turn the campaign around in the last weeks. It finally turned to Charles Black, the "last bare-knuckle brawler" left in the Bush campaign, to run his own off-the-record opposition research. "We're gonna strip the bark off the bastard," Black had been telling colleagues for months.[39] The silver bullet was going to be Clinton's draft status, his trip to Moscow as a student, and the two antiwar rallies he helped organize during his university days in England. Eventually Gary Maloney, a protégé of Lee Atwater, who was studying for his doctorate at Oxford, was called in to produce photographs of the rallies and, they hoped, discover the mother lode: a bearded, scruffy Clinton at a rally with Vietcong flags flying.[40] Nothing came of this venture, but it demonstrated how desperate the Bush campaign team had become to find anything to tarnish Clinton.[41]

The personal problems of Bill Clinton, his antiwar record, his days at Oxford, his years as governor of Arkansas—none of this seemed to matter. The critical issue in 1992 was not "trust" or "character"; voters had moved on to "change" as the key issue.[42] No amount of damaging information about Clinton's character or personal failures dug up by the Republican opposition research team was going to matter.

In 1996, the Dole campaign was experiencing a familiar sinking feeling. No matter what character faults Bill Clinton possessed, people really did not care.[43] There was plenty of character-related ammunition amassed during four years of the Clinton White House (and this was before the Monica Lewinsky scandal), but focus groups and polling results gave a different message: Clinton was doing a not-half-bad job and character did not really matter. By 1996, Americans had lowered their expectations for presidential behavior and accomplishments.[44]

Clinton pollster Mark Penn's research had led to a similar conclusion. On the matter of personal character and integrity, Bob Dole easily beat Bill Clinton. As long as Clinton wrapped himself in the public values that people believed in "voters would forgive or forget about his personal life." Mark Penn's observation—that "public values trump private character"[45]—served Clinton well, not only in 1996, but during the long, sordid scandal that culminated in an impeachment trial. In the bizarre circumstance of an impeached president delivering his State of the Union address in early 1999, Americans strongly disapproved of Clinton's personal behavior, but gave him high marks for his articulation of values and programs they held dear.

Research conducted in the heat of a campaign often brushes up against ethical boundaries and the tolerance of the voting public. In the 2000 Republican presidential primaries, George W. Bush had just lost the critical New Hampshire primary by a stunning nineteen points to fast-rising Senator John McCain. In South Carolina, the next primary battle, a desperate Bush campaign, along with the Christian right and its allies, pulled out all stops to draw blood. A professor from the fundamentalist Bob Jones University circulated an email charging that McCain "chose to sire children without marriage." Flyers by the thousands were placed under the windshields of automobiles in church parking lots and old folks homes, claiming that McCain had fathered a black child. Then came the whispering campaign and anonymous telephone calls: McCain's wife was a drug addict, McCain became mentally imbalanced from being in a Vietnamese prison so long, and he was the favorite candidate of homosexuals. None of this happened to be true, but that did not matter. McCain was defeated in South Carolina and could never recover thereafter. While the Bush campaign and Karl Rove claimed they had nothing to do with these actions, they, nonetheless, did nothing to condemn them.

In the 2005 New Jersey gubernatorial contest between Democrat Jon Corzine and Republican Doug Forrester, the Forrester campaign launched an ad challenging the character and dependability of Corzine. In the closing days of the campaign, the Forrester ad featured a comment made by Corzine's bitter ex-wife the day before, and contrasted it to the happy, dependable relationship of the Forrester family. On a black screen, with no music and no voice-over, came this ad:

> *New York Times*, 11/2/05, *Joanne Corzine*: When I saw the campaign ad where Andrea Forrester said, "Doug has never let his family down and he won't let New Jersey down," all I could think was that Jon did let his family down, and he'll probably let New Jersey down, too.[46]

Guilt by Political Association: Guilt by association has been a well-worn theme in campaign research for decades. For example, for many years Republican Jesse Helms and Democrat Edward Kennedy were seen as the Senate's ideological polestars, and political researchers would match up their Senate candidate or opponent to see how closely they aligned with either Helms or Kennedy. Then along came Newt Gingrich as the right-wing bogeyman of the 1990s, then George W. Bush during much of the 2000s, and now senators Ted Cruz and Rand Paul are the right-wing poster boys. Taking Ted Kennedy's place have been congresswoman Nancy Pelosi, Senator Harry Reid, Barack Obama, and Hillary Clinton.

During the 1994 congressional elections, an often-repeated tactic was to portray Democratic legislators as being hand-in-glove with the then unpopular and damaged President Clinton. *Congressional Quarterly's* "Roll Call" series conveniently lists votes that have presidential support, and it is just one step farther for a campaign to charge that a freshman Democratic congressman voted 95 percent of the time with President Clinton, and is "just in Washington to do liberal Bill Clinton's bidding." Many Republican challengers wrapped the unwelcome mantle of Bill Clinton over their Democratic opponents. Vulnerable Democrats tried as hard as they could to distance themselves from the president, but many were caught in the political undertow.

The guilt-by-association tactic can play in any direction. In the 1996 presidential campaign, it was difficult at times to determine whether Jack Kemp or Newt Gingrich was Bob Dole's running mate. Democrats were delighted any time they could link the highly unpopular Gingrich with the Dole–Kemp presidential campaign, and Republican incumbents and challengers were tagged with the label "Gingrich clones." A decade later, in the 2006 campaign for the U.S. Senate in Virginia, the campaign of incumbent Republican George F. Allen, Jr. charged that opponent, James H. Webb, Jr., (and former Reagan administration official) was beholden to liberal Washington senators and was "firmly on the side of John Kerry, Ted Kennedy, and Charles Schumer." Jerry Falwell, longtime evangelical preacher and leader of the once-powerful Moral Majority, told a private audience in 2006 that nothing would more motivate conservative evangelicals than having Senator Hillary Clinton run for the presidency in 2008, not even Satan. "I hope she's the candidate. Because nothing will energize my [constituency] like Hillary Clinton ... If Lucifer ran, he wouldn't."[47] Clinton ran; however, it was not Satan who beat her but Barack Obama in the 2008 Democratic Party primaries.[48]

Half-Truths and Innuendo: Much political advertising is built on solid research but unsupportable conclusions. This is the world of half-truths and innuendo. In one striking example, Jim Courter, running for governor of New Jersey in 1989, was attacked in campaign advertising by his opponent James Florio, whose ads charged that Courter had illegally stored a hazardous environmental substance in his backyard. "Imagine," began the ad, "it's almost unbelievable—a candidate for governor with toxic waste barrels on his own property." The television ad, produced by Squier/Eskew Communications, failed to mention that the hazardous substance was actually several barrels of home heating oil stored on land owned by Courter and his brother.[49] In a state sensitive to environmental degradation, this half-truth was all the more devastating.

Presidential candidate Michael Dukakis was accused in 1988 of doing nothing when he was governor to clean up the pollution of Boston harbor. The Bush campaign hammered him for his failures, but nowhere mentioned that cleanup of the harbor was primarily a federal, not state, responsibility.

Both the Dole and Clinton campaigns engaged in half-truths. In one Dole commercial, Clinton stated: "I will not raise taxes on the middle class." Then the narrator took over. "But he gave the middle class the largest tax increase in history—higher taxes on your salary, gasoline, Social Security. Clinton even tried higher taxes on heating your home. Two hundred fifty-five proposed tax and fee increases in all ... Sorry, Mr. Clinton. Actions do speak louder than words." As media critic Howard Kurtz pointed out, the bulk of the two hundred and fifty-five proposed tax and fee hikes were levies on industries and individuals for services they use, such as dredging permits, haddock fees, and grazing fees. The ad also failed to mention that Clinton's income tax increase targeted the wealthiest 1 percent of taxpayers, and the Social Security tax hit the most affluent 13 percent.[50]

Through viral emails, talk radio, blog sites, text messaging, and through television advertising, Barack Obama was the target of an extraordinary barrage of false rumors and smears in the 2008 presidential campaign. Through television advertising, the National Rifle Association falsely charged that Obama would ban hunting rifles. Rumors spread that he was not a Christian, but a Muslim; that he was a socialist; that he "palled around" with "terrorist" William Ayers, the one-time 1960s radical; that he did not go to Harvard Law School on his own merits.

The John McCain–Sarah Palin campaign and the RNC were so inspired that they sent this robo-call (automated telephone call) to hundreds of thousands of voters:

> Hello. I'm calling for John McCain and the RNC because you need to know that Barack Obama has worked closely with domestic terrorist Bill Ayers, whose organization bombed the U.S. Capitol, the Pentagon, a judge's home, and killed Americans. And Democrats will enact an extreme leftist agenda if they take control of Washington. Barack Obama and his Democratic allies lack the judgment to lead our country. This call was paid for by McCain-Palin 2008 and the Republican National Committee, at 202-863-8500.[51]

How Personal? Floyd Brown's aggressive research tactics during the 1992 presidential campaign illustrate the seamy side of opposition research. Brown was involved in the creation of the Willie Horton commercials in 1988, in 1992, he headed the Presidential Victory Committee, an independent group that backed George Bush. A CBS News report in July 1992, filed by reporter Eric Engberg, charged that Floyd Brown aggressively tried to substantiate a story that a woman named Susan Coleman had an affair fifteen years earlier with her then law professor, Bill Clinton, and had committed suicide when the romance ended. The CBS report stated that the Coleman family maintained there was no truth to the story and that reporters who had investigated it found that an anonymous and false letter was sent to news organizations. Despite all this, Brown hired private detectives to try to substantiate the story and hounded the Coleman family with unwanted telephone calls and visits. The sister of the suicide victim said on the CBS interview: "To think that they have a right to just foster this type of grief on a family and then dredge up something like this." CBS correspondent Engberg said on the air: "When we confronted Floyd Brown, he asserted a special right to track down sleaze and use it to blackmail candidates."[52]

Brown clearly and flagrantly crossed the ethical line of valid, fair, and public research. President Bush had earlier insisted that Brown not air a television ad that raised questions about Clinton's character and invited viewers to call an 800 number to listen to alleged conversations between Clinton and Gennifer Flowers, a woman who claimed to have had an affair with Clinton. The Bush–Quayle campaign eventually filed a complaint with the FEC against Floyd Brown after President Bush read a transcript of the CBS interview. Press secretary Marlin Fitzwater said in announcing the complaint filed with the FEC, "as the president has said, Floyd Brown's activities are despicable and have no place in the American political system."[53] The late-filed complaint, of course, did nothing to change the tone of the presidential debate, but did give the Bush campaign momentary cover. Floyd Brown, unbowed, became chairman of Citizens United, a conservative organization that claims 150,000 members, had his own talk show in Seattle, and appeared frequently on television as a political commentator.[54]

What's Fair? What will the public tolerate when it comes to opposition research, attack ads, and "gotcha" politics? Voters have been exposed to raw, visceral attack commercials based on campaign research. Sometimes the ads work, many times they fail. Voters are not fools and understand when campaign commercials have crossed the line of fairness. One recent study of Virginia citizens concluded that voters are "savvy enough to make assessments about the fairness" of campaign charges and "will punish" candidates whom they consider to be most unfair.[55] Researchers from the Sorensen Institute for Political Leadership at the University of Virginia found that the voters surveyed considered "fair" the charges that criticize opponents for talking one way and voting another, or for the opponent's voting record or business practices, or for taking money from special interests. The voters surveyed felt that charges were "unfair" when they deal with past extramarital affairs, past personal troubles with drugs or alcohol, the personal lives of the opponent's party leaders, or the behavior of family members.[56]

Drawing the Line

In the heat of the battle, campaigns are tempted to use whatever damaging material might be available to them. But certain lines should be drawn, for both practical and ethical reasons. On a purely practical point, no research should be conducted on an opponent that can come back to embarrass the other campaign. Hiring a detective agency to dig up dirt on a candidate's high-school or college years, badgering friends and neighbors of the candidate for titillating information, publicizing a campaign hotline that asks people to spread gossip and innuendo—all of this can easily backfire. Apart from their ethical shortcomings, such actions announce to the world that a campaign is willing to look under any rock against its opponent.

A campaign should not give to the press or some other third party material that it is not willing to defend and make public itself. If a campaign has damaging evidence against an opponent and is convinced that this material is relevant to the character or actions of that opponent and that the public should know about it, then the campaign has the obligation to make that information known itself, not use a third party as a cover.

As an ethical matter, evidence against an opponent should be relevant to the office, particularly if it borders on questions of character and personal life.[57] Perhaps more as a tactical point than an ethical one, the Clinton–Gore reelection campaign charged Senator Bob Dole with having an extramarital affair some thirty years ago. To the credit of the *Washington Post*, which had confirmed Dole's extramarital relations, it did not make those details front-page news. The executive editor of the *Post*, Leonard Downie, Jr., explained the newspaper's decision: "After completion of our reporting and extensive discussion with senior editors and reporters, I decided that this information we had about this personal relationship twenty-eight years ago was not relevant to Robert J. Dole's current candidacy for president and did not meet our standards for the publication of information about the private lives of public officials."[58]

Along with determining whether an issue is relevant, campaign research should recognize and respect a statute of limitations on both personal and political conduct. Unless the actions that took place fifteen or thirty years ago were outrageous and beyond societal norms, they should be considered a closed book. Looking for a bearded picture of student Bill Clinton holding a Vietcong flag or wishing to make a trip to the Soviet Union should be out of bounds. Not only is it not relevant to the questions of character and qualification for the presidency, but from a political and tactical point of view probably has little significance.

In addition, carefully assembled facts should not lead to widely distorted conclusions. While campaigning often looks like a shouting match or a mud-throwing contest, research needs to be reined in and conclusions should not be drawn that cannot be supported by factual evidence. This does not mean that political researchers have to adapt the norms and disciplines of social science research, but that they must draw the line. When the evidence does not support bald conclusions, the research specialist must make that point emphatically. If the point is not made by the researcher when turning over the materials, it is almost guaranteed to be distorted even further once it is in the hands of the media advertising specialists.

Finally, and most important, innocent third parties should not be harmed. When candidates thrust themselves into the political arena, they know that their lives and careers will be put under the microscope. However, the privacy and reputations of innocent spouses, ex-spouses, children, colleagues, and associates should be spared from the bruises and spotlight of harsh campaign attack ads.

It is no wonder that many decent and honorable civic-minded individuals refuse to run for elective office. They know that the moment their names surface as possible candidates, the opposition party, a potential primary opponent, or even a freelance investigator will be digging through public records, compiling information on business and personal matters, and searching vast electronic databases. In the often brutal world of modern professional campaigning, this is the inevitable price that candidates must pay.

Notes

1   From a conversation with James Carville, August 1982.

2   John Brady, *Bad Boy: The Life and Politics of Lee Atwater* (Reading, Mass.: Addison Wesley, 1997), 171.

3   Douglas Frantz, "Plenty of Dirty Jobs in Politics and a New Breed of Diggers," *New York Times*, July 6, 1999, A16.

4   Janet Buttolph Johnson and Richard A. Joslyn, *Political Science Research Methods,* 3rd ed. (Washington, D.C.: CQ Press, 1995), 41ff.

5   Cooler heads prevailed, and I was hired to be research director for a 1982 Senate campaign under the general direction of James Carville, his first major job as a campaign manager. Our candidate, Lieutenant Governor Richard J. Davis of Virginia, lost by just over two percentage points to three-term congressman Paul Trible. Over the course of the next ten years, I periodically worked as research specialist for (and against) Carville in several statewide campaigns.

6   The Chambliss attack ad can be found on *YouTube* at www.youtube.com/watch?v=tKFYpd0q9nE (accessed February 15, 2015); the Dole attack ad can be found on *YouTube* at www.youtube.com/watch?v=Gb_k9qCxhGo (accessed February 15, 2015).

7   Barbara Boxer for U.S. Senate campaign, produced by Greer, Margolis, Mitchell, Burns. Cited in "The Campaign's Dirty Dozen," 2738–9.

8   For examples of the use of staff for campaign purposes, see Larry J. Sabato and Glenn R. Simpson, *Dirty Little Secrets* (New York: Times Books, 1996), ch. 8.

9   Samuel L. Popkin, *The Reasoning Voter: Communication and Persuasion in Presidential Campaigns* (Chicago, Ill.: University of Chicago Press, 1991), 12. Popkin notes that the basic question for candidates and campaigns is: "What have you done for us lately?"

10   Conrad appeared to waver on his pledge not to run again, joking in early 1992 that he had written the pledge under the influence of a 104-degree fever. He finally kept his word, announcing his retirement in April 1992 with this explanation: "There is a tremendous air of cynicism in the country, and I do not want to contribute to it." Phil Duncan, ed., *Congressional Quarterly's Politics in America, 1994: The 103rd Congress* (Washington, D.C.: CQ Press, 1993), 1158–9.

11   Reprinted in Karen S. Johnson-Cartree and Gary A. Copeland, *Negative Political Advertising* (Hillsdale, N.J.: Lawrence Erlbaum Associates, 1991), 87.

12   See, for example, the responses of focus group participants in the analysis of the National Focus Groups Report, April 25–29, 1992, prepared by Market Strategies Inc., for the Bush-Quayle reelection campaign. Peter Goldman et al., *The Quest for the Presidency: 1992* (College Station, T.X.: Texas A&M University Press, 1994), Appendix: "The Campaign Papers," 666–75.

13   It is ironic that the biggest policy promise (and failure) that Bill Clinton made during his first administration—to create comprehensive national health care reform—never came back as an issue against him in the 1996 reelection.

14   Popkin notes that a campaign is effective only if voters see three connections: "(1) between the issue and the office, (2) between the issue and the candidate, and (3) between the issue and the benefits they care about." Popkin, *The Reasoning Voter*, 100.

15 The "Mike DeWine for Senate" ad was produced by Stevens Reed Curcio & Potholm, and debuted on July 14, 2006. *National Journal* "Ad Spotlight," www.nationaljournal.com.

16 The ad was produced by Brabender Cox and first appeared on September 15, 2006.

17 Members of Congress, until the late 1980s, were able to collect honoraria up to the amount of 30 percent of their salary for speaking engagements and appearances.

18 Being very meticulous, one congressional staffer listed all magazine subscriptions received by a member's office in the quarterly report required by the clerk of the House of Representatives. Listed for all to see, and for the opponent's campaign to pounce upon, was a subscription to *Playboy* magazine.

19 Terry Cooper, "Negative Image," *Campaigns and Elections,* September 1991, 18.

20 Brady, *Bad Boy,* 171–2.

21 Mark Shields, "GOP Chastity Belt," *Washington Post*, January 13, 1999, A23.

22 Insights Corporate Selection Systems, Inc., a company that specializes in background checks, preemployment surveys, and substance abuse issues, offers several online services: lists of bankruptcies, federal, state, and county tax liens, and judgments; bankruptcy filings; real estate transfers and ownership; business and professional licenses; municipal court rulings, felony or misdemeanor cases; business ownership; and other state and federal databases. CBD Infotech provides financial information on individuals; Auto Track finds current and previous addresses, connecting people to cars and property, bankruptcy records, and professional licenses. See David Samuels, "The White House Shamus," *New York Times Magazine*, August 2, 1998, 38ff.

23 See Sabato and Simpson, *Dirty Little Secrets,* 174–7, for examples of unwarranted and illegal uses of credit records against candidates and their families.

24 Rebecca Fairley Raney, "For Speculators, a Potential Gold Mine," *New York Times*, January 2, 1999, A7.

25 Hershman states that he does not accept this kind of work, primarily because of ethical concerns, but also for financial reasons—campaigns just do not have enough money to pay for investigatory research. "Semi-Private Dicks," *Capital Style*, September 1998, 13.

26 Even before presidential campaigns, the fight to ratify the Constitution in 1787–88 showed that negative attacks were prevalent. See William Riker, "Why Negative Campaigning Is Rational: The Rhetoric of the Ratification Campaign of 1787–1788" (paper delivered at the annual meeting of the American Political Science Association, Atlanta, August 1989), cited in Darrell M. West, *Air Wars: Television Advertising in Election Campaigns, 1952–1992* (Washington, D.C.: Congressional Quarterly, 1993), 47 n. 39. See also Johnson-Cartree and Copeland, *Negative Political Advertising,* 4–7; Kathleen Hall Jamieson, *Dirty Politics: Deception, Distraction, Democracy* (New York: Oxford University Press, 1992); and Victor Kamber, *Poison Politics: Are Negative Campaigns Destroying Democracy?* (New York: Insight Books, 1997).

27 Edwin Diamond and Stephen Bates, *The Spot: The Rise of Political Advertising on Television,* 3rd ed. (Cambridge, Mass.: MIT Press, 1992), 379.

28 West, *Air Wars,* 45–51.

29 I owe this observation to my colleague Michael B. Cornfield; see also Larry J. Sabato, *Feeding Frenzy* (New York: Free Press, 1991).

30 Martin Schram, *Running for President 1976: The Carter Campaign* (New York: Stein and Day, 1977), 326–7. On the history of campaign ads in presidential elections, see Kathleen Hall Jamieson, *Packaging the Presidency,* 2nd ed. (New York: Oxford University Press, 1992); Diamond and Bates, *The Spot*; Darrell M. West, *Air Wars*; and Myron A. Levine, *Presidential Campaigns and Elections: Issues, Images, and Partisanship,* 2nd. ed. (Itasca, Ill.: F.E. Peacock, 1992).

31 The effort was led by James Pinkerton and Don Todd, director of opposition research at the Republican National Committee.

32 John F. Persinos, "Gotcha! Why Opposition Research Is Becoming More Important and How It Is Changing Campaigns," *Campaigns and Elections*, August 1994, 20. The Perot campaign in 1992 reportedly spent more than $1 million in opposition research. According to research consultant Kevin Spillane, "that amount doesn't include the top-secret money he spent on private investigators to look into his own people. We'll never know the true extent of his oppo research expenditures."

33 Goldman et al., *The Quest far the Presidency,* 525. The RNC research unit was run by David Tell through 1991. Tell then moved on to the Bush-Quayle campaign in a similar role of opposition research director.

34 Ibid.

35 See Lorraine Adams, "The Script of Scandal," *Washington Post Magazine*, August 9, 1998, 12; and Michael Isikoff, *Uncovering Clinton: A Reporter's Story* (New York: Crown, 1999), 32–3.

36 Goldman et al., *The Quest for the Presidency*, 526.

37 Ibid.

38 Ibid.

39 Ibid.

40 Ibid., 528ff.

41 Goldman et al. note that the Bush campaign, desperate to find anything on Clinton, continued searching nearly to the end of the campaign. Whitewater looked like a "dry hole," and the focus was on sex and the draft. The sleuthing is illustrated in the "Case of the Preacher's Daughter" (an elusive young black woman who claimed to have had sex with Clinton) and the "Case of the Gun-Shy Marine" (the Marine colonel who allegedly heard Bill Clinton say, while at Oxford, that he had decided to renounce his U.S. citizenship and move to Sweden). When this quest for a "doomsday weapon" ended in failure, the Bush campaign had to return to their more conventional charges against Clinton's character. *The Quest for the Presidency*, 588–91.

42 I owe this observation to my colleague Don Walter.

43 Samuels, "The White House Shamus," 38.

44 Evan Thomas et al., *Back from the Dead: How Clinton Survived the Republican Revolution* (New York: Atlantic Monthly Press, 1997), 110.

45   Ibid., 88.

46   National Journal AdWatch, 2005 Political Ads: New Jersey Governor. The Forrester ad was produced by Stevens, Reed, Curcio & Potholm.

47   Peter Wallsten, "Falwell Says Hillary Better Motivation Than Satan," *Washington Post*, September 24, 2006, A13.

48   See Dennis W. Johnson, "An Election Like No Other," in *Campaigning for President 2008: Strategy and Tactics, New Voices and New Techniques*, ed. Dennis W. Johnson (New York: Routledge, 2009), 14–15.

49   Phil Galey, "Campaigning Turns Downright Dirty with Innuendo and Rumors," *St. Petersburg Times*, November 2, 1989. Not to be outdone, Courter, within days of the Florio attack, aired an ad of "dubious veracity" implying that Florio was linked to organized crime through union contributions. See David Broder, "Deep in Mud in New Jersey," *Washington Post*, October 18, 1989, A31.

50   Michael Oreskes, "'Attack' Politics, Rife in '88 Election, Comes into Its Own for Lesser Stakes," *New York Times*, October 2, 1989, A24.

51   Dennis W. Johnson, "An Election Like No Other."

52   Howard Kurtz, "Dole and Clinton Use Each Other's Words in New Ads," *Washington Post*, October 9, 1996, A20.

53   Thomas Ferraro, "Bush Files FEC Complaint against 'Willie Horton' Creator," *United Press International*, July 15, 1992.

54   Ibid.

55   Paul Freedman, William Wood, and Dale Lawton, "Do's and Don'ts of Negative Ads: What Voters Say," *Campaigns and Elections*, October/ November 1999, 25.

56   Ibid. "Fair" charges were seen as "very fair" or "somewhat fair" by 70 percent or more of those sampled; "unfair charges" were those seen as "very fair" or "somewhat fair" by less than 37 percent of the respondents.

57   Sabato, *Feeding Frenzy*, 218ff, develops guidelines for press reporting of candidates and politicians that are useful for any political researcher. Sabato argues that certain areas of private life should be shielded from publication and broadcast: nonlegal matters involving a candidate's underage children; current extramarital sexual activity "as long as it is discreet, noncompulsive, and the official's partner(s) are not connected to his or her public responsibilities and are not minors," and all past sexual activities and personal relationships occurring years ago; sexual orientation per se, "unless compulsive behavior or minors are involved"; drug or alcohol abuse when young; and internal family matters and nonfinancial relationships with relatives and nonpolitical friends.

58   Blaine Harden, "A Seething Dole Intensifies Attack," *Washington Post*, October 26, 1996, A1.

5

Testing Public Opinion

Politics without polling has become as unthinkable as aviation without radar.

—Daniel S. Greenberg, editor of *Science and Government Report*[1]

Pollsters have overused "focus groups," in which civilians are carefully, demographically selected and wantonly encouraged to whine.

—Joe Klein, Newsweek reporter and author of *Primary Colors*[2]

Pete Dawkins had everything going for him—good looks, charm, a telegenic family, and a storybook resume, as well as Heisman Trophy winner, All-American football player at West Point, Rhodes Scholar, one of the youngest generals in the army, and a successful Wall Street financier. In the 1988 New Jersey Senate election, he challenged one-term incumbent Frank Lautenberg. The national Republican Party had committed money and energy to target the New Jersey Senate seat for victory. But Dawkins had one glaring vulnerability. He was perceived as an opportunistic newcomer. He had moved to New Jersey just before announcing his candidacy, and he had been mentioned as a possible candidate for elective office in about nine other states in the few years since he had retired from the military. The Dawkins strategy was to take on this issue from the start. In his announcement speech, Dawkins, surrounded by his family, talked about his dreams and hopes for America and, with a smile and confident look, he stated, "I moved around a lot. I lived in a lot of places. But I have to tell you that throughout all those years, in all those places, I never found a single place that had as good people or as much promise as I found right here in our Garden State."

The Lautenberg campaign had a videotape of the announcement speech and the more times media consultant Carter Eskew rewound the tape, the more he was convinced something was there. Pollster Paul Maslin and general consultant James Carville agreed. New Jersey voters are a tough, cynical lot. Focus groups throughout the two New Jersey major media markets (New York and Philadelphia) were shown the clip from the Dawkins announcement speech. Paul Maslin, who conducted the focus group sessions, then asked the lunchbucket Democrats and Reagan supporters for their reactions to the Dawkins announcement tape: "He's a phony," "He's got some nerve talking about New Jersey" "Beautiful Garden State—hell, I'd get out of here if I had the chance!"[3] Citizens from New Jersey, who had spent their lives coping with pollution, mind-boggling traffic congestion, heavy tax burdens, a rising crime rate, grinding local corruption, and an ingrained inferiority complex, were not buying Pete Dawkins and his treacly homage to their native soil.

From the focus group research[4] developed one of the most controversial and inventive campaign ads of the 1988 season. The barrage of campaign ads did not start until Labor Day weekend, mostly because of the enormous expense of buying ads in the largest (New York) and fourth largest (Philadelphia) television markets in the country. Carter Eskew's first ad far the Lautenberg campaign was a direct attack on the credibility and motives of Dawkins. With a still frame of Dawkins smiling in the background, a voice-over asked, "Why did Pete Dawkins move to New Jersey last year? Because he likes us so much?" Then twenty-one seconds of Pete Dawkins, smile on his face, uttering the words from his announcement speech: "I moved around a lot. I lived in a lot of places. But I have to tell you that throughout all those years, in all those places, I never found a single place that had as good people or as much promise as I found right here in our Garden State." The screen went totally black for two seconds, then the voice-over intoned scornfully: "Come on, Pete, be real."

This totally unorthodox first ad never mentioned Senator Frank Lautenberg and gave his opponent thirty seconds of free air time. But it devastatingly drove home the point: Dawkins came across as an opportunist and a phony. The rest of the campaign featured nasty attack ad countering even nastier attack ad. Only in the last week, with Dawkins out of funds, was the Lautenberg campaign able to field its effective positive accomplishment ads. Republican George Bush and Democrat Frank Lautenberg both won handily in New Jersey. On election day, fewer than half of the eligible New Jersey voters participated, a turnout that political scientist Clifford Zukin blamed on a "very serious dysfunctional cynicism about politics."[5]

Professionally run campaign focus groups were just coming of age in the late 1980s, and the Lautenberg campaign took advantage of this form of qualitative analysis to test the opponent's credibility and motivations. The New Jersey voters gave the campaign strategists the ammunition needed to launch their controversial ad campaign.

Polling and Campaigns

In the private business sector, public opinion research is a multi-billion-dollar enterprise, where increasingly sophisticated techniques determine what the public thinks, wants, fears, and desires. Businesses use survey research, focus groups, and other forms of qualitative and quantitative analysis to determine customer satisfaction and product acceptability. Consumer testing tells us what colors and shapes are most appealing, what slogan has the greatest believability, and which beer "tastes great" and is "less filling." Survey research will tell a company to use the word "kids" in its ads instead of "children" because kids is a warmer, friendlier word. Dial-meter research tells us that one candidate for a local television anchor position has more credibility and warmth than another, which TV soap opera cast member should be killed off, and how movies should end so as to attract the biggest audiences.

Many of the same opinion research techniques are used in campaigning, policy formation, and governing. Tracking polls told the Clinton White House that Attorney General Janet Reno would be a credible voice after the Branch Davidian disaster in 1993, and later told Clinton policymakers that most Americans would support bombing Iraq.[6] The Clinton White House made focus group and public opinion testing a major factor in every public pronouncement and decision. Clinton "polls as often as he breathes," observed political consultant Dick Morris.[7] Every State of the Union

speech, every presidential address, and every major campaign announcement was pretested, topics were emphasized or disregarded, words and
phrases were stressed or avoided, depending upon what the public wanted
to hear. Polls and focus groups concluded that Clinton's affair with Monica
Lewinsky was a private matter; when it was finally time to address the
nation, six times in a four-minute speech, Bill Clinton uttered the resonating word "private". Undoubtedly, polls and focus groups told the White
House that the public did not want the president to talk about the
Lewinsky affair during his 1999 State of the Union speech. While
Republicans stewed, Clinton, in his natural element, never mentioned
Monica and spoke at length about just what was on peoples' minds. In poll
after poll, a significant majority of citizens said that the president addressed
the important concerns of the nation in his speech. Indeed he did, thanks
to the White House's exacting attention to what the public wanted to hear.

George W. Bush repeatedly pledged during the 2000 presidential campaign that his administration would be different: "I really don't care what
polls and focus groups say. What I care about is doing what I think is
right," he said. There would be no in-house pollster like Patrick Caddell
(Carter), Robert Teeter (Nixon, Ford, Bush I), Richard Wirthlin (Reagan),
Stanley Greenberg (Clinton) or Mark Penn (Clinton). But, George W. Bush,
like all presidents in modern history, did hire pollsters and has been a
frequent user of private public opinion polls and focus group analysis; he
is just not as open about it. Bush's principal pollster is the very low-keyed
Jan van Lohuizen, while Fred Steeper runs his focus group research. When
Bush unveiled his plan to privatize Social Security in February 2002, he
chose his words very carefully. He did not talk about "Social" Security, but
about "retirement" security. In his speech, the president emphasized
"choice" (three times), "opportunity" (nine times), and "savings" (eighteen
times). Focus groups and survey research had told the researchers that
certain words and ideas resonated positively with the public, and others
were to avoided at all costs.[8]

Barack Obama also relied on his senior campaign pollster, Joel Benenson.
Working through the Democratic National Committee, Benenson supplied
the White House with polling data, giving the president and his senior
advisers a sense of what the public would support, and helping the White
House tailor its message more effectively. David Binder, a pollster who also
worked on the Obama presidential campaigns, provided the White House
with vital information emerging from focus group sessions.

More than ever before, public opinion testing is key to nearly every facet of campaigning and office holding. In an era when many voters say that politicians are out of touch with the American people, candidates and officeholders increasingly rely on the weathervane of public opinion to point to the mood of the public, adjust to its nuances, and use the public as a sounding board for campaign and policy themes. Veteran Democratic pollster William R. Hamilton described polling as the "central nervous system" of modern political campaigns.[9]

In earlier years of professional consulting, the campaign manager or general consultant would bring in a pollster and the media consultant, with each working more or less separately on his or her own specialties. But in the past thirty years, survey research has moved to center stage, and the pollster, media consultant, and campaign manager now form the strategic core of the campaign.

Private campaign survey research varies widely, depending upon the competitiveness of the race, the funds available, whether or not there is a primary opponent, the size of the electorate, the demography of the voting population, and the overall dynamics of the campaign. In addition to private polling, which is usually paid for directly by the campaign or the political party, there may be other polls conducted throughout the campaign, including those conducted by the news media and universities. Presidential campaigns take polling to a whole new order of magnitude, both in the private polls conducted by the campaigns and in the enormous variety of independent trend polls, debate reaction surveys, tracking polls, and, ultimately, exit polls.

A well-financed statewide campaign would conduct its own private public opinion studies at various stages of the campaign. Some of these might include:

- *Focus Group Analysis*: These studies are conducted in each of the state's major media markets perhaps twelve to fourteen months before the election. Assuming that the state has three major media markets, there will be four or five focus group sessions for each market. Each focus group will have eight to twelve participants. Focus group analysis together with candidate and opposition research provides basic information used in creating the benchmark survey.
- *Benchmark Survey*: This first poll taken by the campaign gives a detailed analysis of the strengths and weaknesses, opportunities and dangers of

the campaign ahead. The benchmark survey might be taken ten to twelve months before the election, with five hundred to twelve hundred voters participating.

- *Focus Group Analysis After the Benchmark*: Small group analysis, with eight to twelve participants in several focus groups, explores in greater depth the responses given in the benchmark survey.
- *Trend Surveys*: Taken perhaps four or five months after the benchmark poll, when there has been movement or change in the campaign, such as commercials run by the opponent, trend surveys have roughly the same size of sample, five hundred to twelve hundred voters, but there are fewer questions asked than in a benchmark poll.
- *Dial-Meter Analysis*: Used to test-market candidate (and hypothetical opponent) commercials before they are aired; thirty to forty participants might be involved in each dial meter session.
- *Tracking Polls*: In the last few weeks of the campaign, tracking polls are taken to determine late trends and movements of public preference. A rolling average of four hundred voters is used, with one hundred added each night and one hundred dropped from previous nights.

Presidential candidates for the major parties use all of these tools. So, too, do multi-million-dollar campaigns, such as a growing number of Senate, gubernatorial, and ballot issue contests. Other campaigns, such as a typical congressional contest with a million-dollar budget, might be lucky to have a benchmark poll, one trend survey, and perhaps limited tracking polls.

The benchmark or baseline poll is the first survey taken by a candidate for office, and serves as the basic tool for campaign planning and strategy. Democratic pollster Mark Mellman and his colleagues note that polling "is at its best when it is testing the relative merit of competing ideas, hypotheses, and theories."[10] The key feature is that the benchmark is a projective exercise; it introduces both positive and negative information about the candidate. The benchmark poll gives information on the candidate's name recognition, electoral strength, and voter evaluation.[11] The survey results are used to decide whether a candidate should run or to test the vulnerability of an incumbent or the strength of other candidates. Benchmark polls help determine whether the campaign should target a different set of voters, adjust the basic campaign message, develop different press events, or adjust its spending of resources.[12] Benchmark surveys are often preceded by a series of focus group interviews to help determine the questions that go into the benchmark or baseline survey.[13] Candidate and opposition research also yields critical information for survey questions. Nearly all benchmark polls are conducted by telephone and with a fairly large sample (five hundred to twelve hundred for a statewide race, four hundred to five hundred for congressional districts) asking ninety to one hundred questions.[14] A typical benchmark poll lasts fifteen to eighteen minutes, with some running twenty-two to twenty-four minutes. With longer benchmark surveys, pollsters run the risk of losing respondents, who might be tempted to hang up before the questions are completed. For smaller races, a benchmark poll of twelve minutes and correspondingly fewer questions might be what a client can afford.[15]

Timing of the benchmark poll is an important judgment call. If it is conducted too soon, the public may not have any interest in the campaign and have very low recognition level of the candidates. If held too late, candidates may miss important public trends, use faulty assumptions to begin their campaigns, and start out on the wrong foot without benefit of solid survey research information.

The end product of the survey is the analysis, together with the raw data in cross-tabulation tables. Here, the pollster explains the candidate's strengths and weaknesses, how he or she compares with the opposition, and what is on the minds of voters. The best of benchmark poll analysis requires perception and insight so that the data come alive. The benchmark analysis must accurately reflect the data, but above all, the data, and thus the survey analysis, are valid only when exacting social science survey research methodology is carefully employed.

During the middle of the campaign, the pollster will use trend surveys, shortened versions of the benchmark poll, to evaluate the twists and turns of a campaign to see if the candidate or the opponent's message is getting through, to determine what has changed since the benchmark survey, to test new issues, and, generally, whenever there has been a change in the dynamics of the race. A trend survey usually has the same sample size as a benchmark poll, but the number of questions asked is fewer, in the twenty-five to thirty-five range.[16]

Tracking polls were devised in the early 1970s to determine voter trends and preferences in the last crucial weeks of the primary or general election. During those weeks, campaigns kick into high gear. Voters are bombarded with campaign advertising, nightly television news features clips of candidates as they go from event to event, and voters start paying some

attention to the elections. Through tracking polls, a campaign can determine if its advertising is working or if the opponents' ads are having any
impact. By the late 1970s, a new technique, rolling averages, was introduced separately by V. Lance Tarrance and William Hamilton. During four
consecutive evenings, one hundred voters are interviewed. The four
hundred total responses are then analyzed. On the fifth night, another one
hundred voters are interviewed and the first night's one hundred responses
are replaced. Then on the sixth night, another one hundred voters are
interviewed, and the second day's responses are dropped. In this way, a
reliable sample of four hundred persons would yield results that could be
tracked from day to day.[17]

With sophisticated telephone and survey technology, polling data collected
at 10:00 p.m. one night can be analyzed and delivered to the campaign the
next morning. With overnight information, a campaign can make quick
decisions on advertising and on where to spend precious last-minute dollars
and in which markets, and can determine which ads, especially negative ads,
are working. Tracking is so important to the Tarrance Group's work that this
Republican polling firm stays open twenty-four hours a day for the last six
weeks of the campaign cycle. It may be conducting tracking polls for up to
one hundred clients. Tracking ends at 11:00 p.m. and written reports are
available to clients the next day at 7:00 a.m.[18]

A variant of the tracking poll, but not involving continuous polling, is
the "brushfire" poll. Republican pollster Gary Ferguson described the
survey, used principally in congressional or other nonstatewide races—three
hundred interviews over two nights, then seven to ten days later another
survey, then a week later, another three hundred interviews.[19]

In a typical statewide race, and certainly in presidential races, news
organizations and national polling firms also conduct surveys. News organizations conduct trial heat surveys that typically ask: "If the election were
held today, who would you vote for?" Pollsters conduct cross-sectional
surveys in which a sample of adults (or likely voters) is asked about the
candidates or issues; another poll is taken some time later, asking another
sample, of equal size, the same questions. Cross-sectional surveys have the
advantage of telling what overall changes have occurred in preference, but
do not explain what internal changes may have occurred from one survey
to another.[20] Panel surveys, which feature interviews of the same individuals, are also used by news organizations and national polling firms to
determine how the dynamics of the election have impacted voter attitudes.

Tracking polls have become especially important in presidential contests. While tracking polls have been used in earlier presidential races, the Democratic polling firm Lake Research Partners and the Republican firm the Tarrance Group have been instrumental in developing nationwide tracking polls through their "Battleground" series, conducting nightly tracking of public opinion from September 1 through November 1. Finally, election-day exit polls are conducted at carefully selected voting precincts to determine how voters actually voted, what influenced them, and other election-day issues that the media wish to explore.[21]

Polling technology has advanced dramatically in the past two decades. At one time, polls were conducted with pencils and paper, with interviewers filling in answer grids and later punch cards; detailed reports were written and the results given back to the client several weeks after the survey. It was also standard practice to administer polls in the field through personal interviews and the survey results might not be known for two weeks. Nearly all interviews are now conducted by telephone, taking advantage of the enormous changes in telecommunications and computer technology—low-cost, long-distance charges, speed dialing, random digit dialing, and computer-assisted telephone interviewing (CATI). With a CATI system, interviewers sit before a video terminal and feed answers into the computer as the respondent is giving them. In the earlier days of CATI, and before the revolution in personal computers, expensive mainframe computers were required to handle the number crunching. Today, however, personal computers easily do the job; CATI systems are more sophisticated, better able to handle large quantities of data, and cost far less to operate.[22] Further, random digit dialing has been replaced in the last decade by clustered random sampling from voter registration files. Now, instead of just calling any number, campaigns can focus on persons who have actually voted in previous elections.

Several of the major polling firms do not conduct their own interviewing, but leave it to professional phone bank firms. The subcontracting to phone bank firms is done primarily as a cost factor; a sophisticated phone operation may mean a capital investment easily over a million dollars and a considerable personnel overhead in trained interviewers. By using an outside phone bank, noted Democratic pollster Kirk Brown, his firm can conduct surveys for clients at the right time, not having to schedule surveys around the times available for an in-house operation.[23] An outside phone bank company is useful because it puts a further screen between the candidate and those being surveyed, providing another filter against survey bias.[24] It is not unusual for telephones to ring in homes in Colorado, the respondents answering questions read to them by interviewers in Kentucky, who are working from scripts prepared by a polling firm based in Washington.

Bill Hamilton has noted several related trends in polling. First is the adaptation of a technique used in market research of testing television spots by having one hundred or so people watch a rerun program on an independent station, with the campaign commercial and other commercials inserted in the program. The ads are viewed in a natural setting, at home, the way voters see ads, woven into commercial breaks. A second trend is the testing of radio spots or audio tracks from television commercials during a telephone interview. Another trend is the use of a new kind of sampling, before moving into the tracking phase, that asks a very small number of questions to a very large population. This has the advantage of quickly determining the reactions from a much broader number of participants and participant subgroups, so that media messages can be targeted with nearly pinpoint accuracy.[25]

A variation of this technique is marketed as a "bullet" poll. These polls are generated solely by computer, and will have a sound similar to automated voice mail systems. The person answering the telephone is given a short recorded message (*In the election for governor in 2016, there are two candidates, William Smith, the Republican, and Alice Jones, the Democrat*). Then, the person answering the telephone is asked to choose (*Press 1 if you are for William Smith; press 2 if you are for Alice Jones*). This kind of poll is truly bullet-like in its speed; answers can be tabulated and reported within hours. Further, bullet polls are relatively cheap; automation replaces humans sitting at terminals asking questions. The major problem with bullet polls, however, is the inability to control who answers the telephone when it rings. Bullet polls may ask if a person is registered to vote or if a person is of voting age. But, without human judgment in the screening process, there is no way of telling if children are screened out, if too many women or too few elderly people answer the telephone, or other problems.

The Problem with Numbers

Polling is seductive. Any poll will generate answers. Those answers can always be turned into numbers and look very scientific. Add a decimal point and it looks like real, hard science.

Mark Mellman and colleagues[26]

Of all the skills in the field of political consulting, survey research stands nearly alone in demanding adherence to well-developed social science methodology. Errors can arise in three major areas of public opinion surveys—in sampling error, when the sample selected is not representative of a relevant population; in measurement error, when questions are poorly designed or badly arranged; and in specification error, when a theory is inappropriate for the opinion that the poll is trying to measure.[27] Social scientists Henry A. Brady and Gary R. Orren see the latter two, measurement and specification errors, as the most serious and fundamental problems. If errors do occur in these areas, the validity of the entire poll can be affected.[28]

Is public opinion being sampled? Social scientist Russell Neuman observes that mass public opinion is stratified along a sophisticated continuum.[29] On most issues, the great majority of citizens are uninformed and inattentive. He sees three separate publics. First, the bottom stratum, roughly 20 percent, who do not monitor politics and are unlikely to be mobilized to political action, even to vote. Second is the attentive and active 5 percent, who for political matters may be only a fraction of 1 percent of the entire population. Most people fall into the third stratum, the half-attentive vast middle. Their responses represent "quasi-attitudes"—somewhere between an attitude and a nonattitude. Neuman sees citizen responses as a "mixture of carefully thought out, stable opinions, half-hearted opinions, misunderstandings, and purely random responses."[30]

When a busy parent, trying to finish the dinner dishes before tucking in the kids, picks up the telephone, the last thing on her mind might be whether the Republican plan for immigration reform is good for the country or whether the administration's policy toward Iran is working. Daniel Greenberg observes that what pollsters are collecting under such circumstances are "intellectually undigested responses to issues of the moment, which is quite different from deliberately arrived at opinion."[31]

At one time, it was almost a unique experience to be asked for an opinion by a stranger over the telephone. Now it is just one more annoyance in the frazzled lives of busy people. Just as junk mail floods peoples' mailboxes, junk phone calls pester people during the evening. This presents the

pollster with two fundamental problems: individuals will refuse to participate in a poll or, more frustrating, will become impatient and hang up
before the interview is complete.

Republican pollster Ed Goeas has noted that the refusal rate closely
parallels how people feel about government. When citizens are fairly
content with government, the refusal rate goes down; when irritated and
exasperated, the refusal rate goes up.[32] Today, citizens are beyond annoyed
and irritated. Kirk Brown sees refusals and terminations as a "tremendous
problem," particularly in urban areas of California, New York, and New
Jersey. One estimate is that the national refusal rate is around 72 percent,
and in New York City and southern California, it jumps to nine out of ten
persons contacted refusing to participate.[33] Given the surly mood of many
citizens, it becomes very difficult to complete a twenty-minute telephone
poll. This puts pressure on the pollster to devise poll questions that are
neither too long nor too complicated, that are interesting and sound
unbiased while still fitting the requirements of a legitimate survey, and to
find a representative sample willing to respond. Answering machines add
another layer of disconnectedness between the surveyor and the respondent.

Another major concern of pollsters is the fact that two out of every three
Americans use a cell phone and cell phones are steadily replacing landlines.
This is particularly true for young, single, and childless voters. In addition,
pollsters worry about the quality of cell phone interviews. The person being
interviewed could be anywhere—in a crowded coffee shop, on a bus, stuck
in traffic, in a noisy restaurant. Who could be candid, give thoughtful
answers, and be able to concentrate when a pollster calls them under those
conditions? There is also a problem of geography. It used to be simple: call
persons who live in a particular area code. But so many people, particularly
college students, will live in one part of the country and have their cell
phone number reflecting their home state. Further, calling someone on a
cell phone can cost four to five times more than a landline call. The reason?
Federal law prohibits automatic dialing of cell phones; they must be dialed
manually, and that adds to the cost of the survey. There is also the concern
that young voters, who are the most heavily invested in cell phones, might
be under-represented when polling is done just through landlines. Pollsters
are trying to adjust to these realities of cell phone usage and figure out how
to accurately and efficiently reach all segments of the voting population.

Even slight nuances in the way questions are posed can lead to major
changes in the public's response. Questions must be clear, with no

overlapping alternatives and no false premises; they cannot pose two or more questions in one; and questions cannot be emotionally charged, embarrassing, overly technical, or leading to a particular answer.[34] Further, questions must permit alternative answers, such as "don't know," or "stay the same." Pollster Albert Cantril argues that well-conducted interviews have a "pace and rhythm; they possess a beginning, middle, and end; they evolve as a rapport is established between respondent and interviewer." In this context, question order can be an important consideration, and questions may have to be rotated to remove the impact of one question upon a succeeding one.

Do individuals lie to pollsters? Sometimes they do, and pollsters try to make adjustments by modifying the question order and using variations of the same question to screen out inconsistencies or false statements. Sometimes these adjustments simply do not work, especially when sensitive or controversial subjects are considered. For example, a poll taken just days before the 1990 Louisiana Senate primary showed that 22 to 28 percent of the voters preferred white-supremacist David Duke; he ended up with 44 percent of the vote.[35] Assuming that the poll was an accurate reflection of the Louisiana voting population, many individuals were either not telling the truth to the interviewers or had an unusual last-minute change of mind.

Sampling errors cannot account for some of the discrepancies found, particularly in elections in which race could be an issue. In 1989, three African Americans were elected to prominent positions—David Dinkins, mayor of New York City, Norman B. Rice, mayor of Seattle, and Douglas Wilder, governor of Virginia. In each election, the three winners barely won, but the late tracking polls and exit polls showed them with substantial leads of at least ten percentage points. There is considerable evidence that whites who state they are undecided in a black–white election end up voting overwhelmingly for the white candidate. In New York and Virginia, a major black candidate would draw in a new set of voters, many of whom have not been previously identified. In exit polls, Wilder and Dinkins voters were more enthusiastic than their rivals, turning out earlier in the day to vote, which led to early numbers showing both candidates comfortably ahead. When it came to Barack Obama and the 2008 presidential election, the Bradley effect did not apply. There was no evident pattern that people would tell pollsters they would vote for an African American for president, but then fail to support him in the voting booth. "The unambiguous answers is that there was no Bradley effect," concluded Mark Blumenthal, editor of Pollster.com.[36]

Polling is an inexact science and results can vary widely. For example, on the eve of the 1992 presidential election, national polls were showing quite different results. Two weeks before the election, a *Wall Street Journal*–ABC poll reported a nineteen percentage point Clinton lead, while other surveys were showing Clinton leads of about half that size. One week before the election, the Gallup poll conducted for CNN and *USA Today* had a Clinton lead of just two points, while at least four national polls had Clinton leads of between seven and eleven points. George Bush, who earlier urged voters to ignore those "nutty" polls, pointed to the convenient Gallup poll as evidence that Clinton's lead was collapsing.[37] The uncertainty and volatility of the 1992 race led pundits to call it a "pollercoaster." At the same time, the Tarrance Group and Lake Research were claiming unparalleled accuracy with their Battleground '92 nationwide tracking polls.[38]

One of the biggest problems, wrote Richard Morin, was trying to determine who really would vote. Some people do not tell the truth about their voting intentions and young people typically have a lower voting rate than other adults. Pollsters use questions to screen out the probable nonvoter, but this is far more of an art than a science. MTV and the "Rock the Vote" campaign targeted young people, urging them to vote. Pollsters could only guess what the impact of these efforts would be on young voters, who were more attracted to Obama than to Romney. Turnout is even more difficult to predict in midterm elections and primaries, when it is historically lower.

Another difficulty was the steady but persistent buildup for Ross Perot and the erosion of support for both Clinton and Bush. In the Battleground '92 tracking survey, Perot started with just 3 percent favoring him in the first week of the tracking (September 6). Over the next seven weeks, Perot gained steadily, ending with 19 percent of the vote.[39] The popularity of Ross Perot represents an anomaly in American politics. Political scientist Raymond Wolfinger noted that Perot represented neither the model of a standard-bearer of a sectarian party nor a major political figure who had been disappointed by his party.[40]

Veteran political observer Charles Cook notes the wide discrepancies in polls during the late summer and early fall of the 1996 presidential campaign. He writes that private polls conducted on behalf of candidates and parties are "by definition, biased and unreliable" in the view of many observers. Polls taken by newspapers or university-sponsored polls should be more impartial and reliable, but "some of the shoddiest, most superficial polls" are often commissioned by local news organizations that pay a fraction of the going cost for such a poll, often conducted by "fly-by-night" firms. Cook observes that university-based surveys sometimes suffer because of the lack of adequate supervision over student-run polls. What troubles Cook most are the erratic numbers released by reputable firms. Polls can come from anywhere and, during the election season, they are far more numerous than at any other time. Attentive voters must be their own best editors, exercising a healthy skepticism about polling results and taking the findings with a grain of salt.

Cook's advice was certainly needed during the final days of the 2012 presidential election. Conservative pundits, mostly on Fox News and talk shows, were convinced that Romney would win, even win handily. Their own internal polling was telling them that, and wishful thinking was helping propel them into public declarations of the certain defeat of Barack Obama. Nate Silver, one-time professional gambler and developer of sophisticated statistical analyses for baseball, in 2012 was working for the *New York Times*, and through his aggregating of data from private and public polls, had accurately predicted the outcome of forty-nine out of the fifty states results. Throughout the general election, he was telling readers that Obama would win, but he was roundly criticized and even ridiculed by conservative pundits.[41]

Pseudo-Polls: The term "pseudo-polls" refers to the growing phenomenon of public opinion surveys that are devoid of methodological safeguards.[42] Newspaper columnists, talk-show hosts, television shows like *American Idol,* and a growing number of candidates are asking readers or viewers to mail in a sample ballot, call an 800 or 900 number, post responses on an Internet site, through text messaging, or Twitter. The results are sometimes enthusiastically announced as public opinion, but in no way do such "polls" accurately measure the public at large.

Increasingly, 800 and 900 numbers are used by the media to get a sense of the pulse of the American people. But 800 and 900 number polls are wholly unrepresentative; they are nothing more than the comments of people who care enough to respond. Unless this fact is explained deliberately and often, viewers or readers develop the false sense that the results actually reflect reality. The media do a fairly poor job of reporting legitimate, scientific polls,[43] and there is little to suggest that they will vigilantly point out the unreliability of pseudo-polls.

One example of press vigilance and good reporting clearly reveals how pseudo polling, left unchecked, can distort reality. Long before he became a television celebrity, *USA Today* asked its readers in June 1990 if Donald Trump symbolized what was right or wrong with the United States. Eighty-one percent of the 6,406 people who called an 800 number said that Trump was great and 19 percent said he was bad for the country. But there was an organized effort to fix the numbers. It turned out that 72 percent of the telephone calls came from two phone numbers.[44] Had this fact not been reported, readers would never have known that these results were cooked.

Online Polling: It was inevitable that the Internet and online polling would come to political campaigns. One of the first was conducted in early 1996 in the 26th congressional district of New York. Online viewers were able to examine the issue positions of Representative Maurice Hinchey and his two challengers and then cast their preferences online. By the end of the 1996 cycle, online polling had become commonplace, much of it done by news organizations and some by political campaigns. One study found fifty-seven political website polls operating that year, many of them simply "horse race" polls and some oriented toward policy issues; most, however, were nothing more than junk polls, permitting people to cast preferences more than once and lacking any safeguards for random sampling.[45]

For critics of online polling, the biggest problem concerns the inability to obtain random sampling. If all citizens were wired, the problems of sampling would be mitigated; but all citizens are not, and in all probability many may never have access to the Internet or email. For some time to come, there will be some 30 percent of the U.S. population who do not have online access or capabilities, especially the elderly, poor, and those with modest levels of formal education. Resolving the issues of online sampling presents some of the most important obstacles to using the Web for serious political survey research. Political scientist Alan J. Rosenblatt argues that sampling online is faced with many problems unique to the Internet and that such sampling can be a "nightmare filled with ghosts and avatars."[46] Among the problems is the seemingly simple collection of email addresses. Email lists are proprietary information, some available to the public and others not; there is a multiplicity of email addresses, with no standard format, and there is no central directory of such addresses.

Some polling firms are undeterred by the obstacles of using online survey research. Harris Interactive, Polimetrix, Knowledge Networks, Global Marketing Insite, and others, have carved out online polling niches for corporate and nonprofit clients. Some have ventured into politics and have achieved demonstrable successes. In 2000, the Harris Interactive poll did better than most traditional telephone polls in predicting the presidential outcome. During the 2003 gubernatorial recall in California, Knowledge Networks, a firm that specializes in corporate, nonprofit, and academic clients, conducted online polls that accurately showed that the recall would easily pass and that Arnold Schwarzenegger would readily defeat governor Gray Davis. In the 2004 presidential campaign, Zogby Interactive accurately predicted the results, concluding that Bush would defeat Kerry by 50 percent to 49 percent, while the actual percentage was 51 percent to 48 percent.[47] John Zogby is an enthusiastic backer of online polling, including campaign polling, and has compiled a database of several hundred thousand voters, encompassing all demographic variables. He draws upon this vast pool along with traditional telephone interviews. But private pollsters are by and large still leery of relying on online poll results. The primary concern is that only 70 percent of the adult population is online, and one of the key voting groups, the elderly, could readily be overlooked in such polls. Many private pollsters see traditional telephone polling, despite its inherent problems of refusal rates, fairly high expenses, and inability to reach cell phone users, as the far more accurate measurement of public opinion.

Online polling is bound, however, to make inroads. It is cheaper and faster than telephone polling, larger pools of individuals can be reached in a shorter period of time, the turnaround is quicker, video and audio files can be appended to the online poll, and the problem of large refusal rates is resolved by permitting respondents to answer at their pace and time schedule. With passage of time, the next generation's elderly will be thoroughly comfortable using the many platforms of online communication.

Growing Use of Focus Groups

For decades, focus group research has been used in the commercial marketplace, testing and measuring consumer preferences for services and products.[48] Inevitably, political campaigns caught on, and by the mid-1980s, focus group research became commonplace in major elections.[49] Focus groups are now standard research tools in nearly every statewide race and were used heavily in recent presidential campaigns. Focus groups, and their electronic cousins, dial-meter groups, reveal much about attitudes, fears, and preferences of small groups of carefully selected individuals, but very little about public opinion at large. They are tempting substitutes for the real thing: scientifically based survey research.

The focus group is a structured conversation. Eight to twelve individuals, carefully chosen to fit a targeted demographic or political cluster, are asked both general and specific questions by a moderator adept at bringing out participants' responses through open-ended questions and associational techniques. Under ideal circumstances, focus groups are held in each of the competitive media markets in a statewide race, with four or five different sessions per market. Focus group sessions are held in special market research rooms, commonly found on the upper floors of shopping malls that have one-way mirrors and audio- and videotape capabilities. Often, focus groups are segregated by gender or by race; typically, a woman will moderate an all-female group or an African American will moderate an all-black group. Pollster Stanley Greenberg observed that the key to an effective focus group is homogeneity of the participants: "The more homogeneity, the more revealing" the answers.[50] Homogeneity appears to allow for a freer conversation without the added constraints of race, sex, party preference, or class that might come with a more diverse group.

Small-group participation and dynamics are important features of focus groups. But no matter how carefully the participants are chosen, inevitably some individuals will present problems. Social scientist Richard Krueger identified several: the self-appointed expert, the know-it-all who thinks he knows everything about politics; the dominant talker, who cannot keep quiet; the shy participant, who has nothing to contribute; and the rambler, who cannot get to the point and drifts off on irrelevant tangents.[51] Veteran Republican focus group moderator Brian Tringali found another problem type—the Oprah Winfrey participant, who deviates from the conversation to bring in personal problems, wanting to share them with the group.[52]

Potential problems are generally spotted in the reception room before participants assemble in the focus group session. For example, participants who are C-SPAN junkies may be screened out because they probably fit into the self-appointed expert category. Also screened out are strong partisans, or, especially late in a campaign, individuals who have definitely made up their minds. Once inside, the moderator must be able to control the flow of conversation, quieting those who tend to dominate and opening up those who say little. Pollster Kirk Brown sees the know-it-all as the biggest problem. While this individual is often clearly wrong about a set of facts, other focus group members have a strong tendency to believe him or her rather than the moderator, particularly when the moderator tries to correct factually wrong information. The moderator, Brown observed, has a difficult, if not impossible, task of changing a clearly factually wrong view.[53]

The focus group moderator works from a carefully prepared script, drawing out responses from participants in a variety of ways. Brian Tringali follows a general format when probing responses from focus group participants. First, ground rules are established. At the outset, participants are told what is expected of them, that everyone's views are important, that the session is confidential, and that it is being video- and audiotaped. Next, the environment is established. Participants introduce themselves and tell a little about their families and where they work. Questions then move on to more contextual concerns. In their everyday lives, what are they worried about, what are their big concerns in life? The third stage tests levels of political and issue awareness. Open-ended questions are asked about politics and public issues, probing levels of general knowledge about office-holders and issues. The fourth stage tests image information. Participants might be shown a campaign advertisement or a news clip of some relevant event and asked to discuss it. The fifth stage probes the participants' appraisals of the job performance of the incumbent or challenger.

The sixth stage seeks more specific and directed information. For example, the moderator might hold up a newspaper article or comment on something in the news, then get the participants to fill in the details and get reactions.

Finally, there is a set of what-if scenarios, presenting participants with a variety of hypotheticals that fit into the overall message and campaign strategies of the candidates. Throughout the focus group sessions, which generally last up to two hours, the moderator must remember that the goal is not to educate the focus group participants, but to discover their opinions, attitudes, biases, and viewpoints.[54]

Focus group research can be highly useful to a campaign, especially as a means of unearthing new information. When a policy or campaign issue first appears or emerges in a different context, it is often tested in a focus group before being addressed in a benchmark poll. For example, when immigration reform and the war on terrorism became important issues, pollsters needed first to determine what voters knew and understood, and what language should be used later in the survey research questions. Focus group research helps determine what citizens know, what they comprehend, and the language that will fit their understanding. Focus group research is also very useful when analyzing attitudes in states or regions that have high growth rates, such as Florida, where many new voters have arrived since the last election cycle and where there is no reliable current history on voter demographics and preferences.[55]

Focus group research adds a human dimension that cannot be matched by traditional survey research methods. Participants are recorded and their reactions are carefully observed and measured. Their answers to open-ended questions can give campaign researchers valuable information; participants are free to express themselves, to complain, and to vent their anger. The moderator can also guide participants through several sets of facts, situations, or scenarios to understand how opinion is molded and changed.

One well-known example of this was the focus group research conducted in Paramus, New Jersey, during the early stages of the 1988 presidential campaign. The Bush campaign's decision to go on the offensive with a blistering attack against Michael Dukakis came over Memorial Day weekend when the results of several focus groups were analyzed and the videotapes shown to George Bush. There was urgency in the Bush camp: a just-published Gallup poll showed that Michael Dukakis was 16 points ahead.[56] The Bush campaign conducted focus groups around the country in areas considered to be hotly contested; one such area was northern New Jersey. In Paramus, two sessions were held with conservative Democrats who had supported Reagan in 1984, but were leaning toward Dukakis in 1988. The moderator asked questions about Dukakis: What do you think of Dukakis if he opposed capital punishment? If he vetoed legislation as governor that would allow teachers to lead schoolchildren in the pledge of allegiance? If he permitted murderers to have weekend passes from prison?

The reactions were strong and fierce. According to Bush campaign pollster Fred Steeper, "majorities favoring [Dukakis] became majorities opposing him, he was fingered as a liberal." When approached one at a time, each of the negatives about Dukakis could be rationalized away by the focus group participants, but the cumulative effect was devastating. "It took all four or five [issues]," said Steeper, "you could literally see the tearing, the ripping going on."[57] Whatever positive attributes people had identified in Dukakis soon turned to anger and resentment.[58] "I realized right there that we had the wherewithal to win ... and that the sky was the limit on Dukakis' negatives," campaign manager Lee Atwater concluded.[59]

Bush was shown the videotapes of the Paramus focus groups and given a choice by Atwater—attack Dukakis now or attack him later. Bush chose now, and one of the ugliest presidential media campaigns was soon under way. Such dirty work, however, is usually left to surrogates, not presidential candidates. "We knew that if we left [the attack against Dukakis] to surrogates, it wouldn't have the impact," Atwater said. "Plus, Bush didn't have an image of personal meanness, so we knew he would be credible."[60]

Focus group participants are often asked to comment on certain words or phrases in candidate speeches and potential wording of referendum ballots, and as a pretest for policy statements. In preparing for the 1994 fall congressional elections, Representative Newt Gingrich and House Republican leaders launched their ten-point "Contract with America" with an announcement on the Capitol steps and a nationwide advertisement in *TV Guide.* The carefully prepared and worded contract was to set the agenda for the new session of Congress and became even more important when the Republicans captured the House of Representatives. House Minority Whip Newt Gingrich, representatives Dick Armey of Texas, Bill Paxon of New York, Robert Walker of Pennsylvania, Tom DeLay of Texas, and other Republicans, had earlier in 1994 come up with the idea of a ten-point legislative agenda that an overwhelming majority of Republican incumbents and challengers would sign onto and that could be brought to the House floor within one hundred days.

In order to craft the succinct Republican message and legislative agenda, Representative DeLay consulted with more than a hundred business groups concerned with regulatory relief. In addition, all House Republican incumbents and challengers were given an eight-page questionnaire with sixty-seven specific items to be tested.[61]

Republican pollster Ed Goeas conducted three focus groups, showing participants eight television ads that had been prepared. "The one thing that jumped out was that voters were looking for a mechanism to hold elected officials more accountable," Goeas said. "The most important thing about the contract is the accountability of signing a pledge."[62] Words and phrases were tested in the focus groups conducted by Goeas and later by pollster Frank Luntz. In fact, the "contract" in "Contract with America" came from observations of focus group participants. The term "empowerment" was scrapped because participants did not understand it, replaced with the phrase "individual choice". The term "citizen legislator" was used to explain the concept of term limits, and even the word "Republican" was avoided because of negative reaction from focus group participants.[63]

Increasingly, focus groups serve as prescreeners for campaign commercials. Before a multi-million-dollar television buy, a campaign may want to test the reaction of focus group viewers. Polling pioneer George Gallup first used the instant reaction meter technique in the 1940s to learn what an audience felt while watching motion pictures, and later Gallup used a device called the Hopkins Televote machine to monitor public response to the 1960 Kennedy–Nixon presidential debates.[64] Campaigns now pretest commercials using electronic and standard focus groups techniques. Those commercials receiving a favorable reaction from the participants will have a better chance of being aired; those that receive merely a lukewarm reception may not see the light of day. Participants become critics—they don't like the flashy tie that Ron Paul is wearing, they don't want Ted Cruz to say bad things about his opponent, and don't like the way Hillary Clinton is being picked on by her male opponents.

Pretesting inevitably leads to friction between media consultants who use their skill and artistry to create the commercials, and pollsters armed with focus group research results. The media consultants think they have a creative, hard-hitting ad; the focus groups criticize the harsh tone of the commercials. When thirty-second spots are previewed before focus groups, particularly dial groups, and reactions are minutely observed, the creativity of the media team is immediately scrutinized. Left to the preferences of focus group participants, campaign commercials would be far more bland and would lose their critical and creative edge. Republican consultant Mike Murphy argues that focus groups "reflect a make-believe world of politics where you never say anything bad about your opponent."[65] Media consultants sometimes view this screening procedure as nothing more than ill-informed second-guessing, making television critics out of focus group participants and diluting their craft.

Focus group analysis can provide a campaign with information that is overlooked or misread by the campaign team. For example, in a Senate race several cycles ago, the consultants for the Democratic incumbent thought they had a winning issue. The Republican challenger opposed a hike in the minimum wage. In this heavily industrial, unionized state, reasoned the consultants, Democrats will go crazy when they hear this. Yet the consultants were cautious enough to pretest the minimum wage issue with the focus group. The participants, blue-collar Democrats, were told that the

Republican candidate did not support a hike in the federal minimum wage. There was no outcry, really no visible reaction—certainly not the visceral and heated response the consultants were expecting. In focus group after focus group, the reaction was the same: Who cares? So what? Two focus group participants best summed up the reaction: "Look, everybody in my family and my friends are all working and have got decent jobs." Another said: "My neighbor's kid works down at McDonald's, and they're paying two bucks an hour more than minimum. Who cares?" Minimum wage, typically a bread-and-butter Democratic issue, had no salience with these blue-collar Democrats—they were doing just fine, and their friends were doing okay, too. Minimum wage went no farther as an issue in the campaign; it never made it to the benchmark poll because the issue fell flat on its face in the focus groups.

The order for focus groups and benchmark polls can be reversed. With survey research conducted first, focus group analysis can later explain and amplify survey findings. Republican pollster Whit Ayres often uses this method.[66] Starting first with solid survey research findings, tested through a benchmark poll, Ayres then moves to focus group analysis for extended analysis. Ayres will hone in on focus group participants whose views represent a larger group of voters and will probe in detail interesting and unusual findings of the survey research.

Campaign focus groups hit their stride in the 1990s. Audio- and video-taped recordings provide nuance and human expression. Focus groups are fluid, the questions are often open ended, and the moderator can probe farther and deeper into areas of inquiry. Political scientists Michael X. Delli Carpini and Bruce Williams note that focus groups are valuable "in revealing the *process* of opinion formation, in providing glimpses of usually latent aspects of this process, and in demonstrating the *social* nature of public opinion."[67] Finally, focus groups are relatively inexpensive, about one-third the cost (if two are conducted in one night) of a traditional poll. Focus groups are a seductive alternative to survey research.

The biggest problem with focus group research is the temptation to extrapolate the results to the general population. These are the views of twelve focus group participants, carefully chosen, usually with the goal of some kind of demographic homogeneity. "There is no escaping the fact," observes veteran pollster Albert H. Cantril, "that a dozen individuals, no matter how carefully selected, cannot be looked to as a microcosm of a larger population."[68] This is a reality that faces pollsters and candidates who may mistake compatible focus group results with public opinion reality. When thirty-four participants in three focus groups think your candidate is a pretty decent fellow, this information may be comforting, but it is no sure reflection of what the rest of the public may be thinking. The media faces similar problems. When focus group findings are controversial and newsworthy, or fit into the larger story being prepared, it is tempting to report the findings, failing to mention that this is not a true representation of public opinion.

Long-time Republican operative Roger Ailes, at the end of his consulting career, caustically denounced the increased reliance on focus groups. A focus group, he said, "is five professionals in a room who say, 'We don't know what to do, so let's get twenty amateurs to tell us what to do'."[69]

A frustrated Mike Murphy, Republican media consultant who resigned from the 1996 Dole campaign with less than two months to go before the election, wrote in the conservative magazine the *Weekly Standard* a blistering memo to Bob Dole called "How to Win." His first piece of advice was to "stop all the useless polling and focus groups. Dole for President has polled and focus-grouped its way to disaster. Any poll taken today will give the same toxic advice—be more like Clinton. Worse, polls and focus groups are behind the really numbskull ideas like 'mention the Internet in your big debate close.' You deserve better."[70]

Electronic Focus Groups and Mall Testing

Another tool in the qualitative research arsenal is the electronic focus group, variously called dial meters, instant-reaction meters, or people-meter groups. Electronic focus groups take research to another plane of response, testing fears, beliefs, and prejudices, and charting them on a computer printout. Saturday night television variety shows back in the 1950s used "applause meters" to measure audience approval of the talent on stage; the louder and longer the applause, the farther the needle jumped to the right on the audiometer. Now, campaigns do a more sophisticated version with "perception analyzers" (hand-held dial meters), and computers graphing the information, showing spikes of approval or flat lines of disinterest and boredom. The results tell campaigns early on what parts of a candidate's "appearance, delivery, phraseology, or message turns voters towards or against a candidate."[71] Electronic focus groups, which first appeared in the 1976 presidential election, are now a standard feature in virtually every presidential and statewide race, and are moving broadly into ballot initiatives and other races.

The participants in electronic focus groups are carefully selected to meet certain demographic and political criteria. For example, they might all be suburbanites in a swing area of the state who had voted for Barack Obama in 2012, but were now disenchanted with the Democratic Party. The group size is typically much bigger than a focus group, perhaps thirty, fifty, or even a hundred participants.

The electronic-focus group participants often sit in an auditorium, watch videotapes or television, and critique what they see. Each participant is given a dial meter, or "perception analyzer," a simple hand-held device with a dial that can be moved left to right, from 0 to 100. Each dial meter is hooked up to a computer that graphs the responses of the participants. The measurement is very crude, but effective. If a participant agrees whole-heartedly with what is said on the television screen, he moves the dial toward 100; with total disagreement, he moves the dial down to zero.

Participants respond to the words and phrases of a speech and the computer displays their collective reactions. Several test sites can be linked together through a central computer, recording the reactions of participants in, for example, Seattle, Dallas, Denver, Buffalo, and Atlanta. A presidential campaign can find out instantaneously, from dial meter test sites through-out the country, which phrases are resonating with voters and which are falling flat.

Electronic focus group analysis can go much farther than standard focus group research by instantaneously measuring reaction to words and phrases. It is far less subtle, far cruder—yes or no, up or down—analysis, but it has the virtue of instantaneous reaction. In one example, the Bush I reelection campaign used electronic focus groups to test-market campaign themes. President Bush's State of the Union speech in January 1992 marked the unofficial kickoff of the presidential campaign season.[72] The campaign themes and messages were far from developed, Patrick Buchanan was embarrassing the president in early primary states, and Democratic challengers were watching eagerly to see what George Bush would say. The Bush campaign assembled an electronic focus group of about thirty voters from the Chicago suburbs who had voted for Bush in 1988, but were undecided in early 1992.

Elizabeth Kolbert noted that, for the first forty minutes of the speech, the dial meters barely moved, not even when the president intoned that "the Cold War didn't end, it was won," or "I know we're in hard times, but I know something else—this will not stand!" or when Bush promised to "get more good American jobs within our own hemisphere through the North American Free Trade Agreement." Bush aides observing the Chicago electronic focus group were distressed. The participants were just not impressed or moved by anything Bush was saying.

Not until the last few minutes did the needles finally leap with approval. When Bush said, "This government is too big and spends too much," the dial needles jumped to an average of 94. The campaign was finally onto something. The very next day, the campaign filmed a new commercial for use in New Hampshire. President Bush, in the Oval Office, outlined his economic plan. "My plan will work without big government spending," he said, looking directly into the camera.[73] Bush had found his words, and they were repeated over and over during the campaign.

In early 1996, the Dole campaign had already done some focus groups and polling, and now wanted to refine Dole's announcement speech by testing it with small groups armed with dial meters. The groups sat for hours listening to different versions of Dole in drafts of his announcement speech and segments from other speeches he had made throughout his career. For a dial-meter group of thirty participants in Atlanta, Dole hit on several well-received themes. He scored 93 on welfare reform— Washington had failed and the federal government had to get out of the way and let the states run welfare programs. He scored 90 on several themes—Dole's charge that, under the Democrats, government demanded more and more authority over our lives; his pledge to pass a balanced budget; his assertion that government had become the enemy of religion; and a call for a simplified tax system and tougher drug enforcement. There it was, the Dole campaign message, wrapped up in the dial-meter high-approval zones. Bill Lacy, campaign manager, had found the Dole message and was adamant, saying, "We are not going to budge from this. You're going to have to kill me, and if you want to kill me, if you want me to leave the campaign, fine."[74]

At the 1996 Republican National Convention, campaign operatives carefully monitored the reaction of dial-meter groups. In a hideaway room below the convention floor, a bank of computers tracked immediate reactions to the speeches of Colin Powell, Nancy Reagan's tribute to her husband, Elizabeth Dole's talk-show-friendly stroll among the delegates, and Bob Dole's acceptance speech. The computers tracked the immediate reactions of participants in electronic focus groups in Atlanta and Denver. Testing was done by Dole pollster Tony Fabrizio, and participants watched the televised speeches, turning dials. Words and phrases were watched carefully to see which caught the imagination and reaction of the focus groups. What Republican opinion strategists were finding was that carefully selected swing voters were responding better to the convention proceedings than the network analysts were reporting.[75]

Despite their increased use, dial meters have several major problems. Albert H. Cantril argues that instant-reaction meters "have all of the worst drawbacks of focus groups and none of the advantages." He notes that the simple plotting of audience responses through dial meters onto a computer screen "tells little about why the audience reacts as it does. Was it the demeanor of the speaker, the content of what was said, the cutaway shot, or some other facet of the presentation?" For Cantril, the principal deficiency is that the instant poll "elevates the immediate reaction to an undeserved level of importance and implicit validity."[76]

Public Opinion at the Shopping Mall: Mall testing (or mall intercepts), a variation of focus group analysis, was used extensively by the 1996 Clinton campaign. Democratic pollster Doug Schoen, together with partner Mark Penn, had doubts about the constant use of focus groups as a mechanism for understanding voter preferences. "A year ago, we saw all the other pollsters holding focus groups, looking for problems. Our sense was that people were more satisfied than not."

Penn and Schoen set up kiosks in shopping malls in sixteen swing states. A participant approached the kiosk, was asked questions about his or her party affiliation and general views of the president. This information was then keyed into a computer. Then the participant viewed different versions of Clinton television commercials and was asked a number of follow-up questions. The whole procedure took about ten minutes, and some two hundred viewer samples could be taken in a single evening. Viewing commercials at a kiosk was similar to the way most people watch television—by themselves.[77] Mall testing is an expensive way of determining voter attitudes, and the extensive use of mall testing by the Clinton team could probably be only replicated at the national level or by candidates with very deep pockets, like 1998 California gubernatorial candidate Al Checchi.

Mall testing removed the element of small group behavior found in focus groups. The mall testers would not have to worry about the impact on the rest of the group of the dominant talker, the know-it-all, or the tendency either to whine or say nothing.

The Clinton media team of Bob Squier, Bill Knapp, and Hank Sheinkopf, produced fake—and very nasty—campaign ads and then tested Clinton response ads with mall voters. Consultant Marius Penczner used an advertising technique called animatics, video rough cuts using dummy images that could be transmitted by computer to the malls where the pollsters were testing the ads. A quick and cheap spot could be created by inserting the image they wanted to test: a scowling Dole, a forceful Clinton, happy children, kindly senior citizens. Using this method, the Clinton response ads were "tested, refined and retested until they actually left voters feeling better about the President than they had before seeing the original Dole attack."[78]

Ethical Dimensions

Political polling is an intensely competitive, pressure-packed business. The specialty is relatively easy to enter; there is often the temptation to cut corners, shave costs, and undercut the competition. There is always the pressure to win, whether it is the contract or the election. Pollsters also bring a certain degree of assuredness to the campaign. Of all the consultants, they are the ones with the numbers, the percentages, the cross tabulations. Looking back on her experience in White House strategy sessions, Reagan speechwriter Peggy Noonan observed, "In every political meeting I have ever been to, if there was a pollster there, his words carried the most weight because he is the only one with hard data, with actual numbers on actual paper."[79] But precise numbers are not the same as accurate numbers; only when methodological safeguards are carefully followed will the findings be valid. No candidate or other consultant should be expected to look over the shoulder of the pollster to assure that all steps and safeguards have been completed. There is no peer review in the heat of the campaign. "There is a huge reservoir of trust in this business," observes Republican pollster Whit Ayres. "When you say you've done the calls, you've actually done them."[80]

It does not happen often, but when data are falsified, it could lead to serious consequences. For example, in 2006, two principals of the polling firm DataUSA pled guilty to participating in a federal wire fraud conspiracy. Their firm, which had been hired by Senator Joe Lieberman, President Bush II, and Connecticut representative Rosa DeLauro, among others, falsified data and failed to complete surveys. When they were up against a deadline and had not met the demographic quotas involving race, gender, and political affiliation, they simply made the data up.[81]

A survey that contains flawed questions does a disservice to the client and is damaging to the reputation of the polling firm. If questions are faulty, or poorly worded and easily misinterpreted, the responses distort the population sample. A disturbing trend is the practice of push polling, in which anonymous telephone surveyors serve as campaign shills. Under the guise of a legitimate poll, telemarketers call voters and give them damaging or misleading information about a candidate. The tactics of push polling violate the universal rules of survey research: that questions will not mislead or direct a respondent to a certain answer, will not confuse, and will embrace scientific neutrality. They have been roundly condemned by the American Association of Political Consultants, the American Association of Public Opinion Research and other professional societies. The abuses of push polling are detailed in Chapter 7.

Another ethical problem is the overselling of public opinion research. Candidates generally understand the need for both qualitative and quantitative research; they know it is expensive but necessary for an aggressive and successful campaign. But how much polling should be done? A candidate should not be frightened into spending for more research than necessary. Like direct mail or media consultants, pollsters are competing for scarce campaign dollars, but they cannot push for more and more surveys unless justified by the dynamics of the campaign.

A related problem is promising more than can be delivered. Pollsters might promise thorough scientific methodology in conducting and analyzing survey data, but then fail to deliver. An example of this would be a firm that undercuts the competition in its fee, gets the contract, then cuts corners by not conducting the critical but expensive call-backs to achieve an accurate sampling or using telephone numbers from a phone book rather than random digit dialing. Accurate survey research demands methodological integrity and does not come cheap.

Other problems arise when consultants give clients incomplete or inaccurate data. In the heat of the battle, candidates can rely only on the measured analysis of their pollsters. It is wrong to scare clients with nothing but bad news when, in fact, the poll results show positive information as well. Even worse is to tell clients only what they want to hear, though the pressure to do so can be intense.

Finally, there is the problem of giving out information about a poll without the client's permission. The findings and analysis of a poll belong to the client who paid for it. It is wholly unethical for a pollster to give out such information without the permission of the client.

Survey research, done right, is "light years ahead of political consulting when it comes to formal standards and mechanisms for ensuring public accountability."[82] When conducted properly, survey research results can tell a candidate with considerable accuracy and objectivity what is on voters' minds. This level of social science integrity comes only through carefully developed questions, rigorous application of methodological standards and sampling techniques, and a sound analysis of results. Focus group research adds another layer of concern. Because focus group analysis is qualitative analysis, it requires solid, objective judgment, summarization, and measurement of open-ended comments. When done poorly, polling yields inaccurate results, which are often difficult to spot and do a disservice to a consultant's client and ultimately to the business of survey research.

Notes

1   Daniel S. Greenberg, "Why Voters Should Just Say No to the Plague of Political Polling," *Chicago Tribune*, October 24, 1990, 19.

2   Joe Klein, "Where the Anger Went," *Newsweek*, November 4, 1996, 33.

3   Comments of focus group participants are as recalled by the author, who was sitting in the observation room behind the participants. Maslin recalled, "People were climbing the walls. They were hooting [Dawkins] down, saying things like, 'I mean, I like New Jersey, too, but who the hell does he think he's kidding?'" Lloyd Grove, "How Experts Fueled a Race with Vitriol," *Washington Post*, January 18, 1989, A1.

4   A second set of focus groups was scheduled because Carville thought the first groups' reaction was anomalous. Correspondence with Harrison Hickman, senior partner of the Democratic polling firm that conducted the Lautenberg campaign's research, May 1, 1998.

5   Grove, "How Experts Fueled a Race with Vitriol." Zukin was polling director for Rutgers University's Eagleton Institute of Politics.

6   Paul Bedard, "Living, Dying by the Polls; Numbers Do Lie, Clinton Finds Out," *Washington Times*, April 30, 1993, A1. For a description of poll usage in the early

Clinton administration, see Elizabeth Drew, *On the Edge: The Clinton Presidency* (New York: Simon and Schuster, 1994), and Bob Woodward, *The Agenda: Inside the Clinton White House* (New York: Simon and Schuster, 1994).

7   Transcript, *60 Minutes*, CBS Television, December 13, 1998.

8   Joshua Green, "The Other War Room," *Washington Monthly*, April 2002; and Kathryn Dunn Tenpas, "Words vs. Deeds: President George W. Bush and Polling," *Brookings Review*, Summer 2003, 33–5.

9   William R. Hamilton, "Political Polling: From the Beginning to the Center," in *Campaigns and Elections: American Style*, ed. James A. Thurber and Candice J. Nelson (Boulder, Colo.: Westview, 1995), 178.

10   Mark Mellman, Edward Lazarus, Allan Rivlin, and Lisa Grove, "Benchmark Basics and Beyond," *Campaigns and Elections*, May 1991, 22 and 24.

11   Herbert Asher, *Polling and the Public*, 2d ed. (Washington, D.C.: CQ Press, 1992), 96–7; and correspondence with Kirk Brown, partner, Hickman-Brown Public Opinion Research, Washington, D.C., May 1, 1998.

12   Asher, *Polling and the Public*, 23.

13   William R. Hamilton noted that several pollsters, including himself, have developed programs using the content analysis technique on voters' responses to open-ended questions. This procedure is a substitute for early focus groups. While the pollster cannot actually view the interaction among voters, this technique has the advantage of spreading out responses across a larger constituency and is less expensive than conducting separate focus groups. Hamilton, "Political Polling," 173.

14   Hamilton, "Political Polling," 172–3.

15   Telephone interview with John Anzalone, president, Anzalone Research, Montgomery, Alabama, March 23, 1998.

16   Hamilton, "Political Polling," 174.

17   Ibid; see also Asher, *Polling and the Public*, 98–9. On the application and interpretation of tracking polls, see Bruce W. Blakeman, "Tracking Polls: How to Do Them," and Glen Bolger and Bill McInturf, "Tracking Polls: Avoiding Mistakes," both in *Campaigns and Elections*, August 1995, 25ff; and Donald P. Green and Alan Gerber, "How to Interpret Tracking Polls," *Campaigns and Elections*, August 1998, 23ff.

18   Interview with Edward A. Goeas III, president, the Tarrance Group, Alexandria, Virginia, July 19, 1995.

19   Interview with Gary Ferguson, vice president, American Viewpoint, conducted by Marco Althaus, Alexandria, Virginia, December 6, 1994.

20   See Asher, *Polling and the Public*, 96–104, for a useful synopsis of election polls.

21   The Lake–Tarrance battleground poll is now the George Washington University Battleground Poll; see Warren Mitofsky, "A Short History of Exit Polls," in *Polling and Presidential Election Coverage*, eds. Paul J. Lavrakas and Jack H. Holley (Newbury Park, Calif.: Sage, 1991), 88ff; and Kathleen A. Frankovic, "Technology and Media Polls," in *Media Polls in American Politics*, ed. Thomas E. Mann and Gary R. Orren (Washington, D.C.: Brookings Institution, 1992), 32–54.

22 On CATI technology, see Gary W. Selnow, *High-Tech Campaigns: Computer Technology in Political Communications* (Westport, Conn.: Praeger, 1994), 54–64.

23 Interview with Kirk Brown, partner, Hickman-Brown Public Opinion Research, Washington, D.C., June 13, 1995.

24 Anzalone interview.

25 Hamilton, "Political Polling," 171–7. See also Brian C. Tringali, "Three Trends to Watch in Political Polling," *Campaigns and Elections*, August 1995, 20–1.

26 Mellman et al., "Benchmark Basics and Beyond," 32. On polling and politics in general, Herbert Asher, *Polling and the Public: What Every Citizen Should Know*, 6th ed. (Washington, D.C.: CQ Press, 2004); Jeffrey M. Stonecash, *Political Polling: Strategic Information in Campaigns* (Lanham, Md.: Rowman and Littlefield, 2003); Robert M. Eisinger, *The Evolution of Presidential Polling* (New York: Cambridge University Press, 2003); and Susan Herbst, *Numbered Voices: How Opinion Polling has Shaped American Politics* (Chicago, Ill.: University of Chicago Press, 1993).

27 Henry A. Brady and Gary R. Orren, "Polling Pitfalls: Sources of Error in Public Opinion Surveys," in Mann and Orren, *Media Polls*, 58ff.

28 Albert H. Cantril, *The Opinion Connection: Polling, Politics, and the Press* (Washington, D.C.: CQ Press, 1991), 91.

29 W. Russell Neuman, *The Paradox of Mass Politics: Knowledge and Opinion in the American Electorate* (Cambridge, Mass.: Harvard University Press, 1986).

30 Ibid., 184. See also Samuel L. Popkin, *The Reasoning Voter: Communication and Persuasion in Presidential Campaigns* (Chicago, Ill.: University of Chicago Press, 1991); and John R. Zaller, *The Nature and Origins of Mass Opinion* (New York: Cambridge University Press, 1992).

31 Greenberg, "Why Voters Should Just Say No," 19.

32 Goeas interview.

33 Brown interview; J. Todd Foster, "Is Online Polling A. Representative, B. Accurate, C. Efficient, D. Don't Know Yet?" *Campaigns and Elections*, September 2006, 33.

34 Brady and Orren, "Polling Pitfalls," 71.

35 Greenberg, "Why Voters Should Just Say No."

36 Blumenthal quoted in Katherine Zernike and Dalia Sussman, "For Pollsters, The Racial Effect That Wasn't," *New York Times*, November 5, 2008. Adam Clymer, "Election Day Shows What the Opinion Polls Can't Do," *New York Times*, November 12, 1989, sec. 4, 4. See also Michael Traugott and Vincent Price, "Exit Polls in the 1989 Virginia Gubernatorial Race: Where Did They Go Wrong?" *Public Opinion Quarterly* 56 (summer 1992): 245–53; and Asher, *Polling and the Public*, 116. The tendency of polls to overestimate a black candidate's share of the vote is called the "Bradley effect:" Los Angeles mayor Tom Bradley was predicated by all published polls in California to defeat George Deukmejian for governor of California in 1982, but lost in a very close race. Cited in Brady and Orren, "Polling Pitfalls," 83.

37 Richard Morin, "On Election-Eve 'Pollercoaster,' Voter Is the Switch," *Washington Post,* October 30, 1992, A16.

38   Tarrance Group promotional literature.

39   Battleground '92 Tracking Poll in Peter Goldman et al., *The Quest for the Presidency*: 1992 (College Station, T.X.: Texas A&M Press, 1994), 733–5.

40   Raymond E. Wolfinger, "The Promising Adolescence of Surveys," in *Campaigns and Elections: American Style*, 186–90, quotation from page 190.

41   Charles E. Cook, "Political Silly Season Arrives, Bringing Wild New Polling Numbers," *Roll Call*, September 19, 1996, 8. Nate Silver and conservative punditry in Dennis W. Johnson, "The Election of 2012," in *Campaigning for President 2012: Strategy and Tactics*, ed. Dennis W. Johnson (New York: Routledge, 2013), 18–19.

42   Barry Orton, "Phony Polls: The Pollster's Nemesis," *Public Opinion* 5 (June/July 1982): 56–60.

43   See David L. Paletz, et al., "Polls in the Media: Content, Credibility, and Consequences," *Public Opinion Quarterly* 44, no. 4 (Winter 1980): 495–513; and Brady and Orren, "Polling Pitfalls," 55–94.

44   Amitai Etzioni, "Teledemocracy: Ross Perot Left the Residue of a Good Idea behind Him: The Electronic Town Meeting," *The Atlantic* 270, no. 4 (October 1992), 34, citing the reporting of Richard Morin, polling director of *Washington Post*.

45   Wei Wu and David Weaver, "On-line Democracy or On-line Demagoguery? Public Opinion 'Polls' on the Internet," *Harvard International Journal of Press/Politics* 2, no. 4 (Fall 1997): 71–86.

46   Alan J. Rosenblatt, "On-line Polling: Methodological Limitations and Implications for Electronic Democracy," *Harvard International Journal of Press/Politics* 4 (Spring 1999): 30–44, at 39.

47   Alan Wirzbicki, "Once Derided as Servants of British Tabloids and Dog-Food Marketers, Internet Pollsters Say the 2004 Election May Belong to Them," *Boston Globe*, September 5, 2005, D1.

48   See David L. Morgan, *Focus Groups as Qualitative Research* (Beverly Hills, Calif.: Sage, 1988), 11–4, for a historical perspective. See also Robert K. Merton and Patricia L. Kendall, "The Focused Interview," *American Journal of Sociology* 51 (1946): 541–57; Robert K. Merton, Marjorie Fiske, and Patricia L. Kendall, *The Focused Interview,* 2nd ed. (New York: Free Press, 1990); and Paul Lazarsfeld, *Qualitative Research: Historical and Critical Essays* (Boston: Allyn and Bacon, 1972).

49   Republicans were the first to see the possibilities of focus groups. Republican pollster Fred Steeper remembered hooking focus group participants to dial meters during the 1976 presidential debates between Jimmy Carter and Gerald Ford. President Ford made his infamous gaffe, asserting that Poland and Eastern Europe were not under Soviet domination. This clear misstatement did not even register with the dial-group participants monitored by Steeper. President Ford was not hurt in public opinion polls until the media picked up on his error and reported it widely. Dial groups, or electronic focus groups, are variants of the standard focus group and are described below. Elizabeth Kolbert, "Test-Marketing a President," *New York Times Magazine*, August 30, 1992.

50   Ibid.

51   Richard A. Krueger, *Focus Groups: A Practical Guide for Applied Research*, 2nd ed. (Thousand Oaks, Calif.: Sage, 1994), 117ff.

52   Telephone interview with Brian Tringali, senior vice president, the Tarrance Group, Arlington, Virginia, June 12, 1995.

53   Brown interview.

54   Tringali interview.

55   Brown interview.

56   Paul Taylor and David S. Broder, "Evolution of the TV Era's Nastiest Presidential Race: Bush Team Test-Marketed Negative Themes," *Washington Post*, October 28, 1988, A1. See also Jack W. Germond and Jules Witcover, *Whose Broad Stripes and Bright Stars?* (New York: Warner, 1989), 154–65.

57   Kolbert, "Test-Marketing a President."

58   Christine M. Black and Thomas Oliphant, *All by Myself: The Unmaking of a Presidential Campaign* (Chester, Conn: Globe Pequot Press, 1989), 140.

59   Taylor and Broder, "Evolution of the TV Era's Nastiest Presidential Race."

60   Ibid. The Paramus focus group has been widely noted, in Roger Simon, *Road Show: In America Anyone Can Become President, It's One of the Risks We Take* (New York: Farrar, Strauss, and Giroux, 1990), 214–17; Peter Goldman, et al., *The Quest for the Presidency: 1988* (New York: Simon and Schuster, 1989), 299–303; and Myron Levine, *Presidential Campaigns and Elections: Issues, Images, and Partisanship* (Itasca, Ill.: Peacock, 1995), 200–3.

61   Dan Balz, "GOP 'Contract' Pledges 10 Tough Acts to Follow," *Washington Post*, November 20, 1994, A1.

62   Ibid.

63   Goeas interview. Jacob Weisberg, "The Conformist: Republican Pollster Frank Luntz," *New York Magazine*, January 9, 1995, 16. Luntz was formally reprimanded by the American Association for Public Opinion Research in 1997 for refusing to disclose the wording of poll questions and other details of his surveys conducted for the 1994 "Contract with America." Luntz stated that his surveys showed that at least 60 percent of the public favored each of the elements in the Republican contract, but he refused to provide basic information about the survey results. The American Association for Public Opinion Research (AAPOR), the nation's leading professional polling association, holds that researchers must disclose, or make available for public disclosure, the wording of questions and other methodological details. Luntz, not a member of AAPOR, held that he was only protecting the confidentiality of his client. *Campaign Insider*, April 30, 1997, 1.

64   Cantril, *The Opinion Connection*, 141.

65   Quoted in Howard Kurtz, "Campaign '96—When Candidate Turns Negative, Voters May Too," *Washington Post*, October 16, 1996, A13. Kirk Brown observes that focus groups can make negative ads even more effective by pointing out their objections to ominous music, unflattering pictures of opponents, or undocumented claims. Correspondence with Kirk Brown, May 1, 1998.

66 Telephone interview with Q. Whitfield Ayres, president, Ayres and Associates, Roswell, Georgia, March 23, 1998.

67 Michael X. Delli Carpini and Bruce Williams, "The Method Is the Message," *Research in Micropolitics* 4 (1994): 57–85.

68 Cantril, *The Opinion Connection*, 140.

69 Roger Simon, "The Killer and the Candidate: How Willie Horton and George Bush Rewrote the Rules on Political Advertising," *Regardies Magazine*, October 1990, 80ff.

70 Mike Murphy, "How to Win," *Weekly Standard*, October 21, 1998, 18.

71 Richard Maullin and Christine Quirk, "Audience Response Systems," *Campaigns and Elections*, August 1995, 27.

72 Kolbert, "Test-Marketing a President.

73 Ibid.

74 Bob Woodward, *The Choice* (New York: Simon and Schuster, 1996), 158–9.

75 David Maraniss, "Image-Makers Produced Virtual Reality Convention," *Washington Post*, August 17, 1996, Al.

76 Cantril, *The Opinion Connection*, 141–2.

77 Richard Stengel and Eric Pooley, "Masters of the Message: Inside the High-Tech Machine That Set Clinton and Dole Polls Apart," *Time*, November 18, 1996, 6ff.

78 Ibid.

79 Peggy Noonan, *What I Saw at the Reagan Revolution* (New York: Random House, 1990), 249, cited in John F. Geer, *From Tea Leaves to Opinion Polls: A Theory of Democratic Leadership* (New York: Columbia University Press, 1996), 130.

80 Ayres interview.

81 Michael P. Mayko, "Polling Firm Officer Admits Faking Data," *Connecticut Online*, September 20, 2006, www.connpost.com. Darryl Hilton and Tracy Costin pled guilty; the firm is now known as Viewpoint USA.

82 Cantril, *The Opinion Connection,* 183.

6

The Media: Old and New

The year 2012 will be remembered as the year advertising dollars shattered spending records, the *Citizens United* decision fueled Super PAC advertising, the line between traditional and social media blurred, and paid communications produced fewer results than ever before.

—Consultant Evan Tracey, 2013[1]

For decades, the dominance of broadcast television has served to push grassroots participation out of politics. The Internet has brought the grassroots back.

—Chuck DeFeo of Townhall.com, 2006[2]

Campaigns have never had so many ways to communicate with the public, and never had so many challenges in reaching their audiences. Television, the prime vehicle for campaign messages, has undergone extraordinary changes in the past three decades. Networks continue to lose market share, cable television has proliferated, and new technologies, like TiVo, have created additional challenges for candidates and their appeals.[3] Further, campaigns are faced with an increasingly disinterested public; local and national television news reporting that gives little attention to campaigns and less attention to issues; pressure to mount expensive media buys to offset the loss of free media opportunities; and a television culture that highlights the sensational, turns news into tabloid fodder, and cheapens public discourse. Thrown into this mix comes the next wave of communication: online, unfettered, and transforming our whole system of communication.

The Ferocity of the Airwaves

Political consultants and reporters were amazed at the amount and ferocity of television advertising during the 1996 presidential elections. They marveled at the sixteen-month-long barrage of commercials unleashed by the Clinton reelection campaign and at the saturation of television ads by Republican candidates as they vied for their party's nomination. Clinton media consultant Bill Knapp estimated that the Republicans spent roughly $60 million, and the Republican firm National Media estimated that the Clinton–Gore and Democratic National Committee spent some $70.2 million during that same time in television spots.[4] The Clinton–Gore campaign and the Democratic National Committee bought over 93,000 television advertisements, mostly thirty-second spots, in the seventy-five largest media markets, while the Dole–Kemp campaign and Republicans purchased nearly 75,000 spots.

But 1996 paled in comparison with the 2000 and 2004 elections. In 2000, more than $840 million was spent on campaign commercials for all candidates, and, in 2004, some $620 million was spent on presidential candidates, with a total of $1.45 billion spent on behalf of all presidential, federal, state and local candidates, and ballot issues.[5]

The battle for the 2004 Democratic nomination was fiercely fought over the airwaves. During the crucial Iowa Democratic caucus, candidates Howard Dean, Richard Gephardt, and John Kerry poured millions into television advertising. Kerry's surprising victory in Iowa came about through a concerted grassroots effort, but also through a powerful television commercial that helped introduce Kerry to Iowa Democrats. The spot, "Courage," produced by media consultant Jim Margolis, portrayed Kerry as a young Vietnam veteran testifying before Congress and now as a presidential candidate.

[On screen: Senate Foreign Relations Committee, 1971; Lt. John Kerry (Ret.)]

John Kerry [testifying before the committee]: How do you ask a man to be the last man to die in Vietnam? How do you ask a man to be the last man to die for a mistake?

[Voice-over]: John Kerry. The 25-year-old swift boat commander who won three Purple Hearts and the Silver Star for bravery, then came home and helped rally the nation against that war.

Ever since, he's been on the front lines of the fights that matter. The new senator who defended a woman's right to choose...

[On screen: Sen. John Kerry, Senate Foreign Relations Committee]

... sounded the alarm on terrorism years before 9/11 ...

[On screen: cover of Kerry's book, *The New War: The Web of Crime That Threatens America's Security*]

... stopped George Bush and the oil companies from drilling in the Arctic Wildlife Refuge.

[Headline on screen: "Kerry takes on Bush over Arctic drilling"—Boston Herald, 1/23/02]

... Now he's running for president.

John Kerry: We need to get some things done in this country-affordable health care, rolling back tax cuts for the wealthy, really investing in our kids.

[On screen: John Kerry; JohnKerry.com]

John Kerry: But right now, too many in politics are afraid to take on the powerful interests, or they're like George Bush and are working hand-in-hand with them. I believe the courage of Americans can change this country.

[On screen: The courage to do what's right for America]

John Kerry: I'm John Kerry, and that's why I approve this message.

[On screen: Approved by John Kerry. Paid for by Kerry for President; JohnKerry.com]

Soon, however, Jim Margolis was brushed aside, and another veteran Democratic media consultant, Robert Shrum, became the primary creative voice for the Kerry team.[6] Communications scholar L. Patrick Devlin noted that the Kerry media team produced and played more television commercials than any other campaign in American presidential history. Altogether, there were one hundred and sixty different ads, one hundred and twenty-four of which were by the Kerry campaign, with the remaining being hybrid ads paid for by Kerry and the Democratic National Committee.[7] This was nearly twice the number of ads that the Bush campaign produced, with the Kerry strategy focusing on commercials tailored to local issues in battleground states.

The great bulk of the television commercials for both Kerry and Bush heavily targeted seventeen battleground states. Voters living in the Washington, D.C. media market probably wondered if a presidential election were going on. Washington, Chicago, Boston, Los Angeles, Houston, and New York, and many smaller media markets received less attention because the outcome for electoral votes was far more certain than in the critical battleground states.

Despite all the money spent in presidential campaigns trying to persuade voters, throughout the years, many citizens said that the commercials were not very helpful. According to one survey, in the 1992 presidential campaign, 38 percent of the voters felt that the presidential campaign commercials were helpful, while 59 percent felt that the commercials were not helpful. By contrast, in 1996 campaign, only 25 percent of the voters felt that campaign commercials were helpful, and 73 percent said they were not helpful. Dole voters were the least satisfied with the information found in campaign ads. In 2000, some 34 percent thought that there was too much mudslinging and negativity in campaign commercials, but that percentage rose dramatically in 2004, with 72 percent of voters in a survey saying there was more negativity than in past elections.[8]

If voters were disheartened by the barrage of advertising in 1996, 2000, or 2004, they would have to be astounded by what came in 2008 and 2012, and what promises to come in future presidential, congressional, and major statewide contests. In 2008, the Campaign Media Analysis Group tracked three hundred and eighty distinct television ads that were aired from early April to November 5, 2008, by the McCain and Obama campaigns. As in past presidential campaigns, some battleground markets were inundated with ads, particularly the Philadelphia, Cleveland, Denver, major Florida markets. Washington, D.C. was also a heavily advertised market because it reached into northern Virginia, which was a battleground state. But there was very little advertising in Seattle, Los Angeles, or Dallas: Washington state and California were solidly Democratic, and Texas was comfortably Republican. Why waste the television dollars trying to persuade voters? Altogether, the McCain campaign spent about $125 million on television advertising, while the Obama campaign spent $236 million.[9]

One of the unusual features of the 2008 presidential campaign was Obama's thirty-minute prime-time television commercial on the networks and leading cable outlets. No one had tried a lengthy piece like this since Ross Perot did in 1992 and 1996 when he ran as a third-party candidate. It costs the Obama campaign about $4 or $5 million, but it was seen by 33.5 million people, nearly one in five homes in the top television markets, making it the most watched political commercial in presidential history.

During the 2012 presidential election, Republicans outspent Democrats on television ads. In all, over $1 billion was spent, with Republicans spending $580 million and Democrats spending $470 million. Altogether, 474 unique presidential ads were aired, up 40 percent from 2008. Probably the one ad that stands out from the rest, which the *Los Angeles Times* and *Politico* both said was the best in the campaign, was called "47 Percent." Produced by Democratic media consultant Mark Putnam for the Obama team, this thirty-second commercial took Romney's infamous depiction of "47 percent of American people," and contrasted those words with a montage of elderly veterans and working men and women, shot in black and white, facing the camera, and definitely not smiling:

> There are 47 percent of the people who will vote for the president, no matter what, who are dependent on the government, who believe they are victims, who believe government has a responsibility to care for them, who believe they are entitled to health care, to food, to housing—you name it. And they will vote for this president no matter what. And so my job is to not worry about those people—I'll never

convince them that they should take personal responsibility and care for their lives.[10]

The 2014 midterm elections saw an extraordinary amount of television advertising, particularly aimed at Democratic incumbents, and paid for by outside interest groups. But with more ads, there is evidence that voters are just tuning them out. Political consultant John Brabender saw this in the results of focus group discussions. "Ads are having much less impact than they did a decade ago. I find this in focus groups. People are so skeptical about political ads."[11]

Issue Advocacy Ads Flooding the Airwaves: Third-party issue advocacy ads have become a weapon of choice after their widespread use in the 1996 elections. Political scientist Darrell M. West observed that "what started as a trickle of ads over the past several decades has become a torrent on almost every conceivable topic ... Once the exception more than the rule, television ads have become the latest form of political volleyball on policy issues."[12] The Annenberg Public Policy Center found that in the 1996 election cycle, issue ads were the favorite form of delivering pure attack against an opponent. Both sides were doing it, with nearly the same number of ads supporting Republicans as supporting Democrats and roughly one out of four issue ads focused on Medicare.[13]

Issue ads flourished in campaigns during the 2000s. Fueled in great part by soft money contributions during the 2000 presidential campaign, more than $500 million was spent on television and radio commercials for issue ads.[14] One rather mysterious organization, calling itself Republicans for Clean Air, attacked Senator John McCain's environmental record with a $2.5 million television blitz over a six-day period in three Republican primary states. The so-called environmental group turned out to be Texas billionaires Sam and Charles Wyly, both of whom had given hundreds of thousands of dollars to McCain's rival, George W. Bush. McCain, understandably, was outraged at not only the ferocity of the attack, but also the anonymity of the front group. This spurred McCain to introduce federal legislation requiring 527 groups to file with the IRS and to have the disclosure reports made available through the IRS website.[15]

Then following passage of the Bipartisan Campaign Reform Act in 2002, soft money was banned, and spending on issue ads by 527 advocacy groups became more prevalent. Thanks to the loophole in the IRS code, 527 nonprofit groups were permitted to spend as much money as they wanted on campaign commercials, providing a billion-dollar-plus windfall for television stations and adding an important new set of voices.

Probably the most widely remembered issue ads in the 2004 election were a series sponsored by a 527 organization, Swift Boat Veterans for Truth.[16] John Kerry emphasized his service in Vietnam, and when he mounted the Democratic National Convention podium on July 29, 2004, to accept his party's nomination, he introduced himself to the world: "I'm John Kerry, and I'm reporting for duty." There were plenty of Vietnam veterans angry with Kerry, particularly when he very publicly became the leading voice of Vietnam veterans against the war. Kerry's detractors became more upset when he won the Iowa caucus, was surrounded by admiring Vietnam vets who had served with him, and in May 2004 launched a $25 million advertising campaign emphasizing his heroism and courage.

The Swift Boat Veterans set out to present another picture of Kerry. They registered as a 527 group, but at first had little money to get their message out. Then wealthy supporters of Bush opened their wallets. Bob J. Perry, a friend of Bush and Karl Rove, contributed $4.5 million; Harold Simmons' Contrans Corporation contributed $3 million and Boone Pickens chipped in $2 million. Altogether, Swift Boat Veterans received over $17 million in donations.[17] The Swift Boaters turned to Republican media consultant Chris LaCivita for assistance and the media firm of Stevens, Reed, Curcio and Potholm of Alexandria, Virginia, which made the first ad, called "Any Questions?"

John Edwards: *If you* have any questions about what John Kerry is made of, just spend three minutes with the men who served with him.

[On screen appear, one after another, thirteen Vietnam veterans, each standing before a backdrop showing his picture when in Vietnam; each picture has his name and accompanying rank and service medals. The first is Al French.]

Al French: I served with John Kerry.

Bob Elder: I served with John Kerry.

George Elliott: John Kerry has not been honest about what happened in Vietnam.

Al French: He is lying about his record.

Louis Letson: I know John Kerry is lying about his first Purple Heart because I treated him for that injury.

Van O Dell: John Kerry lied to get his bronze star. I know, I was there, I saw what happened.

Jack Chenoweth: His account of what happened and what actually happened are the difference between night and day ...

Bob Elder: He is no war hero.

Grant Hibbard: He betrayed all his ship mates ... he lied before the Senate ...

Bob Hildreth: I served with John Kerry...

Bob Hildreth [off camera]: John Kerry cannot be trusted.

Independent media sources and Kerry supporters roundly criticized the ad, but soon it took on a life of its own. The ad was first released on August 5, 2004, during a lull period, after the Democratic convention and before the September Republican convention. The ad was placed in just three battleground states for a modest $546,000 in air time. What it received, however, thanks to its explosive message, was millions of dollars worth of free media exposure. The Swift Boat Vets went on to make six other commercials, all questioning Kerry's credibility and fitness to serve, which aired from August through mid-October.[18]

Long-time observer of presidential ad campaigns Patrick Devlin concluded that in the 2004 contest, the Kerry campaign both started and finished with positive commercials, leaving the negative advertising up to 527 groups sympathetic to Kerry. In May of that year, Moveon.org launched a $10 million anti-Bush ad campaign that ran in seventeen battleground states. One of the ads, entitled "Fire Rumsfeld," depicted a hooded Statue of Liberty, reminding viewers of the abuse of prisoners in the Iraq war. While Kerry let others rip into the president, the Bush campaign from the very beginning launched negative ads, spending over $60 million beginning in March, charging Kerry with being indecisive, soft on defense, a "flip-flopper," and unfit to run for office. The Bush media team immediately jumped on an unguarded comment made by Kerry before a veterans' organization, "I actually did vote for the $87 billion before I voted against it." Devlin argues that the Bush team ran the "most negative campaign in presidential history."[19]

While the Bush campaign advertisements were hard hitting and negative, they also presented a more consistent portrait of the president's positions, qualities, and overall image. While the Kerry media team produced many more ads than the Bush team, they were roundly criticized as being unfocused, failing to present a clear, consistent image of the candidate and his positions. Media critic Bob Garfield railed against Kerry's media team: "Not since George H. W. Bush's failed in the 1992 reelection campaign have we witnessed such fecklessness, such indecision, such flailing to define a candidate's positions, his qualities, and his overall brand image."[20]

Media consultants added one new wrinkle to their commercials in the 2004 presidential race, called "tracking" or "pre-buttal" ads. The Bush media team made the first tracking ad using Kerry's infamous line, "I actually did vote for the $87 billion ...," and showing it in cities where Kerry was scheduled to speak. The Democrats soon caught on. The Democratic National Committee produced a series of quick ads that shadowed Bush. For example, just before the president was supposed to speak in Scranton, Pennsylvania, the Democrats featured an ad that reminded Scranton viewers that Bush had promised four years earlier to bring quality health care to every senior citizen, but that now that he was running for reelection, he had failed to deliver. That same ad was reconfigured for stops in Milwaukee, Wisconsin, Cedar Rapids, Iowa, and Erie, Pennsylvania, Cleveland, Ohio, and in West Virginia. All of the spots had the same punch line: "Now Bush is back. But around here, we remember Bush's broken promises."[21] The ads probably would not win any awards for ingenuity or aesthetic appeal. They were produced in a hurry, looked fairly crude, but were placed on the air just in time.

Outside interest groups were not as active during the 2008 campaign as they were in 2004. Both John McCain and Barack Obama asked outside groups, like 527s, political action committees, and 501(c)(4) "social welfare" organizations, to refrain from adding their voices to the election debate.[22] Nonetheless, a number of third party players jumped in, including top spender Service Employees International Union (SEIU), spending over $29 million to support Obama, the National Rifle Association, nearly $7 million to defeat Obama, National Republican Trust PAC, $6.5 million to defeat Obama, and MoveOn, $5.4 million to support Obama.[23]

But 2012 was a much different story. In early 2010, the U.S. Supreme Court ruled in *Citizens United v. Federal Election Commission* that the federal government could not ban political spending by corporations in candidate elections. Barack Obama called the decision a "major victory for big oil, Wall Street banks, health insurance companies, and other powerful interests that marshal their power every day in Washington to drown out the voices of everyday Americans."[24] The floodgates were now open, Super PACs and 501(c) organizations were created and reenergized, and other outside groups took on the role of attack machines, hammering away at Obama and Romney, unleashing advertisements that the candidates themselves would dare not launch. Of all the pro-Republican ads in the campaign, just 36 percent were directly controlled by the Romney campaign; 66 percent of Democratic ads were controlled by the Obama campaign. On the Democratic side, the most active outside groups were Priorities USA Action, SEIU, and the American Federal of State, County, and Municipal Employees. On the Republican side were Restore Our Future (Romney's PAC), American Crossroads and Crossroads GPS (Karl Rove), Americans for Prosperity (Koch brothers), and American Energy Alliance (Koch brothers and others). Political scientist Lawrence Jacobs characterized the outside groups as "basically nameless, faceless assassins who come in at night to take out the opponents."[25]

Journalist Dan Balz of the *Washington Post* wrote that the "most egregious example of a campaign out of bounds" and the most dishonest campaign ad came from Priorities USA, the pro-Obama Super PAC.[26] Called "Understands," it featured a GST Steel Company employee named Joe Soptic, who had lost his job when Bain Capital, Mitt Romney's old firm, shut it down.

Joe Soptic [facing the camera]: I don't think Mitt Romney understands what he's doing by closing the plant. I don't think he realized that peoples' lives completely changed.

[Text: Mitt Romney and Bain Capital made millions for themselves and then closed this steel plant.]

Soptic: When Mitt Romney and Bain closed the plant, I lost my health care and my family lost their health care.

[Soptic explained that his wife became ill; she had terminal cancer.]

Soptic: I don't think Mitt Romney realizes what he's done to anyone and furthermore, I do not think that Mitt Romney is concerned.

This ad only appeared twice, but it caused an immediate uproar from the Romney campaign. It unfairly suggested that a working man's wife had died of cancer because of actions taken by Romney. This ad crossed the line; Obama was irritated that this third party ad had taken the focus away from the issues he was trying to emphasize.

During the 2012 campaign, the Koch brothers, Charles and David, and their network of political action committees, Super PACs and allies, had spent at least $407 million trying to defeat Obama. While their side lost, the Kochs continued to play a significant role in the 2014 midterm elections, and promised to do even more during the 2016 presidential election, vowing to spent nearly $900 million.[27]

Anatomy of a Television Commercial

Television commercials are extraordinarily important vehicles for conveying messages about candidates. Millions of dollars in television time might be committed to a particular campaign spot. While ads depend heavily on the skill and creativity of the ad team that puts them together, much more goes into the preparation of today's political commercials.

The following is a hypothetical example of a high-quality, carefully researched and developed campaign commercial for a candidate in a gubernatorial race. Approximately $2 million will eventually be spent on television advertising for this gubernatorial campaign, and the first commercial prepared is a sixty-second biographical piece.

The gubernatorial race is for an open seat, and the commercial will be for Jim Bennister, the current lieutenant governor. Bennister won the lieutenant governor's race three years ago and he received more votes than any other statewide candidate that year. Yet, Bennister is largely unknown to voters today. He has been overshadowed by the governor, has not used free media as effectively as he should have, and as a result he has relatively low name recognition.

The media team advises Bennister that the first commercial needs to be a biographical, soft piece—one that reintroduces him to voters. That decision came through a lengthy process involving research, market testing, and campaign instinct. Nine distinct phases are involved: research, buying decisions, ad concept, ad creation, testing, final production, launching the ad, airing the ad, and, finally, impact analysis.

1. Research

Information and analysis come from four sources: candidate research, focus group analysis, the benchmark survey, and targeting analysis.

Candidate Research: The research consultant has been conducting candidate research for almost four months. Lieutenant governors typically have little to do, and this state is no exception—Bennister presides over the state Senate and casts a rare tie vote when necessary. Bennister is also chairman of a commission on state homeland security and terrorism prevention. The research consultant has little to work with, but does come up with six achievements by Bennister that he thinks will become good thematic material:

- Bennister has led the fight to protect the state and its citizens against acts of terrorism and has worked closely with state and federal law enforcement officials. (Little has been accomplished, but at least Bennister can point to his leadership of this important-sounding, but relatively insignificant, committee. The consultants are anxious not to tie Bennister's work with that of the immigration and border patrol enforcement, which is getting poor ratings in recent polls.)
- He has achieved a perfect voting/attendance record while in office (this is somewhat disingenuous because the researcher has to dip back to his days as state delegate).
- He fought to roll back the taxes on personal property (also somewhat disingenuous; Bennister did this eight years ago while in the state assembly and rode this issue hard to get elected as lieutenant governor).

- He is a proven crime fighter (actually, the only "proof" is some noncontroversial votes during his assembly years and an early endorsement from the state Fraternal Order of Police).
- He promises to make public education the highest priority in his gubernatorial administration (not an accomplishment, just a promise of what he'd like to do).
- He promises to bring back decency and civility to state government.

In truth, the candidate research yields very little in the way of accomplishments, but these are the best that the research can come up with. Total cost for candidate research thus far in the campaign: $15,000.

Focus Group Analysis: The state is divided politically and culturally between the big urban media market and the four much smaller markets downstate. About three million people live in the urban media market and nearly two million live in the four smaller markets. Bennister and his consultants know that they must carry the four smaller markets handily and make a very decent showing in the urban market in order to win. Altogether there are eight focus group sessions: four in the large urban market and two each in two of the smaller markets.

Focus groups are shown video clips of Bennister, old commercials made when he was running for lieutenant governor four years ago, and the focus groups answer questions from a prepared script, which incorporates the six themes from the candidate research plus much more in open-ended and associational questions. The focus group sessions tell the campaign the following:

- Though he was the biggest vote getter in the last election, only sixteen out of eighty-four focus group participants could identify Bennister's name without prompting, just seventeen could identify his picture, and only eleven could identify both the picture and the name.
- After being told who the lieutenant governor was and shown some fairly recent television clips of his presiding over the state Senate, fifty-five out of the eighty-four participants agreed that Bennister looked like a trustworthy, decent individual. Ten more agreed when shown informal scenes at home with his wife and two teenage daughters. Those participants who were not too impressed all came from the urban media market.
- The general mood of the focus group participants was weariness with politicians and political promises, but general contentment with their

own lives. The economy has bounced back and has been relatively strong during the past several years; participants were generally pleased, but saw individual achievement and actions, not government, as the cause of the contentment. Especially in the urban media market, participants were not buying politicians promising them great things. Bennister's boast of being tough on immigration fell flat in the urban media focus groups and only mildly interested participants in the other markets.

- By far the most compelling issue was the rollback of the personal property tax. It did not matter to most that this issue was eight years old, but hardly anyone knew that Bennister had anything to do with the issue. Total cost for eight focus group sessions: $48,000.

Benchmark Survey: The benchmark poll gives the consulting team more valuable information:

- The current governor was well respected and liked, especially in the smaller media markets.
- Only 32 percent of respondents could identify Bennister; of those who could, 41 percent had a favorable view of him, 15 percent had an unfavorable view, and the remaining 42 percent had no opinion or were neutral. He was best known in his home region (a small media market) and least known in the major urban market.
- Throughout the state, the biggest issues on people's minds were the high cost of living (54 percent), high taxes (38 percent), and education for their kids (36 percent).
- Bennister was viewed most favorably by high school-educated men thirty-five to fifty years old, small-business owners, and voters in small town and rural areas.
- Total cost of benchmark poll: $31,000.

Targeting Analysis: The consulting firm conducting the targeting analysis has looked at past voting records, demographic data from census information, and other targeting data. From this information, the campaign will be able to determine, down to the city block level, those who are most likely to vote for Bennister. The targeting analysis confirms much of the benchmark findings and goes beyond the benchmark data. Bennister's strongest probable votes come from the small media markets, but there is also a significant opportunity to capture suburban voters in the state's one major media market as well. Total cost for the targeting analysis: $18,000.

2. Buying Decisions

The media firm has an in-house media buyer whose job is to buy commercial time to have maximum impact, reaching the right audience at the optimum price. The campaign consultants want maximum coverage in all the media markets, hoping to have two thousand five hundred gross ratings points of coverage. But budget constraints prohibit an ad-buy this large. The campaign makes a strategic decision, based on the benchmark and targeting analysis, to buy heavily in the major media market, hoping to pull in many of the suburban voters who could make the critical difference. The campaign will buy ads in each of the markets, concentrating its efforts mostly around the late-evening and early-evening local newscasts. They also decide to reach narrower markets by purchasing a considerable amount of advertising time on selected cable stations. Altogether, the campaign will blanket the state's five media markets with two thousand gross ratings points, averaging $745 per sixty-second spot. In all, three hundred and sixty spots will be aired. Total cost: $268,200 for the media buys, plus a 13 percent media consultant fee of $34,866.

3. Ad Concept

The biographical spot concept is developed primarily by the senior media consultant with the help of the general campaign consultant, the pollster, and the candidate. The final spot concept is a product of the research data and analysis plus the artistic skill and political judgment of the senior consultant team. The consultant team decides to put some policy content into this ad as well. The candidate, who expressed considerable interest in the project early on, particularly during the focus group phase, has basically lost interest and wants only to be shown the final product.

4. Ad Creation

The media firm has an in-house production staff and regularly subcontracts additional crew for major jobs, such as this one-day shoot, which will provide the majority of the footage used in the final sixty-second spot. The media firm hires a helicopter and a makeup artist for the shoot. The media advance team has made arrangements to film at sites throughout the state: a senior citizens center, an elementary school, a clean room in a high-tech factory, a farmer's field, and a suburban police department's shooting range, complete with squad cars. Visuals are very important.

The candidate and supporting cast are lined up to be in the shoot. Bennister is filmed with his parents and two children; there are photos of the lieutenant governor as a child, and vintage photos of his family history, going back to pioneer days. The candidate, camera crew, media consultant, and makeup artist all pile into the helicopter.

It is a grueling day that starts at dawn and continues throughout the day at seven different stops. The weather cooperates. Altogether they have traveled eight hundred miles during the day. The footage of the candidate, with his carefully scripted lines, will be the raw material for the commercials created throughout the campaign. Two hours of high-quality film and four hours of videotape are shot.

The media firm rents time at the national party's media production center, saving about $2,000 in production costs. The voice-over is provided by an announcer on retainer from the party's media center. Also coming from the party's media center are the computer-generated graphics, music, and sound effects.

Total cost of ad creation: $67,000 (for the one-day shoot: $45,000).

5. Testing Ads

Three versions of the biographical spot are produced. Three focus groups are shown these spots, along with other campaign material and earlier spots from other races. Spot number two gets the most positive feedback from the focus group participants, who are using a combination of check-off sheets and dial meters to judge the ads. Yet, there are two glaring problems even on this version. Half the focus group participants were confused about something the lieutenant governor said, and nearly half mistook the governor for the state's senior senator. A new visual is added so that

Bennister's point is clear, and a Chyron overlay, clearly stating "Gov. Jim Forster," is put under the governor's face. A scattering of focus group participants did not like this color or that music, but the exasperated media consultant sticks to his artistic guns and the biographical spot goes through. Most of the material from the shoot is not used, and the most effective scenes are the ones shot around the kitchen table in the lieutenant governor's home, with his photogenic wife and two kids. Bennister himself is quite pleased.

6. Final Ad is Produced

The final version of the sixty-second bio spot is ready for public viewing:

[Upbeat background music; shots of Bennister as a child, montage of family photos, turn-of-the-century shots of his grandparents]

[Voice-over]: Jim Bennister's family has lived here for four generations. Jim's been carrying on the family business, raising his kids, making his hometown a better place to live.

[Shot of Bennister, work shirt on, sleeves rolled up, looking up at the camera while carrying sacks of fertilizer in the family's garden and flower store]

Bennister: Dad taught me the value of hard work, and Mom taught me to respect our neighbors.

[Shots of Bannister with family in kitchen]

Bennister: Sally and I love it here, but we worry about our kids' future. Seems like everything costs more today and we end up just paying more taxes. That's not right.

[Bennister in front of state capitol building with the governor]

Bennister: I want to be your next governor and finish the good work done by Jim Forster.

[Voice-over]: Jim Bennister for governor. Good for our families. Good for business. Paid for by Bennister for Governor, Sarah Williams, treasurer.

7. Launching the Ad

The campaign wants maximum favorable publicity as it launches this first ad buy. Journalists are invited for a preview of the commercial and given a full press kit with biographical information, talking points, information about Bennister's accomplishments, and information about when and where the commercial will run. The campaign has sent out Twitter feeds, with links to the first campaign ad. It also has created its own YouTube channel, and has posted the ad there. Bennister is present at the news conference and answers questions, none of which have anything to do with the bio spot. Fortunately, Bennister is well briefed and handles himself fairly adeptly.

8. Airing the Ad

Four days before the ads are to be aired, the campaign deposits the required funds for the buy. Copies of the ad are sent to the television outlets forty-eight hours before they are to be aired. The media buyer is able to stick with the purchasing schedule, and over the course of the next ten days, the ad will be shown three hundred and sixty times throughout the state.

9. Impact Analysis

Three days after the bio has run its cycle, the campaign pollster conducts a short tracking survey. The ads have had some success. Bennister's recognition level has moved up (32 percent of the voters now recognize him, up from 22 percent before the ads ran); further, Bennister's approval rating has improved slightly (now 41 percent approval, as opposed to 37 percent before the ad ran). Most voters, however, still have not focused on this race, do not know Bennister, and have formed no positive or negative impressions of him. Altogether, nearly $490,000 has been spent on the creation and airing of this campaign commercial.

Instant Ads

Certainly not all campaigns have the luxury of time and resources to produce ads like the one outlined above. Especially in the heat of the battle, during the last crucial weeks or in making "tracking" ads, the commercials need to be produced quickly and cannot be fully researched or tested, and the candidate must rely on the skill, creativity, and judgment of the media consultant.

The abrupt change in leadership in the Bob Dole campaign during the 1996 presidential primaries illustrates this point. The Dole media campaign took a sharp turn when it brought in media consultant Don Sipple as its new chief strategist. Up until this point in the primaries, Dole's ads were sharp, negative attacks on his opponents. Sipple immediately called in Stuart Stevens, who had produced Dole's television ads, and said that they had to throw together a positive ad. By the next day, Stevens and Sipple had put together a script entitled "Proud:"

Dole: We have reached a defining moment in America.

Announcer: Americans long for leadership, a strong president with character and courage who shares our conservative values.

Dole: Basic values like honesty and decency and responsibility and self-reliance.

The campaign had no time for focus groups, survey research, or other tools to craft a major advertisement. It was all political instinct, and had a sounding board of just one person, Sipple's wife, who after watching the ad said, "That's really nice. He has dignity." Sipple pulled all negative ads and replaced them immediately with "Proud."[28]

Negative Advertising

I shall refrain from false or misleading attacks on an opponent or member of his or her family, and shall do everything in my power to prevent others from using such tactics.

—From the Code of Professional Ethics,
American Association of Political Consultants[29]

The negative campaign ad is one of the central features of modern election-eering. Some of the ads are hard-hitting, factual, determined attacks against their candidates' opponents. They are part of the combat of campaigning and political hardball. Other campaign ads step across the line. They are evasive and misleading, untruthful, replete with hyperbole and innuendo, they kindle voter's resentment, suspicion, or envy, or they manipulate personal tragedy for political gain.

In April 2006, MoveOn.org targeted four vulnerable House Republic-ans, spending a total of $1.3 million to purchase negative ads asserting that the legislators had been caught "red-handed." Here is the example from the ads placed in Connecticut:

Announcer: Congresswoman Nancy Johnson. Seniors relied on her, yet Congresswoman Johnson accepted $400,000 from big drug companies and got caught red-handed voting for a law actually preventing Medicare from negotiating lower drug prices for our seniors.

[Picture of Johnson waving; her hand is painted red. Then pictures of Tom DeLay, with a red hand, another with Dick Cheney and a red hand, then a montage of Jack Abramoff and DeLay, with red hands]

Announcer: Tom DeLay, Dick Cheney, Jack Abramoff, and now Nancy Johnson. Another Republican caught red-handed. With 3.2 million members, MoveOn.org Political Action is responsible for the content of this advertisement.

What do we make of such ads? Congresswoman Johnson shot right back in a television ad calling MoveOn.org a "radical group whose ads have been shameful and misleading" and declaring that "we deserve better than hateful and dishonest attacks from [opponent Chris] Murphy's Washington cronies." An NBC affiliate in Connecticut decided not to air the red-handed spots.[30]

Political consultants generally argue that they will continue using negative ads because they work. Many social scientists have studied the impact of negative ads, concluding that such ads can increase voter know-ledge of issues, sometimes hurt the targeted politician, but at other times create a backlash. The ads tend to be more effective when produced by third parties, and addressed at issues rather than a candidate, and can be blunted by a quick rebuttal. Viewers sometimes regard negative ads as less ethical or less fair.[31]

Political scientist John G. Geer defends negative advertising for its power to sharpen and highlight issue difference between candidates and parties. Geer notes that most negative ads in recent presidential elections have focused on issues rather than on personal attacks and have provided voters with valuable information before they reached the polls.[32] My impression is that negative advertising, however defined and measured, does have a long-term negative impact on voters, particularly on their perceptions of government and candidates. There are plenty of examples of ads that drag up long-forgotten divorces, that blow out of proportion personal idiosyncrasies and past mistakes, which, through raw and blurred images or sarcasm and grating sound effects, paint the candidate's opponent in the worst light. When a candidate's votes or policy preferences are attacked, they are invariably taken out of context, and small issues or votes are pumped up to look like enormous faults. In the long run, all of this in the guerilla theater of modern politics must have some corrosive effect on political discourse and the public's view of politics and public service.

Subtler than blatant negative attacks, but far more pervasive, are the ads that manipulate or distort reality. Today, with sophisticated digital technology, any image can be manipulated,[33] and there is nothing to stop image enhancing of candidates. Photo retouches try to make us look better, covering up blemishes, smoothing out wrinkles. Digital image enhancing can go farther: it can slim away unattractive pounds, add hair, make a somewhat lumpy five-foot-six-incher into a slimmed down, handsome five-foot-niner. Image enhancing can provide candidates with makeovers that nature never could produce.

Not all makeovers make people look good. It is standard practice for media consultants to choose unflattering shots of opponents. In grainy black-and-white shots, candidates are shown with scowls, bags under their eyes, goofy looks on their faces—just plain unattractiveness writ large. Digital imaging that can do wonders can also do a great deal of harm.

This image manipulation has always been a factor in media campaigns. Researchers at the University of Oklahoma's Political Communications Center analyzed more than two thousand commercials from 1952 through 1992, and found that 15 percent contained "some ethically questionable use of technology." A follow-up study for the 1996 presidential campaign found that 28 percent of the one hundred and eighty-eight commercials examined contained questionable use of technology—news conferences that were never held, debates that never took place, use of audio or video tricks to stereotype or ridicule opponents.[34] With digital technology now widely available, there will be greater temptation to alter reality.

Negative advertising and the skullduggery of opposition research also have long-term dampening effects on potential candidates. How many exceptionally talented persons are dissuaded from careers in elective office because they are not willing to have their families, personal lives, and reputations besmirched by thirty-second spots at two thousand gross ratings points? Yet, for campaigns, candidates, and media consultants, thinking of long-term implications is a luxury in which they rarely indulge. The pressure on the campaign to win is enormous. In the heat of the battle, campaigns are operating with precious few dollars left, gambling on a last-ditch media buy, frustrated by the barrage of attack ads from the opponent, with the threat of a last-minute issues advocacy campaign ready to kill them off and a nervous candidate who has spent millions of his own money and does not intend to lose. That is the hard reality of media decisions. Ultimately, however, the decision to launch a barrage of negative advertising rests with the candidate alone.

Michael Steele, the Republican 2006 senatorial candidate in Maryland, took a different approach. His campaign ads were striking because they did not mention his party, his opponents, they did not have him mingling in a crowd of admirers. The candidate, looking slightly bemused, was sitting on a stool, pretending to knock on the viewers' television screen, and gently warning against all those negative ads that they might be subjected to. "Soon your TV will be jammed with negative ads from the Washington crowd. Grainy pictures and spooky music saying 'Steele hates puppies'— or worse. For the record, I love puppies. And I think you deserve better, some real ideas for a change." The ad ended with Steele cuddling a puppy in his arms.

Steele's first ad, normally a biographical piece, abruptly began: "I know what you're thinking. I know what you're feeling. Washington has no clue of what's going on in your life. They blame each other, they work the angles while you're just trying to make today better than yesterday ... Instead of the spin, I'll talk straight about what's wrong in both parties."

The ads, produced by veteran Republican media consultant Brad Todd of OnMessage Inc., drew a lot of attention for their stark ice-blue background, the directness of the messenger, and for what they did not say about the candidate. In a year that would be tough on Republican candidates, Steele, the lieutenant governor, never informed viewers of his political affiliation. The ads created a stir, simply because they were different, warm and fuzzy, and memorable. It took only days, however, for his Democratic opponent, Ben Cardin to strike back with this ad: "Michael Steele: He likes puppies, but he loves George Bush." Then the screen repeatedly flashed Steele's views on key issues: he supported the Iraq war, he opposed abortions, and backed Bush's veto of further stem cell research. The ad concluded with a photo of Bush and Steele framed within a valentine heart. Steele, and his puppy, lost.[35]

Using Free Media

While millions of dollars are spent to produce and air campaign ads, few stand out as truly memorable. The 1964 "Daisy" ad, created by Tony Schwartz for the firm of Doyle, Dane, Bernbach, is probably the most famous (and infamous), strongly suggesting that Republican candidate Barry Goldwater was too trigger-happy with nuclear weapons to be trusted.[36] The 1984 "Bear in the Woods" ad warning about the dangers of the Soviet Union and "Prouder, Stronger, Better" ("It's Morning Again in America"), letting voters feel good about their country, were both written and narrated by Hal Riney. The "Willie Horton" ad in 1988, produced by Larry McCarthy for the National Security PAC, combined racism and fear in an attempt to show Michael Dukakis as soft on crime. The first Swift Boat Veterans commercial in 2004, produced by Rick Reed of the Republican firm Stevens, Reed, Curcio, and Potholm, first aired in just seven television markets, but its message extended exponentially as it was picked up by the press.

Those famous ads, and perhaps a few dozen more, are remembered by voters. But most ads are simply forgotten. Media consultant Don Sipple argues that the best way to get the public's attention is through free media, not political ads.

"Forget ads," Sipple said. "The candidate is the salesperson. *It doesn't work without the salesperson.* It's stage management. The Dole campaign underestimated the importance of the *candidate.*"[37]

Many candidates in the past two decades have seen the value of free media and clearly went after it as a part of their overall communications strategy. Ross Perot announced his presidential bid on the *Larry King Live* show, Arnold Schwarzenegger announced his run for the governorship of California on *The Tonight Show.* Bill Clinton played the saxophone on the *Arsenio Hall Show,* Bob Dole joked around with David Letterman, and, since then, aspiring politicians have tried to soak up as much free publicity as they can. For John McCain, Barack Obama, Mitt Romney, Hillary Clinton, and lesser-known aspirants, appearances on talk shows, late night television, and local news become valuable forms of publicity.

But, sometimes, it is nearly impossible for candidates to obtain free television time or newspaper coverage. In the 1998 California gubernatorial primary, for example, it seemed almost impossible. As Todd Purdum observed, the campaign for governor, one month away from primary day, was "all but invisible on television news and only sporadically [got] front-page newspaper coverage."[38]

That left paid television commercials, and the millions of dollars they require, as the principal medium through which the public gets its information about candidates and issues. "The balance between the paid and unpaid media has never been so great," observed political analyst Sherry Bebitch Jeffe.[39]

In California in 1998, few people seemed interested in elections. Instead of steady, comprehensive coverage of the primaries, television was more interested in the busy May sweeps period (giving viewers a heavy dosage of sensational, visual events), fires, freeway shootings and chases, the effects of *el Niño*—not boring politicians and campaigning. The candidates spent record amounts of money buying television commercials because they were relatively unknown to California voters and because local television just wasn't interested in covering the primary election.[40]

What happened with the press in California goes to the heart of the argument of media critics who complain about the cynicism of the press and the decline in public affairs reporting. Social scientist Robert M. Entman argues that the inability of the press to educate and stimulate the public is demonstrated by the fact that fewer people participate in the political process in an intelligent manner.[41] Journalist James Fallows likewise contends that citizens are choosing to disengage from the political process thereby endangering the health of our democratic institutions. People no longer see the relevance of participating in the public dialogue, and view the work of politicians as meaningless in their lives.[42] The real danger is when politics and campaigning for office are viewed as nothing but an irrelevant sideshow, and the media do not even bother to pay attention.

Not only are free media in jeopardy, so, too, are paid media. While federal candidates for office are guaranteed lowest market rates and unlimited access, state and local candidates do not enjoy such privileges. The 1997 Virginia governor's race may have provided a taste of the cutbacks to come in paid media. The four largest television stations in Washington, D.C. sharply cut sales of inexpensive spots to Virginia political candidates, in profit-boosting moves. In early October, with less than a month to go before the election, the stations informed the gubernatorial candidates that they would limit air-time purchases by roughly 40 percent between then and election day. One station gave this reason: open-market competition and limited audience interest in the Virginia campaigns among Washington and Maryland viewers. The ABC affiliate stated it would no longer sell time to lieutenant governor and attorney general candidates at the customary discounted rates for politicians. The NBC, CBS, and Fox affiliates likewise cut back down-ticket campaigns from discounted ads in lucrative prime time and news slots.

The danger of limiting paid television communications was clear to Ellen S. Miller, executive director of Public Campaign: "If we can't even get them [television stations] to provide paid time, what's the potential for getting free time for debates. It has enormous ramifications for the ability of candidates to make their voices heard in races."[43]

Historically, some of the best platforms for free media in presidential campaigns are the political parties' national conventions. But, over the years, the conventions have become events made for television and, ironically, less watched by audiences. The Democratic convention in 1992 paved the way. Clinton pal and television executive Harry Thomason produced "Man from Hope," the made-for-television biography showing Bill Clinton's rough childhood upbringing and his triumph over despair. Earlier conventions had also been well scripted for television, like Ronald Reagan's "Morning in America" themes in 1984 and the tightly controlled Republican convention in 1968. But there was nothing like the 1996 Republican convention. Staged, scripted, controlled, smoothed over, it was the most made-for-television of all conventions. The quadrennial national political convention itself, which may be nothing more than an antiquarian holdover from earlier days of party domination, became a four-day "infomercial" for the Republican Party. Republican leaders with the highest negative public ratings—Newt Gingrich and Pat Buchanan—were shunted off the center stage and given only minor roles. No more vitriol from Buchanan, who had scored big points with his conservative faithful in Houston in 1992, but hurt the party's image with the larger public. Even protesters were confined to a limited, chain-link fence area and given fifty-five minutes (and no more) to make their statements.

But, ironically, fewer people were watching. The networks had long abandoned gavel-to-gavel coverage, with only the cable stations CNN, C-SPAN, and MSNBC doing full coverage. ABC's Ted Koppel noisily left San Diego after the first day, proclaiming that there was no news to cover. Nielsen Media Research revealed that the San Diego convention drew 22 percent fewer viewers during its four days than the Houston GOP convention had in 1992, and that during Dole's acceptance night the drop-off was even bigger, at 30 percent.[44] The biggest winner of the television night was a rerun of *Seinfeld.*

The Democratic Party convention in 1996 was filled with its moments of pathos—tearful moments with James Brady and Christopher Reeve. It was staged and produced almost to the same level of made-for-television perfection as the Republican convention. Network television covered fewer and fewer events, indeed because there were fewer real events to cover.

The 2000 and 2004 presidential nominating conventions continued the trend: little of substance, much tugging at the heartstrings of the party faithful, and full coverage relegated to cable television watched by increasingly smaller audiences. In 2004, the television networks basically snubbed the first two days of the four-day conventions, ignoring some of the major speeches given early. Viewers who wanted to follow the convention would have to resort to cable and the Internet. Filling the void were Black Entertainment Television, MTV, Comedy Central, ESPN, CSPAN, Fox News Channel, CNN, and MSNBC. While political blogging was just starting during the 2000 presidential campaign, it came into its own in 2004. For the first time, both the Republican and Democratic 2004 conventions credentialed bloggers, giving them working space and access to convention participants.

Interest in the presidential nominating conventions seemed to reappear in 2008 and 2012. The 2008 Democratic convention was capped with the boisterous, enthusiastic reception for Barack Obama, with some eighty thousand in attendance at Denver's Mile High stadium. Republicans were sparked by the vice presidential nomination of Alaska governor Sarah Palin and her energetic acceptance speech. In 2012, Mitt Romney's well-orchestrated convention was marred by an off-the-wall endorsement speech by actor Clint Eastwood, using an empty chair as a prop and substitute for an absent Obama. The Democratic convention was highlighted by strong speeches from Michelle Obama, and particularly from former president Bill Clinton.

For many campaigns, television is the best vehicle for communications. But the costs are high. Campaigns have to hire professional media advisers to design and create television commercials, they have to raise significant amounts of funds to produce and air the advertising, they depend upon advertising slots being available (and affordable), and, when campaigns seek out free media, they must depend upon the whims and priorities of local television newscasts. Many campaigns cannot afford to pay the high price of television and, so, turn to cheaper forms of communication, such as radio advertising or direct mail. But now, with the online revolution, a whole new form of communications is open-at a relatively low cost, with no barriers between the campaign and voters and accessible twenty-four hours a day to anyone who wants to visit a campaign's website. Even more, the online revolution brings mobile phones, text messaging, video and text blogs into play as valuable communication devices.

Online Communications

On the eve of the twenty-first century, many of us were both curious and excited about the revolution in online communications. Would the Internet become the dominant vehicle for political communication? Was the age of television about to be replaced by the age of the Internet? Would there be a fundamental shift in the way campaigns connect with voters? Party strategists, consultants, and candidates, increasingly played this guessing game. In the late 1990s, when television was still the dominant form of campaign communication, some were convinced that we were well into a new era of campaign communications. In the first real use of the Internet in presidential campaigns, in 1996 Clinton and Dole and their respective parties had, for their time, sophisticated, appealing websites loaded with voting and policy information.[45] Patrick Buchanan aggressively recruited volunteers for the "Buchanan Brigade" during the 1996 primary season. James Gilmore, running for governor of Virginia in 1997, invited citizens to calculate directly on his website the amount of money they would save if Gilmore's automobile tax plan were enacted. Later, George W. Bush featured a calculator on his presidential website page so that visitors could figure their savings from his tax plan. By 1998, no candidate for statewide office could be without a campaign website. The site provided useful information, gave it to the voters cheaply, and had the symbolic purpose of saying that this campaign was up to date and technologically sophisticated. In early 1999, Steve Forbes made a second run for the Republican primary and became the first presidential hopeful formally to announce his candidacy on the Internet. Forbes made a conventional announcement on the steps of the New Hampshire state capitol with just fifty people showing up, but his website linked him to potentially millions over cyberspace.[46]

Forbes later used his online connection to let his supporters know bad things about George W. Bush. The Forbes campaign took a press story critical of Bush's younger days, which appeared in an obscure Iowa newspaper, and sent it through email to some fifty-six thousand Forbes supporters. Here was a new communications tool at its best: instantaneous, cheap, interactive, and directed to a very specific audience.

In 1998, the Jesse Ventura campaign for governor of Minnesota credited an online political debate, email, and his campaign website, with helping to build momentum with potential voters, especially younger, first-time voters. Ventura noted that the online debate was "truly made for my campaign. It's reaching a huge amount of people at a very low price."[47] While some have credited Ventura's upset victory to his use of the Internet, in a contest as close as this, there are many possible reasons why he won. Probably more than anything else, Ventura's charisma, bluster, and offbeat personality drew many first-time voters to his side. In the 2000 Republican presidential primaries, John McCain was able to raise over one million dollars overnight, illustrating the incredible potential of online fundraising.

By the 2004 presidential race, online communication had become increasingly important, through the expanded use of email and campaign websites. In July 2004, John Kerry publicly announced his vice-presidential choice, John Edwards, by sending an email announcement to his supporters. In anticipation of that announcement, another 150,000 persons were added to the Kerry campaign's email listserv. The Bush campaign boasted of having the email addresses of six million supporters, dubbed e-citizens, who would be counted on to spread the word, energize others, and assist in get-out-the-vote drives. Political communications scholar Michael Cornfield assessed the relative merits of a campaign website and email as political communications tools, concluding that email would outperform a website "ninety-nine days out of a hundred."[48] Cornfield notes that email is delivered to a defined address (while a website must be searched for), email is read (while websites are navigated), email is easier to respond to (while Web sites "engender frames within frames"); and email is harder for the press and the political opposition to monitor than a website.

The great push, as can be seen in Chapter 7, is for campaigns to link up email addresses with known supporters, matching their demographic information (where they live, age, sex, race) with their voting history.

Campaign websites and online communication in 2004 added several innovations. First, instead of contacting thousands of supporters and volunteers as in years past, the candidates and the political parties were able to recruit millions. Howard Dean's campaign linked up with Meetup.com to arrange hundreds of meetings of Dean supporters throughout the nation. Meetup.com, a private commercial website, was originally designed to help like-minded individuals connect with one another. On the Meetup.com website in February 2004, there were 2,800 Chihuahua lovers and 8,800 fans of the musical group Insane Clown Posse. Also, there were 186,000 supporters of Howard Dean, 66,800 for Wesley Clark, and 45,300 for John Kerry. The year before, Meetup.com ran a test marketing of political candidates and some 400 individuals quickly signed up through the website as Dean supporters. Meetup's Scott Heiferman and Dean campaign's principal consultant Joe Trippi soon realized they were on to a new form of political community building. By February 1, 2004, there were over 1,100 sites registered where Howard Dean supporters could meet, raise money, and work together for their candidate. Virtual connections through the Internet became concrete connections; other campaigns soon took notice of this potential community building tool.[49]

A second innovation in 2004 was the use of political blogs. Howard Dean became the first presidential candidate to use a blog, and was soon followed by other Democratic candidates. The Bush–Cheney campaign had its own blog, but lacked the interactivity of the other sites, and served essentially as a campaign bulletin board. With the blogs came a new campaign specialty, the blogmaster, who was responsible for overseeing the flow of blog comments, and acting as an umpire who filters out inappropriate comments.[50]

Many other blogs, unconnected with the campaigns, were active as well. Yahoo counted forty-eight separate blogs covering the 2004 presidential election, with the five most popular blogs each having more than half a million viewers a day, far more readers than all but the largest metropolitan newspapers. Bloggers range all over the political spectrum: the Daily Kos, Instapundit, New Donkey, RedState.com, Blogs for Bush, Buzzmachine, and scores more. The conservative website Townhall.com now links one of the oldest forms of mass communication, radio, with one of the newest, blogging. Talk radio, emerging in the late 1980s has been a favorite medium for conservative voices, and, in 2006, Salem Communications, the owner of Townhall.com, combined the two. The goal was to get millions of listeners to conservative talk radio to move online and continue the conversation, and to create another new wave of grassroots support.[51]

The third innovation was in fundraising. While the 2000 McCain for President campaign was able to raise a million dollars of online contributions literally overnight, it was the Dean primary campaign in 2004 that demonstrated to skeptics that impressive amounts of money could be raised online. Some $41 million was raised by the Dean campaign, much of it came from online donations in small amounts from persons who had not given money before.

To any candidate attempting to mount a serious campaign, whether at the presidential, state or even local level, a campaign website becomes an important communication tool. At the national level, considerable time, research, and money will go into designing an interactive, vibrant website. A campaign will rely on a website design vendor to create a sophisticated site and employ a team of technologically savvy staffers to update and maintain the site, and to serve as webmaster and blogmaster. Such a website might cost well over $50,000 to design and thousands more to maintain. (By contrast, entertainment sites, such as websites for pop stars, might approach $1 million to create). Low budget local campaigns, relying on a basic design template and volunteer maintenance, can easily create and maintain a campaign website for less than a thousand dollars.

The campaign websites are important additions, but they certainly are not panaceas, and any campaign relying solely on a website for political communication would be bound to fail. Despite all the excitement and hype in 1998 and 2000 about the Internet becoming the dominant force in campaigning, online communication only came into its own during the

2004 and 2006 elections. Howard Dean's campaign, before it famously crashed in the first Democratic primary state, showed enormous promise for its creative use of online communications to raise money, create political communities, and sustain excitement. But there has to be genuine energy and excitement for the candidate for it all to work. We need to remember that the second most online-dependent Democratic candidate in 2004 was Dennis Kucinich, whose campaign barely was visible.

During the 2004 presidential campaign, Internet audio and video files were added to the mix of political communications. In July 2004, JibJab Media launched a website featuring a political parody with cut-out figures of Bush and Kerry singing a version of "This Land Is Your Land." There were over 65 million hits to the Jib Jab website, as this clever animation caught the attention of audiences throughout the world. Millions first heard of the site when CBS and NBC evening news featured it. Jib Jab was just one of many animations, video clips, parody sites, and amateur videos that flooded the Internet. Some were clever, some raunchy, and some made little sense at all.[52]

While attention focused on email, candidate websites, and blogs as political communication tools, the next wave of online communication is now beginning to have an impact. Political activists, scholars, and political consultants are now giving serious attention to two other phenomena: the growing importance of mobile telephones as political communication devices and the harnessing of online social networks and user-generated content in political campaigns.

The political communication implications of mobile phones were just catching on in the United States in the mid-2000s.[53] In several countries, however, mobile communication has proven to be a powerful political tool. In the Philippines, a million citizens were rallied by mobile text messaging in 2001, taking to the streets and urging a popular uprising against president Joseph Estrada, who subsequently resigned. During the so-called "Orange Revolution" in Ukraine, hundreds of thousands of protestors were mobilized through text messages in 2004, demanding an election rematch between candidate Viktor Yushchenko and Prime Minister Viktor Yanukovych. The rock star Bono has enlisted fans and activists at his concerts using mobile phone technology, and the World Trade Organization protestors have coordinated and mobilize their actions through cell phones. Howard Rheingold, a leading authority on the social implications of technology, calls them "smart mobs."[54]

Strapped to one's belt or in one's purse, mobile phones have the most personal connection with individuals and are perfect vehicles for instantaneous response. Urgent fundraising appeals, event schedules, appeals for volunteers, reminders to register to vote, and news updates are easily sent through text messaging. Smart phones, which first appeared in 2007 with the Apple iPhone, have made it even easier for candidates to communicate with staff, loyalists, and voters through campaign "apps." Soon, wristwatch technology will hold the same promise for instant connectivity and communication as mobile phones.

Online communication hit a new plateau during the 2008 presidential election, particularly from the Obama campaign. The numbers alone show the energy and vitality of online communication. The Obama website, MyBarackObama (MyBO) saw two million persons logged in, and through that website, supporters were able to contribute money, urge their friends to contribute, and develop communities of supporters. There were over 2.2 million supporters on several Obama Facebook sites, 800,000 on MySpace, and a significant number on other social media sites as well. The Obama campaign recruited one of the founders of Facebook, Chris Hughes, to help develop its online presence. By election time, Obama had "friended" over seven million supporters. There were over 400,000 blog postings, 35,000 volunteers recruited, and 200,000 off-line events were held. Obama was also able to raise over a half-billion dollars through the campaigns online platforms.[55] The McCain campaign had the same online and social media tools, but the enthusiasm for McCain over these platforms paled in comparison to the activity for Obama. Seven million "friends" on Facebook, of course, doesn't mean that those seven million persons would be eligible to vote, but it does give a solid indication of the enthusiasm behind the campaign.

During the 2012 presidential campaign, both the Romney and the Obama campaigns employed the usual digital platforms—websites, online advertising, social media, web videos, and that old reliable, email.[56] The real revolution in communication, as digital expert Julie Germany explained it, was the ability of the campaigns to integrate the thousands of points of data that were accumulating on individual voters and employing sophisticated algorithms to determine patterns of likely voting. By 2012, Facebook had grown to more than one billion users worldwide; Twitter, which did not exist before 2008, now had over five hundred million users throughout the world. Both the Obama and the Romney campaigns took advantage of the Facebook Exchange, which helped them target users in a much more precise way.

Online advertising, which barely played a part in the 2008 presidential campaign, now became an important tool for capturing voters' attention. With more and more voters using smart phones or other mobile devices while they watched traditional television, media experts have been trying to capture their attention through digital advertising. Just as a growing number of voters have turned away from landline telephones, so too are they turning away from traditional television, getting content from Hulu-Plus, Netflix, through TiVo, or other digital video recording devices. The campaigns turned to other sources, as well, including Internet radio, Pandora, or Xbox. At the close of the 2012 campaign, it was evident that while both Romney and Obama used online advertising extensively, the Obama campaign was more successful in targeting and reaching its intended audiences.[57]

With digital technology giving us new platforms and new opportunities each year, who can predict what the next Big Thing in online communication will be. Whatever that may be, it is clear that no serious campaign can now compete without the full range of digital tools. They join television (network, local, and cable), traditional and talk radio, telephone messages, newspapers, billboards, direct mail, and other print media, in the arsenal of tools that campaigns use to reach and persuade citizens to vote for their candidates.

Notes

1   Evan Tracey, "Political Advertising: When More Meant Less," in *Campaigning for President 2012: Strategy and Tactics*, ed. Dennis W. Johnson (New York: Routledge, 2013)

2   Chuck DeFeo, "Call in Now!" in *Person-to-Person-to-Person: Harnessing the Political Power of Online Social Networks and User-Generated Content*, ed. Julie Barko Germany (Washington, D.C.: George Washington University, Institute for Politics, Democracy & the Internet, 2006), 13.

3   See Lynda Lee Kaid, "Political Advertising," in *The Electoral Challenge: Theory Meets Practice*, ed. Stephen C. Craig (Washington, D.C.: CQ Press, 2006), 79–96, for a survey of the extensive political communications research on the impact of television political commercials. Also, Darrell M. West, *Air Wars: Television Advertising in Election Campaigns, 1952–2004*, 4th ed. (Washington, D.C.: CQ Press, 2005); and Doris A. Graber, Mass *Media and American* Politics, 7th ed. (Washington, D.C.: CQ Press, 2006).

4   James Bennet, "Another Tally in '96 Race: Two Months of TV Ads," *New York Times,* November 13, 1996, D20. This survey covered approximately 80 percent of the television market in the United States, but did not include smaller but still important markets such as Macon, Georgia, and Lafayette, Louisiana. Altogether, there are 216 media markets in the United States.

5   Kaid, "Political Advertising," 79; data from TNS Media Intelligence/CMR, press release. On the airwars of the 2000 presidential campaign, see L. Patrick Devlin, "Contrasts in Presidential Campaign Commercials of 2000," *American Behavioral Scientist,* 44, no. 12 (August 2001): 298–9. On presidential contests and television commercials in general, see Kathleen Hall Jamieson, *Packaging the Presidency,* 3rd ed. (New York: Oxford University Press, 1996); Edwin Diamond and Stephen Bates, *The Spot: The Rise of Political Advertising on Television,* 3rd ed. (Cambridge, Mass.: MIT Press, 1996); and Kathleen Hall Jamieson, *Dirty Politics: Deception, Distraction, and Democracy* (New York: Oxford University Press, 1992).

6   Jim Margolis's firm is GMMB (Greer, Margolis, Mitchell, and Burns); Robert Shrum's firm was Shrum, Devine, and Donilon. They were later joined by the firm of Squier, Knapp, and Dunn. L. Patrick Devlin, "Contrasts in Presidential Campaign Commercials of 2004," *American Behavioral Scientist* 49, no. 2 (October 2005): 298–9.

7   Devlin, "Contrasts in Presidential Campaign Commercials of 2004," 299.

8   Pew Research Center for the People and the Press, "Campaign '96 Gets Lower Grades from Voters," Washington, D.C., November 15, 1996, 2–3; and Pew Research Center for the People and the Press, "Voters Liked Campaign 2004, But Too Much Mudslinging," November 11, 2004.

9   Andrei Scheinkman, G. V. Xaquîn, Alan McLean, and Stephen Weitberg, "The Ad Wars," *New York Times,* May 23, 2012.

10   "47 Percent" ad: PrioritiesUSAction, "Understands," YouTube, August 7, 2012, https://www.youtube.com/watch?v=Nj70XqOxptU (accessed February 17, 2015). On Obama's 30-minute infomercial, see Abdon M. Pallasch, "Obama's 30-Minute Infomercial Covers All Bases," *Chicago Sun-Times,* October 30, 2008. On political advertising spending in 2012, see John C. Tedesco and Scott W. Dunn, "Political Advertising in the 2012 U.S. Presidential Election," in *The 2012 Presidential Campaign: A Communications Perspective,* ed. Robert E. Denton, Jr. (Lanham, Md.: Rowman & Littlefield, 2014), 78; and Tracey, "Political Advertising," 92–106.

11   Brabender quoted in Todd Shields, "Politics as Usual: Spend, Spend, Spend," *Adweek,* December 15, 2003, 20.

12   Darrell M. West, "How Issue Ads Have Reshaped American Politics," Conference on Political Advertising in Election Campaigns, American University, Washington, D.C., April 17, 1998, 5; Darrell M. West and Burdett Loomis, *The Sound of Money: How Political Interests Get What They Want* (New York: W. W. Norton, 1998).

13   Deborah Beck et al., "Issue Advocacy Advertising during the 1996 Campaign," University of Pennsylvania, Annenberg Public Policy Center, Report No. 16,

September 16, 1997. This study looked at the content of television advertising in the 1996 campaigns.

14   Annenberg Public Policy Center, *Issue Advertising in the 1999–2000 Election Cycle* (2004), www.annenbergpublicpolicycenter.org/issue-advertising-in-the-1999-2000-election-cycle (accessed February 17, 2015); and Soontae An, Hyun Seung Jim, and Michael Pfau, "The Effects of Issue Advocacy Advertising on Voters' Candidate Issue Knowledge and Turnout," *Journalism & Mass Communication Quarterly* 83 (1) (Spring 2006): 7–24.

15   Albert L. May, "Swift Boat Vets in 2004: Press Coverage of an Independent Campaign," *First Amendment Law Review* no. 4 (2005): 79.

16   The group registered in April 2004 as a 527 group; in September 2004, it changed its name to Swift Boat Vets and POWs for Truth. May, "Swift Boat Vets in 2004," at 67 n. 5. The analysis of the Swift Boat ads relies heavily on this excellent article, and Kate Zernike and Jim Rutenberg, "Friendly Fire: The Birth of an Attack on Kerry," *New York Times*, August 20, 2004, Al.

17   Center for Responsive Politics, "2004 527 Committee Activity."

18   The ads are available on the Swift Boat Veterans website, www.swiftvets.org.

19   Devlin, "Contrasts in Presidential Campaign Commercials of 2004," 298–9; Ann Cooper, "Gloves Off in the Propaganda Contest for U.S. Presidency," *Campaign*, September 10, 2004, 18; Roy O'Connor, "The Shrum Factor," *Broadcast and Cable*, May 10, 2004, 2.

20   Bob Garfield, "Kerry Serves Up Cacophony of Indecision, Missed Shots," *Advertising Age*, September 13, 2004, 53; O'Connor, "The Shrum Factor," 2; Ira Teinowitz, "Kerry Camp Dropped the Ball on Branding," *Advertising Age*, November 8, 2004, 62; "A Strong Brand Was Bush's Ticket to the White House," *Marketing Week,* December 2, 2004, 30; Kenneth Winneg, Kate Kenski, Kathleen Hall Jamieson, "Directing the Effects of Deceptive Presidential Advertisements in the Spring of 2004," *American Behavioral Scientist*, 49, no. 1 (September 2005): 114–30.

21   Shailagh Murray, "Campaign Tool: Tracking Ads," *The Wall Street Journal*, October 12, 2004, A4.

22   Stephen K. Medvic, "Outside Voices: 527s, Political Parties, and Other Non-Candidate Groups," in *Campaigning for President 2008*, ed. Johnson, 189.

23   Ibid., 199.

24   *Citizens United v. Federal Election Commission*, 558 U.S. 310 (2010), majority opinion by Justice Anthony Kennedy. Obama quoted in Ben Frumin, "Obama: Supreme Court Ruling 'A Major Victory for Big Oil, Wall Street Banks, Health Insurance Companies," *TPM LiveWire*, January 21, 2010.

25   Jacobs quoted in Stephen K. Medvic, "Outside Voices: Super PACs, Parties, and Other Non-Candidate Actors," in *Campaign for President 2012*, ed. Johnson, 152.

26   Dan Balz, "A Most Poisonous Campaign," *Washington Post*, August 12, 2012; PrioritiesUSAction, "Understands."

27   Daniel Fisher, "Inside the Koch Empire: How the Brothers Plan to Reshape America," *Forbes*, December 5, 2012.

28 Howard Kurtz "Campaign '96: When Candidates Turn Negative, Voters May Too," *Washington Post*, October 16, 1996, A13.

29 American Association of Political Consultants, AAPC Code of Professional Ethics, www.theaapc.org/default.asp?contentID=701 (accessed February 17, 2015).

30 Available from National Journal Adwatch, 2006 Elections. Jennifer Koons, "Move On Blasts House Republicans for Energy Ties," *National Journal*, April 4, 2006. The MoveOn.org ads were produced by media consultants Zimmerman and Markman; Johnson's ads were produced by Jamestown Associates.

31 Kaid, "Political Advertising," 90; Richard R. Lau, Lee Sigelman, Caroline Heldman, and Paul Babbitt, "The Effects of Negative Political Advertisements: A Meta-Analytic Assessment," *American Political Science Review*, 93, no. 4 (December 1999): 851–75. See also Richard R. Lau and Gerald M. Pomper, "Effectiveness of Negative Campaigning in U.S. Senate Elections," *American Journal of Political Science*, 46, no. 1 (January, 2002): 47–66.

32 John G. Geer, *In Defense of Negativity: Attack Ads in Presidential Campaigns* (Chicago, Ill.: University of Chicago Press, 2006). Recent works on negative campaigning include David Mark, *Going Dirty: The Art of Negative Campaigning* (Lanham, Md.: Rowman and Littlefield, 2006); and Kerwin C. Swint, *Mudslinging: The Top 25 Negative Political Campaigns of All Time* (Westport, Conn.: Praeger, 2005). On emotional appeals in television advertising, see Ted Bader, *Campaigns for the Hearts and Minds: How Emotional Appeals in Political Ads Work* (Chicago, Ill.: University of Chicago Press, 2006).

33 In the 1997 rerelease of *Star Wars,* several characters were added through digital tricks. The movie *Wag the Dog* featured a fake war in Albania that was shot in Hollywood studios. Forrest Gump met President Kennedy, and in recent television commercials, Fred Astaire danced with a vacuum cleaner and John Wayne barked orders to recruits. As a part of its fiftieth anniversary celebration in May 1998, CBS showed off its digital graphics capability in six television shows. Fran Fine, the "Nanny," visits Lucy Ricardo (*I Love Lucy,* vintage 1960) in a dream sequence; a digital Jack Benny shows up on Cosby; Dick Van Dyke makes a guest appearance on his own shove, *Diagnosis Murder,* as the character Rob Petrie, whom Van Dyke had made famous thirty-five years ago. All this was done using Inferno digital compositing software, the SGI platform, and green-screen techniques. Patricia Brennan, "CBS Puts the Old in with the New," *Washington Post TV Week*, May 10–16, 1998, 9.

34 "Technology Increasingly Mixes up Political Candidates' Images, Reality," *Austin* (Texas) *American-Statesman,* October 27, 1996, A17.

35 Paul Farhi, "Where's the Party? Nowhere to be Found in Steele Ads," *Washington Post*, September 19, 2001, C1.

36 "Daisy" in "The Living Room Candidate" Presidential Campaign Commercials 1952–2012, Museum of the Moving Image. Available online at www.living roomcandidate.org (accessed March 24, 2015).

37 Sipple, quoted in Simon, *Showtime*, 78, emphasis in the original.

38 David Maraniss, "Image-Makers Produced Virtual Reality Convention," *Washington Post,* August 17, 1996, A1.

39 Todd S. Purdum, "Race for California Governor Is Not Necessarily the News," *New York Times*, May 6, 1998, A1.

40 Carla Marinucci, "Old-Fashioned TV Debate Interrupts Political Ad War," *San Francisco Chronicle*, May 11, 1998.

41 Robert M. Entman, *Democracy without Citizens* (New York: Oxford University Press, 1990), 3. Another advocate of public journalism is Jay Rosen, *Getting the Connections Right* (New York: Twentieth Century Fund, 1996).

42 James Fallows, *Breaking the News: How the Media Undermine American Democracy* (New York: Pantheon Books, 1996), 7.

43 Spencer S. Hsu, "TV Stations Curtail Discount Ads for Virginia Campaign," *Washington Post*, October 14, 1997, A1.

44 David Maraniss, "Image-Makers Produced Virtual Reality Convention," *Washington Post*, August 17, 1996, A1.

45 On early political use of Internet, see Michael Cornfield and F. Christopher Arterton, "'Is This for Real?' Democratic Politics and the Internet," in *The Internet as Paradigm* (Washington, D.C.: Institute for Information Studies, 1997); Bruce A. Bimber, *Campaigning Online: The Internet in U.S. Elections* (New York: Cambridge University Press, 2003).

46 The Forbes presidential Web site is www.forbes2000.com. See Richard L. Berke, "Forbes Declares Candidacy on Internet and the Stump," *New York Times*, March 17, 1999, A19.

47 Rebecca Fairley Raney, "In On-Line Debate, Candidates Focus on Issues without Spin," *New York Times*, March 2, 1998. Minnesota E-Democracy is found at (www.e-democracy.org). The Democratic primary in 1998 was loaded with famous Minnesota political names. Hubert H. Humphrey III, Ted Mondale, and Mike Freeman, dubbed "the Three Sons," had plenty of advance name recognition.

48 Michael Cornfield, *Politics Moves Online: Campaigning and the Internet* (New York: Century Foundation, 2004), 27.

49 Dennis W. Johnson, "First Hurdles: The Evolution of the Pre-Primary and Primary Stages of American Presidential Elections," in *Winning Elections with Political Marketing*, eds. Philip John Davies and Bruce I. Newman (New York: Haworth, 2006); and Joe Trippi, *The Revolution Will Not Be Televised: Democracy, the Internet, and the Overthrow of Everything* (New York: Regan Books, 2004).

50 Dennis W. Johnson, "Campaigning on the Internet," in *The Electoral Challenge: Theory Meets Practice*, ed. Stephen C. Craig (Washington, D.C.: CQ Press, 2006), 132–3.

51 DeFeo, "Call in Now!," 29–30.

52 Institute for Politics, Democracy and the Internet, George Washington University, "Under the Radar and Over the Top: Online Political Videos in the 2004 Election," Washington, D.C., February 5, 2004, www.ipdi.org/Uploaded Files/political%20influentials.pdf (accessed February 17, 2015).

53   Julie Barko Germany, *The Politics-To-Go Handbook: A Guide on Using Mobile Technology in Politics* (Washington, D.C.: Institute for Politics, Democracy and the Internet, George Washington University, 2005).

54   Howard Rheingold, *Smart Mobs: The Next Social Revolution* (New York: Perseus Books, 2002); Sarah Toms, "The Philippines' Mobile Politics," *BBC News*, April 1, 2006, http://news.bbc.co.uk/1/hi/programmes/from_our_own_correspondent/4864684.stm (accessed February 17, 2015); Gene J. Koprowski, "Wireless World: The 'Orange Revolution,'" *Space Daily*, December 27, 2004, www.spacedaily.com/news/internet-04zzzzw.html (accessed February 17, 2015).

55   Jose Antonio Vargas, "Obama's Wide Web," *Washington Post*, August 20, 2008; Howard Fineman, "What Have We Created?" *Newsweek*, November 3, 2008, 54; Jose Antonio Vargas, "Obama Raised Half a Billion Online," *Washington Post*, November 20, 2008.

56   Julie Germany, "Advances in Campaign Technology," in *Campaigning for President 2012*, ed. Johnson, 81.

57   Ibid., 84–7.

7

Reaching Out to Voters

It's the database, stupid.

—Reporter Elana Varon, paraphrasing James Carville's
famous observation[1]

This is how elections are won: door to door.

—Andy Stern, President, Service Employees
International Union[2]

Reaching the Right Audience

One of the most important and difficult communications tasks is to reach the right audience with the right message, using limited campaign resources to their fullest.[3] Campaigns communicate through a variety of sources, from local and network television, cable television, radio, telephone, direct mail, and increasingly through the Internet, social media and other forms of online communication. To reach their intended audiences, campaigns use the highly developed resources of targeting specialists. While a thirty-second political commercial on television, scheduled for the 6:00 p.m. local news, may reach the largest audience, it will also reach many who are uninterested or ineligible to vote. Cable television reaches a more tightly defined audience; radio has an even greater focus. For cost-per-message, television is generally the least expensive form of communication, but for efficiency and precision of communication, nothing can beat targeted direct mail, telephone communications, or targeted email.

Direct Mail—Focused Audience, Precise Messages: Targeted direct mail and telemarketing can send out specific messages to a variety of select audiences. For a gubernatorial candidate in Iowa (let's assume she is a Republican), no direct mail would be sent to ineligible voters: nonresidents, children, long-standing Democrats, and those who had not voted in prior elections. Separate mailings would be sent to a variety of targeted audiences, with messages tailored to each constituency's interests: thirty-year-old, college-educated, female, Independent voters; rural families with young children; Iowa members of the National Rifle Association; conservative church goers, and a wide variety of other groupings. As direct mail consultants Richard Schlackman and Jamie "Buster" Douglas observe, when used properly, direct mail is the "most precise weapon in a candidate's arsenal."[4]

Lists, Lists, Lists: Whether the goal is to solicit funds, urge citizens to get out and vote, or persuade them to vote for (or against) a candidate, targeted mailings and telemarketing depend upon accurate, up-to-date lists of names, addresses, voting history, party preferences, and other essential information. In today's direct marketing industry, list development and management are a major commercial enterprise, and for campaigns and elections, list management is a vital subspeciality.

Direct marketing specialist David Himes noted that there are six basic categories of lists available to campaigns.[5] Starting with the best:

1. The house list, maintained by the campaign itself, with files on past contributors and volunteers.
2. Outside lists of contributors to similar candidates or causes.
3. Compiled lists, combining categories of donors, such as doctors, business leaders, and so forth.
4. Commercial or direct response lists, such as lists of those who buy certain magazines or merchandise through direct mail.
5. Universal lists, which list every name and address in a specific area.
6. Voter lists obtained from state or local boards of elections, or from the political parties.

In fundraising, candidates rely on ticketed events (such as barbecues, pig roasts, black-tie dinners, hot dog festivals—invariably accompanied by fatty foods and alcohol), political action committee events, personal calls by the candidate, telephone solicitation, direct mail email and campaign websites.[6] To reach people, campaigns turn to their specialized lists.

The house list is by far the most important list a campaign has. It contains the names, email addresses, and other vital information of individuals who have contributed funds or have volunteered for the candidate in past elections. These are the persons who can most likely be counted on to give again. Their response rate and average contribution will be higher than any other group.[7]

In order to expand a house list, campaigns may have to engage in prospecting, sending out thousands of letters to possible donors, hoping to gather a core of givers. Usually prospecting is left to the political parties or to multi-million-dollar campaigns because it takes a considerable amount of time, requires several remailings, and is a very expensive undertaking, usually losing money during the first round of direct mail solicitation.

Republican direct mail consultant Richard Norman recommends to clients that if they can recoup 70 percent of the costs, they should continue mailing. If, for example, there is a million-piece mailing, the costs of production and postage may be a half-million dollars. The mailing may bring in only twenty thousand checks—a relatively healthy 2 percent response rate. If the campaign receives $350,000 (the 70 percent minimum threshold), it should then continue mailing, and keep targeting those twenty thousand donors. Norman observes that "in a normal campaign with one year to mail, you could expect to generate a half-million dollars in net income by remailing to these contributors."[8] The campaign would then repay the cost of the first prospecting ($150,000), and have a net of $350,000 raised. Then, after the election is over, the list of donors might be rented for an additional $150,000 to $200,000, thus raising the total raised for the campaign to $500,000 to $550,000.

Commercial firms compile lists on nearly every conceivable demographic, lifestyle, and cultural variable. Some of these lists can be generally helpful for fundraising, but more importantly for persuasion and get-out-the-vote drives. They are either compiled lists, which are derived from telephone books, newspapers, public records, retail slips, automobile registration, and other sources. Or they are response lists, proven buyers from mail-order catalogues, paid subscriptions to magazines, subscribers to cable television, and others. Compiled lists tend to be more demographic, and response lists tend to be more psychographic.[9] From such lists, and especially from public-record voter files from state election offices, individuals can be isolated by age, sex, race, lifestyle, gender, party affiliation, frequency of voting, home ownership, marital status, children, and so forth. One such firm, I Rent America, advertises some two hundred and twenty million names on computer files.[10] Clients can rent the names of the 266,302 active donors to Handgun Control, the 154,551 alumni of Outward Bound, the 338,424 millionaires (or the 14,632 multi-millionaires), the 748,213 persons over sixty-five living in Illinois, or the 345,895 subscribers to *Vegetarian Times* magazine.[11]

One list management firm, catering to pro-life, conservative candidates and causes, included the following among the thirty-five lists available: Born Again Doctors Who Vote, Christian Action Network, California Evangelical Political Givers, Evangelical Pro-Life Donors, Texas Christian Activists, Conservative California PAC Donors, and Check Writing Evangelical Activists. Another company rents lists entitled America's High-Income Donors, Conservative Wealthy Arts Donors, Gutsy Jewish Givers, Spanish-Speaking Donors, and Cream of the Crop Jewish Donors.[12]

Targeting by Lifestyle: When first introduced to the campaigns in 1978, the Claritas targeting system was considered the "the new magic."[13] Invented in 1974 by computer scientist Jonathan Robbin, this new targeting technique sorted the country's thirty-six thousand zip codes into forty "lifestyle clusters."[14] The clusters were given clever names—"Furs and Station Wagons," "Golden Ponds," "Norma Rae-Ville"—and gave a powerful explanation of geodemographic factors, using multivariate analysis. Veteran consultant Matt Reese improved upon the Claritas techniques, making them more applicable to political campaigns, but still the "lifestyle" targeting system proved not to be a precise enough tool and was too expensive for most political campaigns.[15] As seen below, the geodemographic databases used for commercial purposes have been enhanced and supplanted by the microtargeting techniques.

List compilation is assisted by U.S. Census Bureau data, which offer a wealth of information based on census blocks of approximately eight hundred households and measuring between thirty and fifty economic, family, ethnic, employment, and neighborhood characteristics. These statistics, coupled with voting and geodemographic data integrated into nine-digit zip codes, gives an extraordinary amount of information for targeting purposes. This information is always fluid, continually in need of updating and purging of extraneous names. One of the leading list management firms, Aristotle Publishing, estimates that the data on one of six voters will be outdated or wrong by the time the next election rolls around.[16]

Targeting Aided by Statistical Analyses: Direct mail and targeting consultant Hal Malchow argues that, despite the improvements in census data, the more important development in targeting is the application of predictive technologies that allow voter contact specialists to evaluate all data available to them.[17] Malchow's firm created a statistical technology called CHAID (chi square automatic interaction detection) that analyzes how different variables may predict voting behavior. This computer program is operated by first conducting a mini-poll, based on five thousand to ten thousand identification phone calls to randomly selected voters, asking them if they intend to vote and for whom. Attached to responses from these selected voters would be all existing data on them, such as voting history, sex, age, religion, ethnicity, and other geodemographic variables. In addition, the nine-digit zip code is used to match each name with twenty-five census block characteristics. The CHAID program builds "trees" of voters contacted, starting at the top with all voters, then spreading out to three separate branches, Republicans, Democrats, and Independents. Sub-branches then look at other variables, such as education levels, percentage of children in neighborhood, and ethnicity.

In its first test, in the 1996 Senate special election in Oregon, Malchow's firm was able to explore more deeply the voting preferences of voters. The CHAID system told the campaign that Independent voters were just slightly more undecided (32 percent) than voters as a whole (30 percent). But, probing farther down the CHAID targeting tree, the campaign found that younger Independents, who lived in neighborhoods with less education and many children, were at an undecided rate nearly double (58 percent) that of the Independent group as a whole. Malchow noted that in every race, except one that his firm was involved with in 1996, the CHAID results could not have been predicted by traditional voting analysis.[18]

Other techniques are available as well and have been applied by commercial firms. New decision-tree technologies using statistical methods such as cluster analysis, discriminate analysis, and regression analysis might prove useful in solving particular targeting problems. Further, commercial firms have employed artificial intelligence software called "neural networks," based on the architecture of the human brain, to better understand predictive consumer behavior. These commercial techniques, however, tend to be expensive, requiring greater statistical training, and have a lengthier time for data preparation and analysis, and have somewhat limited application to demands of elections.[19]

Online communication, through the whole variety of social network sites, the Internet, smart phones and apps, has given targeting specialists access to so much more data, so many more points of information about each of us. Big Data, that ever-expanding collection of information, gives political campaigns far more voter and consumer information than ever before. The Obama campaign in 2012, at the edge of technology in many ways, took advantage of a new source of data: our cable television viewing habits. The system was called the "Optimizer," and it helped direct Obama television ads to often unusual times and second or third tiered cable shows, reaching receptive audiences.[20]

Direct mail

Using the mail to deliver messages to voters or to solicit funds goes back to the early days of the twentieth century. William Jennings Bryan, in his third bid for the presidency, sought one million contributors for his 1916 campaign, but only twenty thousand responded to a mass mailing, and Bryan was barely able to cover the costs of the solicitation.[21] Dwight Eisenhower was the first presidential candidate to use direct mail in an effective way, and twelve years later, the Barry Goldwater 1964 campaign broke through with $4.7 million raised from a mailing to twelve million and created a list of 221,000 contributors.[22] Using information from the Goldwater campaign, political consultant Richard Viguerie compiled the first major donors list, with the names of 12,500 conservatives.[23] It took Democrats some time to catch up, but George McGovern's presidential campaign raised direct mail to "a high art form."[24] McGovern's 1972 mailing list contained the names of 600,000 probable donors. Through this list, he was able to raise $3 million in prenomination money and $12 million in the general election in response to fifteen million pieces of fundraising mail sent out.

Since the 1970s, direct mail has become a potent fundraising tool, voter contact, and persuasion weapon for candidates at all election levels, and has proven to be most important in elections below the statewide level.[25] In 1997, *Campaigns and Elections* magazine calculated that direct mail was the biggest aggregate cost item in campaigns throughout the country. While large statewide campaigns spent more on television than direct mail, when all other races are counted, from school board and other local races to the presidency, direct mail proved to be the biggest cost item, with over $3 billion spent from 1994 through 1997.[26]

Open this Envelope! As mailboxes are increasingly filled with catalogs, fliers, and other forms of unsolicited material, readers have become adept at separating real mail from junk mail. Political direct mailers face stiff competition, and the biggest, first hurdle is to get people to open the envelope. A number of tricks and gimmicks are used to entice people to open the envelope instead of tossing it into the wastebasket, such as:

- **Celebrity name**: The National Resources Defense Council sent a fundraising appeal in a large, plain, white envelope with only the name "Robert Redford" where the return address would normally appear. The Interfaith Alliance used the same ploy with just the name "Walter Cronkite" on its business-sized envelope. Who could resist a "personal" letter from a celebrated movie actor–conservationist or "the Most Trusted Person in America"?
- **Looks official and important**: Both political parties have sent large cardboard envelopes that look almost like U.S. Post Office priority mail, with *urgent, extremely urgent, important document enclosed, rush priority, please hand deliver to addressee*, and other phrases urging citizens to open the envelope.
- **Looks handwritten**: Addresses are even generated by laser printer to look as though they were addressed by hand, complete with smudged letters, numbers or letters crossed out, and irregular printing.
- **Here's the money**: Just about the most irresistible example of this gimmick was an envelope for a National Republican Congressional Committee fundraising appeal in March 1997—a clear plastic, $11^1/_2$-by-8-inch envelope with a real dollar bill inside, plainly in view, paper clipped to a response card. The plastic envelope was sealed with a bright orange warning label. "Warning: Contents of this package are monitored. Any tampering will result in prosecution under Federal Postal regulations." The message inside, from Newt Gingrich, pressed the point-here is a real dollar... "whatever you do, please do not keep this dollar." Send the dollar back, the letter implores, because it is "absolutely critical" to have every dollar to rebuild the Republican campaign effort and by sending you this dollar, you will see how "serious our financial situation is."[27]

The pitch from the party—you are special: All of the national political party organizations have aggressive fundraising strategies to sign up donors, give them a sense of ownership, and keep them as loyal givers. These are nothing more than elemental, solid, fundraising tactics. The National Republican Senatorial Committee (NRSC) was particularly good at this, sending out solicitations to a wide variety of potential donors. Following are examples from some letters sent in the late 1990s by the NRSC inviting potential contributors to join Republican donor organizations.

The Republican Presidential Legion of Merit promises to be the "highest honor of its type" in the Republican Party, and "only the most loyal and committed supporters" are encouraged to maintain their active membership. Members receive a Legion of Merit lapel pin and a membership card with a toll-free private hotline, and have their names inscribed on the Legion of Merit Register and kept forever with the Legion's Presidential Papers. "Perhaps someday," notes the membership brochure, "your grandchildren or great-grandchildren will see your name linked historically with one or more of our great Republican presidents" who are also Legion of Merit members. Donors will also receive "action alerts," letting them know "exactly what action" they must take to help stop "Clinton and his ultraliberal buddies in Congress from pushing his 'hare-brained schemes' through Congress."[28] Membership into the "exclusive" Presidential Legion of Merit is $60 per year or on a convenient $5 per month installment plan.

For $120 a year, donors can join the Republican Presidential Task Force, "one of the most prestigious and influential organizations within the National Republican Party." Members will have their names permanently inscribed on the Ronald Reagan Founders Wall located in the Honor Courtyard at the Ronald Reagan Center in Washington, D.C. "Your name will be seen by every visitor and dignitary who visits the Reagan Center for generations to come, and stand as a testament to the role you have proudly played in moving our Party and our Nation forward."[29]

Donors can then work their way up to the Republican Senatorial Inner Circle, "one of the Republican Party's most influential and active organizations," for $1,000 per person or in $500 semiannual installments. Membership includes an annual dinner and after-dinner show featuring Wayne Newton, along with policy seminars, such as "Education and School Choice" and "Overcoming Liberal Media Bias."

Next comes the Republican Presidential Roundtable, which is "strictly limited to 400 carefully selected members nationwide" who give $5,000 a year. The fundraising letter from NRSC chairman Senator Mitch McConnell, on expensive paper with a Presidential Roundtable gold seal, notes that "now that a vacancy has occurred among the 20 coveted Presidential Roundtable memberships reserved for [your state], I sincerely hope you will consider stepping forward to claim it."[30] Members in this category also receive lapel pins and newsletters, a fancy dinner in Washington with party leaders, plus photo opportunities.

These solicitation letters for the NRSC have several elements in common in trying to woo potential givers, such as:

- **Flattery**: Donors are very special people. "Whereas [donor] has shown the highest caliber of patriotism, commitment and integrity" (Republican Legion of Merit certificate). "It's up to smart, dedicated, concerned Americans like you to make sure our nation chooses the right course" (Republican Presidential Task Force, "American Agenda Survey").
- **Insider status**: Donors will have a special hotline or newsletter that gives them inside, confidential information not available to the general public. "Due to the confidential nature of this report, we must have verification that you—and only you—received your special report. Please sign this Receipt of Verification and return it immediately" (a confidential strategic blueprint for Republicans used to win back the presidency in 2000).
- **Rub shoulders with Republican leaders**: Donors will be invited to Washington for a special dinner with party leaders with the chance of having their pictures taken with the leaders, or they will have their names listed on the special commemorative wall at Republican headquarters in Washington.
- **Fighting the good fight against the Democrats and liberals**: Donors are assured that they are the best and last hope to fight back against the Democrats, Bill Clinton, and their dreaded liberal policies. In a NRSC fundraising letter, which accompanied a pitch for a three-by-five-foot ceremonial NRSC flag, potential donors were told that funds were needed to fight against "rich, left-wing Hollywood activists, powerful labor union bosses, and shadowy sources."
- **Soliciting views, asking for money**: A standard practice, not just of the NRSC, is to send a private poll out to potential donors, ask them to answer ten or fifteen policy questions, and then request $35 to $100 either to help pay for the poll or to provide for a radio commercial or

some other specific event associated with donating money. Pollsters would laugh at the questions asked; many times they are blatantly self-serving and lead to only one conclusion. For example, in this NRSC solicitation sent out with the signature of former vice president Dan Quayle: "Ted Kennedy and the liberals in the Senate are trying to revive the Clinton plan to ration and control health care by hiding it in a bill for 'children.' Should the Republican-led Senate continue to fight this deceptive scheme?"[31] Yet the purpose of these "polls" is not to solicit public opinion, but to make a partisan point and to rally the faithful to give money.

Above all, direct mail fundraising solicitation is about developing a dialogue and a relationship between the party or candidate and the giver. It is far more productive to solicit money from those who have already given and are willing to give again—and are given a sense of participation.

Candidates and Direct Mail: Writing in 1988, political scientist R. Kenneth Godwin found that political party mailings tended to stress traditional party themes, such as loyalty, citizen duty, and party issues, while the more provocative, negative, and emotional appeals tended to come from candidates and their direct mail consultants.[32] While direct mail does not have the aural and visual impact of television or radio commercials, it can be a very powerful weapon. Messages unthinkable or inappropriate for television audiences often appear in the mailbox to be opened in the privacy of the home. Indeed, consultants Richard Schlackman and Jamie Douglas have called direct mail the "silent killer" of the campaign.[33] Candidates use direct mail to solicit funds, persuade voters, and urge them to vote, and to attack their opponents. Richard Viguerie said that direct mail "is like a water moccasin—silent, but deadly."[34] In many cases, these messages are interlaced in a combination of urgency, begging, fear mongering, and castigation.

Jesse Helms, Ollie North, and Their Direct Mail Money Machines: Two public figures, Senator Jesse Helms of North Carolina and former lieutenant colonel Oliver North, have stood out for their fundraising abilities, attracting millions from loyal conservative followers. Throughout his long political career, Senator Jesse Helms raised enormous sums through direct mail appeals, much of it through small contributions from conservative elderly people living outside North Carolina. In the spirited and ugly 1990 Senate fight against former Charlotte mayor Harvey Gantt, Helms employed his well-oiled direct mail machine to fill his campaign coffers. By the time of the midyear report, Helms held nearly ten times more campaign funds ($7.9 million) than Gantt ($0.8 million). Despite that fundraising lead, Helms' campaign told his loyal supporters that he desperately needed more because he was in the fight of his life.

In a September 1990 direct mail appeal, Helms said he didn't want to "cry wolf," but that he desperately needed money for television commercials. "There's never been a time when I've needed your help more than now," Helms' plea read, "The wolf is here. He's at the door. He's loaded with money and politically dangerous." In a statement defending the Helms direct mail appeal, a spokeswoman for Helms said, "Harvey Gantt is receiving the majority of his support from left-wing special interest groups: unions, homosexuals, NARAL, avant-garde artists, and People for the American Way."

Gantt's campaign reached far and wide for financial support, only fueling the fire of the Helms direct mail campaign. Gantt fundraisers were highly visible, hosted by liberal, artistic, feminist, and gay/lesbian organizations in New York, Washington, San Francisco, and Los Angeles—just the ammunition Helms needed to show that conservative North Carolina values were somehow being subverted by outside influences.[35]

Not only was direct mail used to fuel the Helms 1990 reelection campaign, it was also used to suppress voter turnout. According to the U.S. Department of Justice, the Jesse Helms Reelection Campaign in 1990 and the North Carolina Republican party violated the civil rights of the state's African American voters by illegally mailing 125,000 postcards to registered voters in eighty-six predominantly black precincts informing them that they were not eligible to vote and warning them that they could face criminal prosecution if they tried. Those voters would undoubtedly have voted in large numbers for Harvey Gantt, who is African American. The Helms campaign paid $127,021 in legal bills and $25,000 in fines for violations of federal election laws. The campaign maintained that it had no knowledge of the mailings, but tacitly accepted responsibility by agreeing to sign the Justice Department consent decree, which outlined the infractions.[36]

Beginning with the Iran Contra hearings, Oliver North's public career has been marked by confrontation, loyal support from conservative followers, and derision and intense opposition from many, including military veterans. Fueled by his nationally syndicated talk show, North ran unsuccessfully for the U.S. Senate seat in Virginia in 1994. In his bid to unseat Senator Charles Robb,[37] North's campaign set a record for direct mail solicitations. Through his nationwide appeal, North was able to raise $20.3 million in a single year through direct mail, major donors, telemarketing, and fundraising events. Approximately $17 million came from direct mail alone, from 245,000 donors who responded to the more than thirteen million letters mailed out.[38]

North's fundraising appeals were laced with urgency and desperation. One letter, sent by UPS rather than the regular mail, pleaded, "*I have no choice* but to rush you this letter by UPS" and urged the reader to "*rush my campaign* a 'do or die' donation." North said he had to raise *$500,000* during the next five days: "*Our bank account [is] nearly dry ... and tomorrow won't do.*"[39] A total of seventy-nine different letters went out during the campaign, and during the last eight weeks there was a mailing that went out to the entire contributor file every week. During that same time, recounted one of North's direct mail consultants Richard Norman, all the names on the contributor list that had phone numbers, roughly 60 percent of the total, were called three times.[40] The direct mail solicitations were enormously expensive; of the $17 million raised from direct mail, $11 million was spent on fundraising overhead.[41]

North has maintained his incredible network of potential donors after the 1994 Senate loss. To keep the faithful interested and informed, North offered a monthly newsletter, *Ollie North's Front Lines,* for $39.95 a year, accompanied by a "black book" of the "25 most dangerous liberals in Washington" or a "spine-tingling videocassette" of speeches by North and other conservatives.[42]

Direct mail often focuses on enemies, such favorite targets as Ted Cruz, Rand Paul, "Tea Party crazies" on the Right, or Barack Obama, Obamacare, Nancy Pelosi, Hillary Clinton, or "radical liberals." During the 2004 elections, a wide range of conservative organizations and the Republican party mobilized Christian Right voters by blanketing them with direct mail on the horrors of gay marriage, the menace of abortions, the threat to traditional family values, the nomination of conservative judges, and other issues. One Republican party direct mail piece to households in Arkansas and West Virginia charged that "liberals seek to ban the Bible," with an image of the Bible with "banned" stamped on its cover. Another image showed the image of one man proposing marriage to another man, warning that "This will be Arkansas if you don't vote."[43]

Ron Paul, running for president in 2008, based much of his third party candidacy on his ability to reach supporters through direct mail and through the Internet to tap their wallets. On the anniversary of the Boston Tea Party in December 2007, Paul supporters created a "money bomb," donating some $6 million through online donations. Both Paul and his son, Kentucky senator Rand Paul, have relied heavily on direct mail and online support to get their messages across and raise funds.[44]

Direct mail was especially important to Mitt Romney's 2012 presidential campaign, particularly in his attempt to reach older voters who are less likely to look at YouTube videos or pop-up ads. Romney and the Republican National Committee spent at least $100 million on direct mail, compared with $70 million for Obama and the Democratic National Committee. Here is a typical Romney direct mail piece, focused on seniors in Florida: "Florida Seniors CAN'T TRUST President Obama. BARACK OBAMA HAS FAILED OUR SENIORS." The brochure shows a grim looking Obama, a picture of an elderly white couple and an older white woman, Romney and his wife.

At the same time, Obama pamphlets flooded Ohio voters' mailboxes, taking a jab at Romney's wealth and his work as a private equity fund manager. Romney is seen powering his luxury powerboat near his second home in New Hampshire. "A NEW $25,000 Tax Cut for Multi-Millionaires—Like Himself," scoffed one ad. "But up to $2,000 in Tax Hikes on Families like Yours." Then the ad ends, "Not so fast, Mitt."[45]

Tea Party-backed Republican Matt Bevin was trying to unseat U.S. Senator and Minority Leader Mitch McConnell in the 2014 Kentucky Republican primary. The McConnell campaign had sent out a direct mail letter warning voters about Bevin. The envelope said "Fraud Alert" "Sensitive Materials Enclosed. Please Open Immediately." It all looked and sounded very official, like something the government would send out. The letter blasted away at Bevin: he praised the Wall Street bailout; he did not pay his taxes; he lied on his resume. "This information is provided as a public service," said the attack mail piece. Bevin was incensed; called the letter a lie: "It's unbelievable. It's crap … All this is just absolute horse pucky." Bevin, a neophyte politician, was floored by the charges, and was soundly beaten by McConnell in the primary.[46]

Telemarketing

Hardly anyone has escaped the irritating telephone calls, invariably coming at dinner time, that ask customers to switch long-distance service, seek donations for charity, pitch credit cards, or sell sure-fire investment advice. Intrusive telemarketing operations have become a part of the jangle of modern life.[47] Consumers can now block most annoying solicitations by signing up through the Do Not Call Registry, which became effective in January 2005. However, political phone calls, as well as those from charities and pollsters were not affected.

Political telemarketers have added their voices, providing campaigns with services, such as voter persuasion and identification, volunteer recruitment, get-out-the-vote efforts, fundraising, mobilization of community activists, and integration with targeted direct mail.

Telecommunications services will argue that they provide a better vehicle for communications than media or direct mail. Veteran telecommunications consultant Walter Clinton argues, for example, that the telephone "is the only true interactive medium that is based on the most fundamental element of communication—response."[48] This exchange of conversation, according to Clinton, begins a highly personal and effective dialogue between a prospective voter (and donor) and a campaign. To be effective, the dialogue has to go in phases, with repetitive contact and reiteration of the campaign message, and this is what a well-orchestrated telemarketing campaign can offer.

Telecommunications consultants also argue that the telephone is a better communications device for raising campaign funds than direct mail. Professional telemarketing fundraising costs more than a direct mail solicitation, but the return is considerably more productive. According to telecommunications consultant Vicki Ellinger, telephone fundraising generates income over and above direct mail programs, a higher average donation and more revenue, and increased response rate to three to ten times that of direct mail, depending upon the application.[49]

Push-Polling: One telemarketing application that has received considerable criticism in the past several election cycles is push-polling. This is a well-worn campaign tactic. Under the guise of a legitimate poll, anonymous telephone callers feed damaging or misleading information about a candidate, attempting to persuade or change the opinion of the contacted voter.[50] In the waning hours of a campaign, when voters are numb to television and radio commercials, push-polling becomes one final attempt to spread negative information about an opponent. Before television was used in elections and before the term *push-polling* was even coined, campaigns used this tactic. For example, in 1948, Richard Nixon, running against Helen Gahagan Douglas for the U.S. Senate seat in California, had campaign workers make anonymous telephone calls telling voters that Douglas was a communist sympathizer.[51]

Push-polling drew fire in 1994 campaigns in Alaska, Colorado, Maine, Nebraska, Wisconsin, and many other jurisdictions.[52] "A lot of campaigns do it," said Republican pollster Neil Newhouse. "It's a very effective tactic to communicate with voters late in a campaign when you have nothing left to turn to."[53] Push-polling hones in on an opponent's record, often distorting or exaggerating it, attempting to be the last—and definitely negative—message voters receive about an opponent before voting.

The next step in push-polling is voter suppression phone banking. As one Republican consultant stated, "It is one of the last unrevealed dirty secrets of American politics."[54] Legitimate phone banks operate to get out the vote, to urge the faithful to turn out on election day. A suppression phone bank aims to do just the opposite, to discourage targeted segments of voters, such as the elderly, farmers, or African Americans, from voting.

In the 1996 Iowa presidential caucus, vote suppression charges flew back and forth among Republican operatives. But vote suppression operations are hard to detect and almost impossible to prevent. One Dole campaign adviser, on the eve of the Iowa caucus, said that vote suppression campaigns "come in with the fog in the last couple of days and then disappear."[55]

Before the 1996 Iowa presidential caucus, the Dole campaign paid over $1 million to a telemarketing and phone bank firm, Campaign Tel, to run a secret negative campaign against Steve Forbes, attacking his most important campaign theme, the need for a flat federal tax. From notes taken by a Campaign Tel employee, the script for the telemarketers was this:

> My name is _____ and I'm calling with a special message for Iowa's farm families. Iowa's farm bureau has adopted a resolution that opposes the flat tax like the one offered by candidate Steve Forbes. Under the Forbes flat tax, Iowa's farmers would pay an average of $5,000 more in taxes.[56]

An estimated ten- to thirty-thousand anti-Forbes calls were made to Iowa farmers, and the phone bank operation, located in a strip mall in Spring-field, Illinois, also made calls on behalf of the Dole campaign to voters in South Carolina, South Dakota, North Dakota, Georgia, Connecticut, and New York—states with upcoming primary elections. The trouble with the Iowa telephone calls was that the Iowa Farm Bureau never passed a reso-lution condemning the flat tax and that some of the callers indicated that they were representing the Farm Bureau or a nonexistent group called Iowa Farm Families rather than working on behalf of Senator Dole's campaign. Campaign Tel employees were instructed to identify themselves as employees of National Market Research and to not mention the Dole cam-paign. According to the *Wall Street Journal,* the Dole campaign insisted that Campaign Tel's main assignment was to conduct voter identification and positive persuasion, not to spread negative information about other candidates.[57]

Push-polling is not polling, and private pollsters from both parties were alarmed that their craft and reputations were being discredited.[58] Republi-can pollsters Glen Bolger and Bill McInturff wrote an article in the trade magazine *Campaigns and Elections* entitled "'Push-Polling' Stinks."[59] In addition, a bipartisan group of twenty Republican and fifteen Democratic pollsters, representing twenty-three of the top political polling firms, sent a letter to the American Association of Political Consultants (AAPC) point-ing out the fundamental differences between legitimate survey research, which they stated they practiced, and the tactics of push-polling, or, by other names, "negative advocacy" "persuasion calls," or "vote suppression" calls.

Bolger, McInturff, and many of their polling colleagues would condemn "sleazy smear tactics often used in negative advocacy phone banks."[60] Republican pollster Ed Goeas echoed this sentiment, stating that "anony-mously spreading rumor and innuendo through 'push-polls' is sleazy and should have no part in a campaign strategy."[61]

The polling firms that signed the letter stated the following in trying to distinguish between legitimate survey research and push-polling, which is usually conducted by a telemarketing firm. First, callers for survey research firms provide respondents with the correct name of their firm or the telephone research center. Push-polls, they contend, generally use fictitious names. Second, survey research firms interview a scientifically drawn small sample of voters, whereas push-polls contact "many thousands of voters," with the goal of swaying—not measuring—voter opinion. Third, survey research firms conduct interviews that are between five and forty minutes in length; push-polls generally last between thirty and sixty seconds. Fourth, a survey research firm "may legitimately test contrasts or negatives about candidates (both about their clients and their opponents), but it uses honest information that may be used in television ads, radio, or mail. It is not designed to persuade the sample called-only to question them." Push-polls are generally done in the last week of the campaign, with the specific intent of persuading voters. Finally, the pollsters wanted it on record that survey research firms "do not do 'push-polling'."[62]

Bill McInturff, reportedly the leader behind the bipartisan letter from pollsters, must have been particularly worried. His firm, a leading Republican polling firm Public Opinion Strategies, was Bob Dole's official pollster during the early 1996 presidential primaries. The press discovered the massive push-poll operation run by the Dole campaign against Steve Forbes, described above, but Public Opinion Strategies did not conduct the operation.

In June 1996, the board of directors of the bipartisan AAPC, in a very unusual move, deemed the following campaign practices unethical: cloaking "persuasion calls" under the guise of a survey; dispensing information meant to change opinions about candidates without identifying the candidate who is sponsoring the push-poll; and delivering false information about opponents during a survey. The AAPC board condemned push-polling as a "clear violation of the AAPC's code of ethics and a degradation of the political process."[63]

Push-polling was condemned, but not abolished. In 2006, the campaign of Robert L. Ehrlich, Jr., the incumbent governor of Maryland, was accused of using push-polling tactics. His pollster, Glen Bolger of Public Opinion Strategies, vehemently denied using such tactics. While Public Opinion Strategies had listed "push-polling" as one of its research methodologies, it quickly revised its website to declare that the firm "did NOT engage in push-polling."[64] Other campaigns were accused of using push-polling tactics in the final days of the 2006 congressional and gubernatorial campaigns.

Getting out the Vote

Democrats traditionally had the edge in getting voters to the polls. With the help of vast numbers of volunteers, particularly from organized labor, candidates were able to reach out to Democratic voters and get them to the polls. However, by 2002, Republicans were beginning to respond, creating a sophisticated system of identifying likely voters and getting them to the polling stations. The program became known as the 72-Hour Project, headed by Blaise Hazelwood, political director the Republican National Committee. Republican advisers Matthew Dowd, Karl Rove, and Mark McKinnon, all with years of experience in targeting techniques, test marketed ways to appeal to their base and to seek out new Republican voters. They discovered that only about 7 percent of the voting public was undecided, and that the real opportunities were in motivating and persuading their base, rather than in trying to win over undecideds.[65]

Republican strategists were rediscovering the oldest of campaign tactics—the "ground war." They were spending more money and investing more heavily in ways to identify, register, and get voters to the polls. Thanks to concerted efforts to identify, register, and get citizens to vote, voter turnout increased substantially in 2004, both for Democrats and Republicans. Democrats had increased their voters by some 6.8 million, but Republicans gained nearly 10.5 million. Through the 527 group, America Coming Together, Democrats launched the largest get-out-the-vote campaign in American history, spending some $135 million for the 2004 presidential race.[66] But it was not enough. They were simply out-hustled by Republicans, who had invested heavily in the ground war and, in 2004, were seeing the fruits of their investments.

A key part of the Republican efforts came through sophisticated new techniques of microtargeting. By 2004, both Republicans and Democrats had created comprehensive voter databases containing information on each of the 168 million registered American voters. The Republican operation was called Voter Vault and the Democratic database was DataMart. The Voter Vault database permitted Republican campaigns throughout the country to log onto a secured Internet site, download voter information, then after calling or making a personal visit with the voter, to add information to the record.[67] As Republican strategist Matthew Dowd observed, "If you're a voter living in one of the sixteen states that determined the 2004 election, the Bush team had your name on a spreadsheet with your hobbies and habits, vices and virtues, favorite foods, sports, and vacation venues, and many other facts of your life."[68]

In 2006, Republicans reached into their Voter Vault, trying to reach carefully selected Republicans, even Democrats and Independents, who might be sympathetic to their candidates. When Republican Randall "Duke" Cunningham resigned (and was later convicted of bribery and conspiracy), his California congressional district looked vulnerable. Thanks to microtargeting techniques, former Republican congressman Brian P. Bilbray was able to capture the seat in a special election. In a fierce Rhode Island Senate primary election, Republican strategists were able to identify sympathetic Democrats and Independents who would support beleaguered Republican incumbent Lincoln Chafee, who was being challenged by a conservative Republican activist. In Michigan, Republicans created a list of snowmobile owners and barraged them with messages warning that incumbent Democratic senator Deborah Stabenow's views on the environment might cripple their enjoyment of snowmobiling. Where did they find the snowmobilers? Through credit card transactions, magazine subscriptions, warranty files, vehicle registrations, and other sources.[69]

Young voters present a particular problem and opportunity for candidates and political parties. Typically, voters between the ages of eighteen and twenty-one had some of the lowest participation rates in electoral politics, and they were hard to reach through traditional methods. But in the 2004 presidential election, young voter turnout saw its biggest increase since eighteen-year-olds won the right to vote through the Twenty-Sixth Amendment to the Constitution in 1971. The turnout for voters between the ages of eighteen and twenty-four increased by 11 percent, going from 36 percent to 47 percent from the previous presidential election.[70] This was still lower than the voter percentage for adults as a whole, but a substantial improvement. Research has shown that automatic telephone calls ("robo" calls) and direct mail are not cost-effective methods of reaching young voters. Volunteer and professional phone banks that used longer and chattier conversation scripts found that they were able to reach more young people and increase their participation.[71] But campaigns had to do more: they had to communicate with young voters using their tools of communication: social media, Twitter, and other forms of digital communication.

Obama campaign strategists in 2012 were particularly concerned about keeping the allegiance of young voters. They feared that the enthusiasm found in 2008 had dropped off in 2012, that many young voters would either stay at home rather than vote again for Obama. The Obama campaign heavily increased its presence on college campuses and focused on technological solutions. During the 2012 presidential elections, microtargeting and technology took a leap forward in sophistication and use. The

Obama campaign invested heavily in technology, spending over $100 million. While much time and effort had been spent in the 2008 Obama campaign in targeting and identifying potential voters, in 2012 that information was all pulled together so that the Obama campaign would have one coherent set of information, a massive profile of their online activists, volunteers, potential voters, offline and online donors. This was all coupled with a sophisticated email system that carefully tested and refined messages sent out to individuals and groups. The Obama team called its effort Project Narwhal.[72] The Romney campaign had also invested heavily in technology, and had developed a voter-turnout mobile app, called Project Orca, which would have helped some thirty thousand Romney volunteers throughout the country report immediately to Boston campaign headquarters on Election Day. But the app and the system behind it were not tested properly, and it repeatedly crashed, and was ultimately of little use to the campaign.[73]

Candidates and political parties have rediscovered the oldest form of voter persuasion, reaching likely voters one at a time. The methods are sophisticated and expensive, but the goal is simple: identify likely voters, register them, and get them out to the polls. In big, statewide contests, this can be a very costly undertaking, and there could be no way that a candidate could reach all voters personally. But in smaller jurisdictions, with the right amount of time, energy, and shoe leather, it can be done.

One extraordinary example came from the nation's capital. Washington, D.C. city councilman Adrian Fenty scored an unprecedented victory in an eight-candidate Democratic mayoral primary in September 2006. He beat more seasoned politicians and won each of the eight wards and remarkably every one of Washington's 142 precincts.[74] The Fenty campaign aired television commercials toward the end of the primary, but certainly did not saturate the airwaves. The campaign also relied on direct mail and telemarketing, as other candidates did as well. But what stood Fenty apart was his ground game. He connected with voters the old fashioned way, by going door to door. For fifteen months, Fenty and his swarm of volunteers knocked on doors and claimed to have visited every house on every street in the city. In a city often racially polarized on Election Day, his capturing every single precinct is a remarkable testament to campaign fundamentals and person-to-person democracy. But Fenty's charm and determination could not help him in 2010: he was defeated in his reelection bid. Such is the fickle nature of politics and public opinion.

Notes

1   Elana Varon, "IT on the Campaign Trail," *CIO Magazine*, June 1, 2004

2   Graeme Zielinski, "Groups Sell Politics Door to Door," *Milwaukee Journal Sentinel*, August 24, 2004, 131.

3   On campaign targeting, see Sasha Issenberg, *The Victory Lab: The Secret Science of Winning Campaigns* (New York: Crown, 2012); Hal Malchow, *The New Political Targeting* (Washington, D.C.: Campaigns and Elections Magazine, 2003); Daniel M. Shea, *Campaign Craft: The Strategies, Tactics, and Art of Political Campaign Management* (Westport, Conn.: Praeger, 1996), chs. 4 and 5.

4   Richard Schlackman and Jamie "Buster" Douglas, "Attack Mail: The Silent Killer," *Campaigns and Elections*, July 1995, 25.

5   David Himes, "Strategy and Tactics for Campaign Fund-Raising," in *Campaigns and Elections: American Style*, ed. James A. Thurber and Candice J. Nelson (Boulder, Colo.: Westview, 1995), 74.

6   Robert Odell, "Raising Big Bucks," *Campaigns and Elections*, May 1996, 23. Odell is president of Odell, Simms, and Associates, a Republican fundraising firm.

7   Scott Huch, principal of the Delta Group, a Republican fundraising and direct mail firm, notes that in 1996 house file response was 8 to 14 percent since 1994 for his clients. Odell, "Raising Big Bucks," *Campaigns and Elections*, May 1996, 24.

8   Richard Norman, president of Richard Norman Company, was the principal fundraiser for the Oliver North campaign; Odell, "Raising Big Bucks," 26.

9   American List Counsel promotional material.

10   Richard Harwood, "All-Pro Politics," *Washington Post*, March 23, 1996, A15.

11   American List Counsel catalogue, "The Only Mailing List Catalog You Need," 1996.

12   Ad placed by Response Unlimited and the Rich List Company of Leslie Mandel Enterprises, *Campaigns and Elections*, January 1992, 30–1.

13   Jonathan Robbin, "Geodemographics: The New Magic," *Campaigns and Elections*, Spring 1980, 25–45.

14   For an analysis of the forty neighborhood target system, see Michael J. Weiss, *The Clustering of America* (New York: Harper and Row, 1989).

15   Shea, *Campaign Craft*, 62. See also Mark Atlas, "Gambling with Elections," in *Campaigns and Elections: A Reader in Modern American Politics*, ed. Larry J. Sabato (Glenview, Ill.: Scott, Foresman and Company, 1989); and Weiss, *The Clustering of America*, 217–22.

16   Aristotle Publishing can provide clients with a dead voter file that can be used to purge voter files and records.

17   Hal Malchow, "The Targeting Revolution in Political Direct Contact," *Campaigns and Elections*, June 1997, 36.

18   Malchow, "The Targeting Revolution in Political Direct Contact"; further elaboration of CHAID is found in Malchow, *The New Political Targeting*.

19   Malchow, *The New Political Targeting* 102–3.

20   Jim Rutenberg, "The Secret to the Obama Victory? Rerun Watchers, For One Thing," *New York Times*, November 12, 2012.

21   Frank J. Sorauf, *Money in American Elections* (Itasca, Ill.: Scott, Foresman and Company, 1988), 26, citing the research of Herbert Alexander, *Money in Politics* (Washington, D.C.: Public Affairs, 1972), 32–3.

22   Schlackman and Douglas, "Attack Mail," 25.

23   Robert V Friedenberg, *Communication Consultants in Political Campaigns* (Westport, Conn.: Praeger, 1998), 104, citing Richard Viguerie, *The New Right: We're Ready to Lead* (Falls Church, Va.: Viguerie, 1980), 26.

24   Herbert E. Alexander, Financing Politics: *Money, Elections, and Political Reform*, 4th ed. (Washington, D.C.: CQ Press, 1992), 67–8.

25   On the mechanisms of direct mail, see Larry J. Sabato, "How Direct Mail Works," in *Campaigns and Elections: A Reader in Modern American Politics*, ed. Larry J. Sabato (Glenview, Ill.: Scott, Foresman, 1989).

26   "Direct Mail," *Campaigns and Elections*, May 1997, 22.

27   All underlining in these examples is in the originals. The postscript reinforces the message: "Yes, the enclosed dollar bill is very real. My colleagues here at the NRCC doubted the wisdom of sending cash in the mail to prove to you the extremely critical points I've outlined above. But, I have every faith you won't 'take the money and run'—but will prove me right, that I can indeed count on you to do your part when we need you most, by sending this dollar back with the most generous donation you can today." Maryland governor Robert J. Erhlich, Jr., used the same real dollar gimmick in his 2006 reelection bid.

28   Republican Presidential Legion of Merit (National Republican Senatorial Committee) promotional literature.

29   Republican Presidential Task Force (National Republican Senatorial Committee) promotional literature.

30   Republican Presidential Roundtable (National Republican Senatorial Committee) promotional literature.

31   National Republican Senatorial Committee, "United States Senate Performance Review," solicitation sent out by former vice president Dan Quayle.

32   R. Kenneth Godwin, *One Billion Dollars of Influence* (Chatham, N.J.: Chatham House, 1988), 116.

33   Schlackman and Douglas, "Attack Mail," 25.

34   Viguerie quoted in Todd Meredith, "One the Envelope," *Campaigns and Elections*, December 2004, 76.

35   Peter Applebome, "Carolina Race Is Winning the Wallets of America," *New York Times*, October 13, 1990, 8.

36   Dwight Morris, "Staving off Gantt," *Washington Post*, September 23, 1996.

37   The Robb reelection campaign was one of my clients in 1993 and 1994.

38   John F. Persinos, "Ollie, Inc.: How Oliver North Raised over $20 Million in a Losing U.S. Senate Race," *Campaigns and Elections*, June 1995, 30. The direct

mail vendors were Eberle Associates, Right Concepts, American Target Advertising, Direct Mail Communications, Squire and Hartfield, and Richard Norman Co., all located in the northern Virginia suburbs of Washington.

39 Persinos, "Ollie, Inc.," 31–2. Emphasis in the original.

40 Odell, "Raising Big Bucks," 27.

41 Persinos, "Ollie, Inc.," 32. On the costs associated with fundraising and why it is a particularly expensive means of gathering money, see Sabato, *The Rise of Political Consultants*; Sabato, "How Direct Mail Works"; and Richard Armstrong, *The Next Hurrah: The Communications Revolution in American Politics* (New York: William Morrow, 1988).

42 Peter Baker, "North Magnetic when It Comes to Fund Raising," *Washington Post*, August 2, 1995, D1.

43 Richard Schlackman and Jamie "Buster" Douglas, "Caught in the Gingrich Glue," *Campaigns and Elections*, May 1997, 24–5. Pascrell defeated Martini in the 1996 general election, and the "Strings Attached" direct mail piece won a 1997 Pollie award, given by the American Association of Political Consultants.

44 David Weigel, "Paul, Inc.: Could the Shadowy Network of Paul's Old Fundraising Machine Sink His Presidential Ambitions? *Slate*, March 31, 2014, www.slate.com/articles/news_and_politics/politics/2014/03/rand_paul_mike_ro thfeld_and_direct_mail_inside_paul_inc_s_fundraising_machine.html (accessed February 17, 2015).

45 Dan Eggen, "Direct Mail Still a Force in Campaigns," *Washington Post*, October 12, 2012.

46 Peter Hamby, "How Mitch McConnell Crushed the Tea Party," *CNN*, www.cnn.com/interactive/2014/politics/hamby-midterms/ (accessed February 17, 2015).

47 The Federal Trade Commission adopted the Telemarketing Sales Rule, which went into effect at the beginning of 1996, setting restrictions on when telemarketing can take place—9:00 a.m. to 8:00 p.m.—and requiring companies to stop calling customers who indicate they want to be left alone. The rule also details what telemarketers must disclose during a call, such as their identity and the nature of goods or services being offered.

48 Walter Clinton, "Telephone Campaigning: The Interactive Medium," *Campaigns and Elections*, October/November 1995, 33.

49 Vicki Ellinger, "Telephone Fund Raising as Political Activism," *Campaigns and Elections*, July 1994.

50 On push-polling, see Larry J. Sabato and Glenn R. Simpson, *Dirty Little Secrets* (New York: Times Books, 1996), chap. 9, entitled "Reach Out and Slime Someone: The Age of Telephone Sleaze."

51 Gary Nordlinger in "Political Consultants," CQ *Researcher*, 6, no. 37 (October 4, 1996): 883.

52 Sabato and Simpson, in *Dirty Little Secrets*, write that of the forty-five candidates running for Congress in 1994 they interviewed, thirty-four claimed that push-polling was used against them, at 258.

53 John Harwood and Daniel Pearl, "In Waning Campaign Hours, Candidates Turn to Phone 'Push-Polling' to Step Up the Attack," *Wall Street Journal*, November 9, 1994, A24.

54 Ann Devroy, "Push Becomes Shove in Political Polling with Negative Phone-Bank Tactics," *Washington Post*, February 13, 1996, A9.

55 Ibid.

56 Glenn R. Simpson, "Dole Campaign Has Paid Over $1 Million to Firm That Uses Telemarketing to Criticize Opponents," *Wall Street Journal*, March 12, 1996, A20.

57 Ibid.

58 However, some polling firms had been accused of conducting push-polling operations, see Sabato and Simpson, *Dirty Little Secrets*, 262, 265–6.

59 Glen Bolger and Bill McInturff; "'Push Polling' Stinks," *Campaigns and Elections*, August 1996, 70.

60 Ibid.

61 Ibid.

62 Letter from Political Consultants to the American Association of Political Consultants, summarized in Bolger and McInturff.

63 Frank J. Murray, "Group to Condemn 'Push Poll' Methods: Settlement Targets Unethical Moves," *Washington Times*, June 24, 1996, A7.

64 Doug Donovan, "Erhlich Opinion Firm Denies Using 'Push Poll' Tactics," *Baltimore Sun*, October 14, 2006, 5B.

65 Thomas B. Edsall and James Grimaldi, "On Nov. 2, GOP Got More Bang For Its Billion," *Washington Post*, December 30, 2004, A1; and Ron Fournier, Douglas B. Sosnick, and Matthew J. Dowd, *Applebee's America: How Successful Political, Business and Religious Leaders Connect with the New American Community* (New York: Simon and Schuster, 2006), 13.

66 Edsall and Grimaldi, "On Nov. 2, GOP Got More Bang For Its Billion," *Los Angeles Times*, September 24, 2006, A1.

67 Jon Gertner, "The Very, Very Personal is the Political," *New York Times*, February 15, 2005, 43.

68 Tom Hamburger, "GOP Mines Data for Every Tiny Bloc."

69 Fournier, Sosnick, and Dowd, *Applebee's America*, 67.

70 "Young Voter Mobilization Tactics: A Compilation of the Most Recent Research on Traditional and Innovative Voter Turnout Techniques" (Graduate School of Political Management, George Washington University, 2006), compiled with the assistances of the Center for Information and Research on Civic Learning and Engagement, University of Maryland.

71 Ibid. Donald P. Green and Alan S. Gerber, *Get Out the Vote! How to Increase Voter Turnout* (Washington, D.C.: Brookings Institution Press, 2004).

72 Sasha Issenberg, "Obama's White Whale," *Slate*, February 15, 2012; see also, Sasha Issenberg, *The Victory Lab: The Secret Science of Winning Campaigns* (New York: Crown, 2012).

73 Zeynep Tufecki, "Beware the Smart Campaign," *New York Times*, November 176, 2012, A23.

74 Lori Montgomery, "In Sweep, Fenty Draws on Uniting to Conquer," *Washington Post*, September 14, 2006, Al.

8

The Money Chase

We raised a lot of money and mobilized an awful lot of people, and we lost, plain and simple. We're going to study what worked, what didn't work, and improve our efforts in the future. We're not going to roll over and play dead."

—David Koch, whose organizations spent at least $407 million trying to defeat President Obama in 2012[1]

Money is distorting democracy now. Money not only determines who wins, but often who runs. If you've got a good idea and $10,000 and I've got a terrible idea and $1 million, I can convince people that the terrible idea is a good one.

—Bill Bradley[2]

The Spiraling Cost of Running for Office

Running for office has become a far more expensive enterprise than ever before. In order to compete, let alone win, candidates for federal, statewide, and many other offices are having to spend more money and devote more time to raising funds. In many ways, candidates have become more dependent on moneyed interests to help them get elected. In addition, outside groups, often hiding the names of their contributors and the amount they have given, are making a major impact on key federal and statewide races. The race for office has become a race for money.

Running for Congress: The cost of mounting an effective race for Congress has increased steadily during the past three decades (Table 8.1). In 1986,

**TABLE 8.1 AVERAGE COST OF CAMPAIGNS FOR HOUSE AND
SENATE WINNERS, 1986–2012, IN NOMINAL AND 2012 DOLLARS**

| | House winners | | Senate winners | |
	Nominal $	2012 $	Nominal $	2012 $
2012	1,596,953	1,596,953	10,351,556	10,351,556
2010	1,434,760	1,511,799	8,993,945	8,276,415
2008	1,362,239	1,452,718	7,500,052	7,998,198
2006	1,259,791	1,434,762	8,835,416 [a]	10,062,557
2004	1,038,391	1,262,120	7,183,825	8,731,637
2002	911,644	1,163,499	3,728,644	4,758,737
2000	845,907	1,127,876	7,198,423 [b]	9,597,897
1998	677,807	957,751	4,655,806	6,558,117
1996	686,198	1,004,150	3,921,653	5,738,761
1994	541,121	838,336	4,488,195	6,953,371
1992	556,475	910,668	3,351,115	5,487,350
1990	423,245	743,512	3,298,324	5,794,148
1988	400,386	777,081	3,746,225	7,270,780
1986	359,577	753,274	3,067,559	6,426,200

Source: Campaign Finance Institute analysis of FEC data.

[a] Hillary Rodham Clinton (D-N.Y.) had the most expensive Senate race in 2006, at $40.8 million.

[b] Jon Corzine (D-N.J.) spent $63,209,506; Hillary Clinton spent $29,941,194. The remaining Senate winners in 2000 averaged $4,737,365.

the average cost for the winners of U.S. House campaigns cost about $753,000 (in 2012 dollars); by 2012, the average cost for winners was nearly $1.6 million. For the U.S. Senate winners, using the same time frame, we find that the average cost of a winning campaign in 1986 was about $6.4 million (in 2012 dollars), while the average cost in the 2012 contests was $10.3 million. There were also some very expensive contests: when Hillary Clinton ran for U.S. Senate reelection in New York, the campaign cost $40.8 million; in 2000, Jon Corzine spent $63.2 million to win the U.S. Senate seat in New Jersey.

The chances for an incumbent House member to be reelected are very high, and it has been that way for decades. Incumbents have a better than 90 percent chance of being returned to office. In recent times, that number dipped below 90 percent only during the 1992 election (88 percent) and the 2010 Tea Party-backed Republican victory (85 percent).[3] Still, incumbents feel it necessary to raise as much money as they can, to scare off opponents, and to arm themselves with television ads, polls, and consultants. But incumbents, particularly Republicans, have had other reasons to worry: the fear of being challenged in their own primaries. While it was an isolated case, the fate of House Majority Leader Eric Cantor of Virginia haunts mainstream Republicans. Cantor, who had a huge $5 million campaign war chest, was picked off during the 2014 Virginia Republican Party primary by David Brat, a relatively unknown and underfunded ($200,000) college professor, who was enthusiastically backed by local Tea Party groups.[4]

U.S. Senate races are also seeing record amounts spent, by candidates and especially by outside interest groups. In 2014, the contest between Senate Republican leader Mitch McConnell against Democratic opponent Alison Lundergan Grimes was expected to reach more than $100 million, an all-time record for a U.S Senate contest. When Elizabeth Warren and Scott Brown competed in 2012 for the U.S. Senate seat from Massachusetts, some $83 million was spent.[5] In 2014, enormous amounts were spent by candidates and especially by outside organizations which were successful in helping defeat several incumbent Democrats.

Presidential Campaigns: Campaign finance scholar Anthony Corrado characterized the 2008 presidential race as an "unparalleled quest for dollars."[6] In all, Barack Obama and John McCain had gathered over $1.6 billion. Outside spending was not a significant factor in this campaign, with both presidential candidates discouraging use the widespread expenditure of outside funds. McCain decided to accept public funding for the general election, and he received $84 million. Obama, on the contrary, decided against accepting public funds and was able to overwhelm McCain with an unprecedented flow of dollars to his campaign during the general election. It was a lesson learned: public financing gives candidates money, but requires them to forgo their own fundraising. Why handicap your campaign when you need the money the most; why not just try to raise it on your own? As seen in the 2012 contest, public funding for the major candidates was dead: they did not need it and did not want to live with its restrictions.

When it was all over, the 2012 presidential contest between Barack Obama and Mitt Romney proved to be the most expensive in U.S. history, with over $2 billion raised and spent by the candidates, their political parties, and outside groups. This was also the first time that both major candidates chose not to accept public funding and instead relied on their own fundraising prowess.[7] As noted at the top of this chapter, hundreds of millions of dollars were raised by Super PACs and other outside interests to persuade voters. The vast majority of the money came from committees and organizations controlled by the Charles and David Koch, the billionaire brothers who were intent on defeating Obama. Another big spender was Las Vegas casino billionaire Sheldon Adelson, who first helped to prop up Newt Gingrich in the Republican primaries, then aided Mitt Romney, and altogether spent some $150 million hoping to defeat Obama. Undeterred, Adelson vowed to spend more of his money for the 2016 presidential race, and brought together likely Republican candidates in Las Vegas in late March 2014. Critics rightly called this the "Sheldon Primary," presidential hopefuls pressing the flesh, currying favor with plutocrats. The Koch brothers announced that they would spent nearly $900 million during the 2016 presidential election.[8]

Super PACs, the Super Wealthy, and "Dark Money": In early 2010, the U.S. Supreme Court ruled in *Citizens United v. Federal Election Commission* (FEC) that the federal government could not ban political spending by corporations during candidate elections. In writing the opinion, Justice Anthony Kennedy said that the federal bans on corporate spending were a "classic examples of censorship."[9] While many in the business community applauded this decision, others, including President Obama were alarmed. Obama declared in his 2010 State of the Union address that this decision "reversed a century of law that I believe will open the floodgates for special interests."[10]

President Obama was right. Soon, the money began pouring in to newly created organizations called Super PACs. There were a couple of features that made Super PACs attractive: unlimited amounts of money could be given, and the donors (and amounts) did not have to be disclosed to the public. This undisclosed money was soon dubbed "dark money." These two features directly contradicted to pillars of campaign finance law: limits on the amount of money donors could give and disclosure of who gave the money. These features still existed, but they did not apply to Super PACs, these new tax-exempt nonprofit organizations, which did not give directly to candidates, but nonetheless spent their money to influence elections through independent expenditures. Most of the money comes through what are called 527 Groups (named after the provision in the Internal Revenue Code), 501(c)(4) "social welfare" groups, and 501(c)(6) nonprofit trade associations (such as the U.S. Chamber of Commerce).

Many Super PACs came up with innocuous-sounding names: Americans for Tax Reform, American Action Network, Americans for Prosperity, Americans for Responsible Leadership, American Crossroads, or Patriot Majority. One such group, Crossroads GPS (Grassroots Policy Strategy) was created by political operatives Karl Rove and Ed Gillespie. They took advantage of the Court ruling and when asked for the names of their donors and how much they gave, Crossroads GPS crossed out the names of all fifty-three individuals who had given $1 million of more in 2012, and blanked out the names of the 291 donors who had given at least $5,000.[11]

As Table 8.2 indicates, the vast majority of money raised by these groups was aimed at opposing Democrats or supporting Republicans.

The Koch brothers and Sheldon Adelson are the most visible billionaires who are putting their own money at work to advance their candidates and causes. But they are not alone. George Soros, through a wide variety of networks, has given generously to liberal and progressive causes, and billionaire Tom Steyer vowed to spend $100 million in 2014 help candidates who advocate climate change policy. A wealthy group of liberal donors meeting as the Democracy Alliance has poured some $500 million into organizations and causes in its decade of existence.[12]

With wide-open spending, sharp partisan differences, and control of both Congress and the White House at stake, there certainly will be no going back: campaigns will cost more, and much of that money will come from outside groups, dominated by a small number of very rich people. Perhaps this won't be the best thing for our democracy and elections, but it will certainly enrich political consultants.

California—The Golden State: For good or ill, California is definitely the golden state for political consultants. No other state comes close in matching the amount of money spent by candidates or by proponents or opponents of ballot issues. As can be seen in the next chapter, hundreds of millions of dollars have been spent by proponents and opponents of ballot issues in recent years, making California the most lucrative market for political consultants, except during presidential election years. The robust nature of ballot issues in California accounts for the bulk of the spending, but the state has also seen record-breaking amounts spent on gubernatorial contests. Former CEO of eBay and Hewlett-Packard, Meg Whitman, ran for governor in 2010, spending over $176 million, with $144 million coming out of her own resources.[13] She lost to former governor Jerry Brown who spent a "mere" $40 million (and none out of his own pocket).

TABLE 8.2 INDEPENDENT EXPENDITURES OF NON-COMMITTEE FEDERAL ELECTION COMMISSION FILERS, 2011–2012

Organization	Independent expenditure ($)	Main purpose	Amount spent ($ million)
Crossroads Grassroots Policy Strategies	70,586,641	Oppose Democrat	62.4
Americans for Prosperity	33,539,772	Oppose Democrats	33.5
US Chamber of Commerce	32,676,075	Oppose Democrats	27.9
American Future Fund	23,959,072	Support Republicans	12.4
Americans for Job Security	15,872,866	Oppose Democrats	15.2
Americans for Tax Reform	15,794,582	Oppose Democrats	14.4
American Action Network	11,786,129	Oppose Democrats	10.4
League of Conservation Voters	10,897,016	Oppose Republicans	8.6
Americans for Responsible Leadership	9,787,783	Support Republicans	6.5
Patriot Majority	7,509,017	Oppose Republicans	6.6

Source: Federal Election Commission filings and Sunlight Foundation

Statewide contests cost more here: trying to reach 10 million voters spread over fourteen media markets is expensive.

Why it Costs So Much to Run for Office: Several factors account for the spiraling cost of elections at the federal level and in many state and local contests. First, candidates are more willing to arm themselves with the services of professional political consultants. This means more polling, greater use of television advertising, more money on telemarketing, and greater willingness to pay high-priced general consultants and campaign managers for their services. Second, more wealthy candidates are now willing to put up their own money to partially or fully finance their campaigns. Third, there is a greater aggressiveness on the part of candidates, especially incumbents, to accumulate large war chests to discourage competitors and to begin campaigning earlier in the cycle. Fourth, since the Republican takeover of the House of Representatives in 1994, its recapture by the Democrats in 2006, then the Republican recapture in 2010, there has been a concentrated effort to defeat or protect vulnerable freshman members. Finally, corporations, unions, ideological organizations, and individuals have exploited the loopholes in campaign finance laws and taken advantage of Supreme Court rulings to permit 527s, nonprofits, and social welfare organizations armed as Super PACs to spend unprecedented amounts of money to influence elections.

Not all elections are high priced. The cost of campaigning will range widely, depending on several basic factors:

- **The cost of media markets**: Media markets, especially television, vary widely, from the expensive urban markets like New York, Los Angeles, and Chicago, to the inexpensive markets of Billings, Montana or Santa Fe, New Mexico.
- **The competitiveness of the race**: A hard-fought election involving several primary challengers and a tough general election fight will take far more resources than a race with no primary and only token general election opposition.
- **The size of the district**: It is far more expensive to reach a voting population of two million in a statewide race than in a congressional district with perhaps 350,000 voters.

Wealthy Candidates Using Personal Funds: A growing number of candidates for high office have used personal funds to help finance their campaigns.

But no one tops Michael R. Bloomberg, who spent more than $261 million of his own money in running for office.[14] Bloomberg handily won reelection as mayor of New York City in 2005, spending more than $85 million of his own funds; that was on top of the $74 million spent in 2001 when he was first elected mayor. The third time he successfully ran, in 2009, he spent $102 million. Bloomberg is a billionaire, many times over, and for him, the investment in his own campaigns amounted to little more than pocket change. Other super-wealthy candidates have run, pouring millions into their own campaigns, but with mixed results. As seen above, Meg Whitman spent $144 million while losing the California governor's race in 2010. Tom Golisano spent $74 million of his own money running, unsuccessfully, for governor of New York in 2002; for all his money, he only received 14 percent of the primary vote. Jon Corzine invested $60 million of his own funds to become U.S. senator from New Jersey in 2000; then spent $43 million, again his own money, to become governor of New Jersey in 2005, but then lost in 2009 while spent another $27 million of his own funds. Presidential hopeful Steve Forbes spent $37 million of his own money in 1996, and another $30 million in 2000; Ross Perot spent $63 million, losing in 1992, and another $8 million in 1996. Mitt Romney dropped out of the 2008 Republican primary after spending $45 million in personal funds. [15]

More often than not, the rich, but politically inexperienced, candidate ends up spending millions and losing. The Center for Responsive Government, a nonpartisan watchdog organization that tracks money and politics, noted that all of the top ten self-financed candidates in 2002 for the House or the Senate were defeated, and nearly all the candidates who spent $1 million or more of their own money in 2004 federal races were also defeated.[16] Voters somehow have an instinct to see through rich candidates who have never run before, throwing around bags of money and hoping to win their support. When Al Checchi was running in the 1998 Democratic gubernatorial primary in California, the eventual winner, lieutenant governor Gray Davis (with no deep pockets of his own) knifed his free-spending opponents (Checchi—$40 million and Jane Harman—$16 million of her own money) with this slogan: "Davis: Experience money can't buy."

Not every rich candidate loses, as seen with Bloomberg and Corzine. Herb Kohl, two-term senator from Wisconsin, twice ran successfully under the banner of "Nobody's Senator But Yours," accepting only small contributions from individuals and spending a total of $15 million in personal funds. When Jon Corzine first ran during the 2000 New Jersey Democratic primary for the Senate, his opponent, long-time politician Jim Florio, mocked Corzine, calling him the "human ATM machine." Corzine won by 16 percent and was unfazed by Florio's jibes: "Make no mistake, I want to invest in America," said Corzine, "and that's what this campaign will be about." For New Jersey voters, Corzine's wealth did not matter.[17]

Rick Scott poured in $85 million (90 percent his own money) in winning the Florida gubernatorial contest in 2010, and was determined to spend at least $100 million in his reelection bid against former governor Charlie Crist.[18]

It is very tempting for candidates with fat wallets to bypass the time-consuming, tawdry, and sometimes humiliating chase for dollars. It is so much easier to concentrate on the business of campaigning when all fundraising can be done by a signature on a personal check. But as the track record shows, dollars alone are hardly ever the answer to a successful campaign.

Skinflint Approach: Far more rare is the candidate who spends virtually no money on campaigning. Former senator William Proxmire of Wisconsin and former congressman William Natcher of Kentucky, both noted for their frugality, were able to campaign on a shoestring. Natcher insisted on paying his own campaign bills, usually no more than $7,000 per election. "Some people are spending $1 million on House races," Natcher once said. "That's wrong. It's morally wrong. I don't believe they can really represent their people if they are taking money from these groups [political action committees]."[19] In 1990, Natcher was outspent $144,315 to $6,766 and still managed to beat his opponent two to one.

But the Natcher and Proxmire examples occur only under unusual circumstances. Natcher had a safe, demographically and politically stable district; in Proxmire's case, it was more a testament to the candidate's unique personality. Proxmire's successor could not afford the skinflint approach. Herb Kohl blitzed the Democratic primary with $7.5 million of his own money for advertising during the last six months of the campaign.

Despite the poor record of wealthy candidates who spend lavishly out of their own pockets, in most cases, the candidate who spends the most money will win. Research covering 2001 through 2004 for state legislative races indicates that, on the average, 85 percent of the winners had raised the most money in their campaigns.[20] The U.S. House and Senate incumbents on the average enjoy a near ten-to-one fundraising advantage over their challengers. It is no coincidence that 96 to 98 percent of the House members and 85 to 95 percent of Senators are returned to office.[21]

Voting (In)efficiency: What does it cost a candidate to gain one vote? During the 2004 election cycle, the cost per vote varied widely. For all state contests in California, each vote cost an average of $14.83; in Illinois, the cost was $16.60; and in West Virginia, $30.25. On the other hand, the legislative races in Florida that year averaged just $3.10 per vote. For other candidates, votes were very expensive. Each of Tom Golisano's 633,000 votes in the 2002 New York gubernatorial contest cost him $110; John Thune and Tom Daschle spent at total of $40 million in the hard-fought 2004 South Dakota senatorial race, costing roughly $75 per vote. Michael Coles, in his unsuccessful bid to oust Newt Gingrich, spent over $5.5 million (a record amount) with each vote costing $43.26. Michael Bloomberg's second re-election race in New York cost him $174 per vote. Illinois senate hopeful Blair Hull fared even worse. He spent $29 million of his own money in 2004 and dropped out before any votes were cast. Somewhere, old-time, big-city bosses are shaking their heads in dismay, thinking how much cheaper it was in the old days of outright bribery and vote buying.[22]

Raw financial numbers do not tell the entire story. What really matters is not how much money was raised, but when and how wisely it was spent. Some campaigns will spend lavishly on overhead, such as expensive campaign office space and full-time salaried employees raising money during the off years. The 2000 Al Gore for President campaign was roundly criticized for its excessive spending during the 1999 preprimary months, with heavy expenditures on campaign offices, a bloated campaign staff, and a revolving door of expensive consultants. After the election, the campaign came in for even greater criticism. The Gore campaign had over $12 million left in the bank; valuable money that could have been spent wisely and strategically at the last minute in key states to get out the vote.

In 1998, one of the worst examples of inefficiency was the reelection campaign of Democratic senator Carol Moseley-Braun of Illinois, which Dwight Morris called a "finance nightmare."[23] While Moseley-Braun was good at raising money ($4,886,749 since January 1993 when she took office), she had only $590,585 in the bank seven months before the election. Where did all the money go? She had to repay debts from her 1992 campaign ($631,109); she spent $1,969,655 on overhead (staff salaries, taxes, rent, utilities, telephone, computers, travel, meals); $1,188,376 on lawyers and accountants; and $1,704,843 on fundraising costs.[24]

Indeed, the cost of fundraising itself can be considerable for any campaign, and such costs often distort a campaign's financial balance sheet. For example, one of the biggest users of direct mail and other fundraising solicitations was the Oliver North for Senate campaign in 1994. North's campaign brought in approximately $17 million in direct mail and telephone solicitations, yet the cost was very high: $11 million to pay for the fundraising services. The net income to the campaign was only $5 million.

Inefficiency can come through using the wrong tactics, the wrong medium, or the wrong message. Al Checchi had some of the most talented, experienced, and high-priced consultants available. His television ads were well crafted and they blanketed the state; he traveled tirelessly throughout California; he was handsome, energetic, and sincere; even his website sparkled. But his critics, and Monday-morning quarterbacks, were quick to point out that Checchi's message was just flat wrong. Checchi positioned himself as the candidate of change, even telling voters, "If you like the status quo, then don't vote for me." His $40 million campaign was based on the notion that voters were disappointed, disillusioned, and wanted something better. As Checchi observed after his landslide defeat, "In the exit polls, voters 2 to 1 said we don't want change. How the hell do you overcome that?"[25] Voters overwhelmingly favored the most status quo of candidates, lieutenant governor Gray Davis.

In the past few years, it seems that the lid has been blown off any kind of campaign finance reform. Outsiders can spend as much as they want, don't have to divulge it, and can form innocuous-sounding groups to hide their intent. Independent expenditures overwhelm the voices of candidates. How did we get to this point? Let us look briefly at federal campaign finance law.

Federal Election Law

Before the federal campaign finance reforms were enacted in the 1970s, election financing was "cash-and-carry politics"—checks were not required, there were no limits on funds, records were not kept except for internal purposes, and there were no requirements for disclosing sources of funding.[26] Each party relied heavily on generous, wealthy contributors.

Campaign finance expert Herbert Alexander noted that the 1972 presidential campaign was the "high watermark for large donors ."[27] Both Richard Nixon and George McGovern benefited, with three contributors giving a total of $4 million in campaign donations.[28]

In 1974, Congress made major amendments to the Federal Election Campaign Act (FECA) of 1971. For the next twenty-eight years, FECA formed the basic requirements for federal campaign contributions and spending. The law was designed to curb the influence of wealthy donors, to require reporting of funds received and spent, and to put ceilings on the amount of money that could be spent in campaigns. The 1974 legislation also created the FEC to administer and enforce federal campaign finance requirements.[29]

Under this law, certain kinds of contributions were forbidden: cash contributions of more than one hundred dollars, contributions in the name of another person, money from anyone under eighteen,[30] and contributions from people who were not citizens or legal permanent residents. Also prohibited were contributions from labor unions or corporations directly to candidates.

The 1974 amendments also restricted the amount of funds an individual could give each year to a candidate or political party. Individuals could give up to $1,000 per election (primary, runoff, general) to each candidate; $5,000 per year to a political action committee; $20,000 per year to the national political party; and $25,000 total per calendar year. The maximum contributions remained the same for the next twenty-two years and, by 2002, inflation had eaten away about two-thirds of their value.

Political action committees (PACs) were also restricted by the federal campaign law. PACs first appeared in the 1940s when labor unions began soliciting funds from their members. There were relatively few PACs in the early years, but once they became sanctioned by FECA, they grew rapidly in the 1970s and 1980s. The latest figures from the FEC indicate there is a total of 4,016 PACs.[31]

There are three basic kinds of political action committees. First, there are "connected" PACs, which are affiliated with a parent organization, such as a labor union, corporation, or membership organization. This is the most common political action committee, generating by far the most money for candidates. Connected PACs solicit funds from employees, members, and shareholders. Second, there are "unconnected" committees, which have no parent organization. These are often ideological PACs or organizations created by political entrepreneurs. Unconnected PACs are free to solicit funds from any citizen who wants to give money. The third kind is the "leadership" political action committee that was created to give certain members of Congress leverage in helping other candidates who might run for House or Senate committee or leadership positions.[32]

Under the 1974 FECA amendments, political action committees were restricted in the amount of hard money they could give to individuals or political parties during a calendar year: $5,000 per election (primary, runoff, general) to each candidate; $5,000 per year to another political action committee (usually to a leadership PAC); and $15,000 per year to the national political party.

Buckley v. Valeo: Almost immediately after the 1974 amendments became law, Senator James L. Buckley of New York and former Minnesota senator Eugene McCarthy brought a lawsuit challenging their validity. In a 1976 landmark decision, *Buckley v. Valeo*,[33] the U.S. Supreme Court upheld contribution limits in the law, but ruled that there could be no expenditure ceilings on campaigns. This meant that wealthy candidates, like Buckley, were now free to spend as much of their own money as they wished on their own campaign. It also meant that organizations could spend freely on political communication.

The Court ruled that:

A restriction on the amount of money a person or group can spend on political communication during a campaign necessarily reduces the quantity of expression by restricting the number of issues discussed, the depth of their exploration, and the size of the audience reached. This is because virtually every means of communicating ideas in today's mass society requires the expenditure of money.[34]

Because of *Buckley*, individuals, labor unions, corporations, political action committees, and organizations could spend as much money as they wanted to advocate the victory or defeat of a candidate for federal office. The vehicle for express advocacy is called an independent expenditure. Money spent for independent expenditures must be reported to the FEC, and must be made without the knowledge, consultation, or cooperation of any candidate.[35] Independent expenditures had always been possible for groups such as NARAL Pro-Choice America, the National Rifle Association, the Christian Coalition, the Sierra Club, and a host of other organizations that wanted to spend funds to either defeat or to help a candidate. In a fairly new twist, the $8.5 million that paid for the Willie Horton ads in 1988 came through an independent expenditure organization created by a group of Republican consultants.

Independent expenditures were given a much wider meaning because of the 1996 Supreme Court decision *Colorado Republican Federal Campaign Committee v. Federal Election Commission.*[36] The Court, in a deeply divided opinion, ruled that political parties had the right to make unlimited independent expenditures, just as long as there is no coordinated activity with the candidates. This new tool allowed both Democrats and Republican campaign committees to give valuable direct aid to their own candidates. The Republicans were the first to take advantage of this ruling. The day after the Supreme Court decision, the National Republican Senatorial Committee (NRSC) established a new independent expenditure unit. The NRSC began pouring nearly $10 million of hard money into key Senate races above and beyond what it had heretofore been permitted to spend in coordination with candidates. The Democratic Senatorial Campaign Committee was able to spend only $1.5 million during this same period of time.[37] As we have seen, in 2010 the Supreme Court opened the doors wide to corporate independent expenditures in its *Citizens United* decision.

Soft Money and Issue Advocacy: The individual contributions, PAC money, and independent expenditures fall under the jurisdiction of the FECA and must be reported to the FEC. Such money is called hard money.[38] *Soft money* is the name given to funds not covered by the requirements and regulations of federal campaign law and, by 1980, candidates and political parties began in earnest to exploit this new form of unregulated and unreported money. Two federal actions were key in opening up the floodgates of soft money. In 1979, FECA was amended so that national party committees could spend money on "party-building activities" in their state and local parties without having that money count against hard money spending ceilings. National parties' funds could now pour into state and local party grassroots campaign materials (bumper stickers, brochures), voter education and registration activities, and get-out-the-vote drives. Technically, the 1979 amendment did not create soft money. It came about through a FEC administrative action in 1978 that changed the rules governing party fundraising. The FEC determined that a state party could use corporate or union funds (both of which were barred as hard money gifts) to finance a share of its voter registration drives. The share of the costs were undefined, and the funds would not be subject to federal limits.[39]

Soft money came in slowly at first, but by 1996 both national parties were aggressively courting wealthy individuals, unions, and corporations to contribute serious sums of money. This became the ideal vehicle for the wealthy individual who had reached the maximum of $25,000 allowed under hard money restrictions. Now, any amount was possible. The potential of unlimited soft money gave new meaning to the old term "fat cat". As journalists Charles Babcock and Ruth Marcus noted, there had been a "tidal wave of money" gathered through soft money by both the Democratic and Republican parties, giving them a greater role in presidential and congressional races than ever before.[40]

As the parties and candidates prepared for the 2000 presidential election, soft money came pouring in. Wealthy donors were given special status: Republican donors who gave $100,000 were part of the Team 100 donors, and those who donated $250,000 were in a more exclusive group, the Republican Regents. Democrats had their own big money club, Leadership 2000, whose members pledged to give or raise $350,000 each. By the time soft money was banned, a total of seven hundred and twenty-four individuals or organizations had given at least $100,000 each to the national Democratic and Republican parties. In total, Republicans gathered more soft money than Democrats, but wealthy Democrats did not shy away from contributing. The top five soft money sources in 2002 had given Democrats $34.8 million and had given Republicans a mere $42,000.[41]

The Hard Money–Soft Money Shell Game: The distinctions between regulated hard money and unregulated soft money were easily blurred. In a way, the difference amounted to nothing more than an accounting shell game. An analysis by the *Washington Post* in 1998 showed that the Democratic National Committee (DNC), deeply in debt and scrambling to catch up with Republicans, enlisted a dozen state Democratic parties to swap soft money for hard money. The DNC needed hard money for its congressional and senatorial candidates; it had an excess of soft money that could not legally be used for such purposes. In 1997, the DNC raised millions of dollars in soft money from labor unions, wealthy contributors, and corporations. The DNC then swapped funds with state parties, turning over soft money to the state parties, giving them a 10 to 15 percent commission, and getting back from the state parties hard money that could be used to help finance federal elections.[42] Soft money became hard money, and through legal fiction and accounting legerdemain, the DNC was able to gain much-needed hard money funds. Soft and hard money swaps had been done in earlier years, both by Democrats and Republicans, but the 1997–1998 Democratic swap was by far the most aggressive.

"It shows the porousness of the system and exposes the myth that there is some separation between hard and soft money," said Don Simon, executive vice president of Common Cause.[43]

Foreign money: Federal law forbids campaign funds from foreign citizens, corporations, and governments. But like so much else with money in politics, there are exceptions and loopholes. For example, U.S. subsidiaries of foreign-owned companies are permitted to make political action committee and soft money contributions as long as the U.S. affiliate, and not the parent company, makes the decisions on contributions. Contributions can also come from "foreign agents," U.S. citizens registered with the State Department who are lobbyists acting on behalf of foreign governments, businesses, or other associations.

The Center for Responsive Politics identified one hundred and five U.S. subsidiaries of one hundred and one foreign-owned companies, in seventeen different countries, which gave PAC contributions to federal candidates during the 2006 election cycle. These subsidiaries contributed over $7.5 million. The biggest contributors, who gave through their American subsidiaries, were the pharmaceutical company GlaxoSmithKline ($530,000, United Kingdom), accounting firm KPMG ($532,000, Netherlands), and two financial services companies, UBS Americas ($456,000, Switzerland) and HSBC North America ($412,000, United Kingdom). Before soft money was banned, U.S. subsidiaries contributed much more to federal campaigns. For example, in 1996, they gave $12.5 million to federal campaigns, with a little over $8 million as soft money.[44]

When PAC money is given by a subsidiary, is it the funds of the American subsidiary or the parent international company? Is the contribution a part of the political business strategy of the subsidiary or the parent? As former chairman of the FEC, Trevor Potter stated, "While it's possible most of the time to discern whether a company is a subsidiary of a foreign-owned parent, it's virtually impossible to figure out whose money" has been donated.[45]

The issue of foreign money surfaced in full force during the 1996 presidential elections with revelations of vast sums of money coming from foreign individuals and corporations, mostly going into Democratic coffers.

Many foreign contributors were involved, and the Clinton campaign and the Democratic National Committee were compelled to return money illegally given.

Republican critics were fast to pounce on the Democrats and President Clinton. Speaker Newt Gingrich, no slouch himself in both raising money and raising ethical issues, declared that the foreign money controversy was part of a pattern for the Clinton administration "that reeks of corruption. We have never had this large a scandal be a part of the American presidency." During the latter weeks of the presidential campaign, Senator Bob Dole attacked Clinton for taking foreign money, while the Democrats shot back that Dole and the Republicans themselves had accepted $2.4 million from foreign interests.[46]

With much fanfare, the Senate investigated the alleged illegal fund-raising activities of the 1996 campaign, concentrating especially on foreign money going to Clinton and the Democrats. The Senate committee, led by Republican senator Fred Thompson of Tennessee, concluded that the Clinton campaign "eviscerated federal fundraising laws and reduced the White House, key administration offices, and the Presidency itself, to fundraising tools."[47]

Seeing an opportunity both to condemn the president and to raise additional funds, the NRSC sent through a direct mail solicitation a very official-looking "Statement of Support" demanding that Bill Clinton fully disclose all illegal foreign cash activities. To make the point, the letter to potential Republican donors included a fake Chinese one hundred-yuan banknote and asked on its envelope, "Has Bill Clinton Sold Out America For Illegal Foreign Cash?" The letter, signed by Senator Mitch McConnell, warned of a "nightmare scenario" where the "most unethical Administration in my lifetime" could funnel "millions in illegal foreign cash to Liberal Democrats" and even take back the Senate in 1998. The letter implores: "Money laundering. Giving top-secret security clearances and sensitive intelligence to foreign donors and communist Chinese agents. Renting out the White House like a Motel Six. Schmoozing drug dealers and illegal arms dealers."[48] For only thirty-five dollars, enraged donors could sign the NRSC's "Statement of Support."

Foreign money has crept into other campaigns as well. Lalit H. Gadhia, an Indian American lawyer, had "a talent for fundraising," especially for receiving small amounts of money from waiters, busboys, and kitchen workers in Indian restaurants in Baltimore. Gadhia collected $46,000 in

1994, all to go to members of Congress considered sympathetic to India on issues, such as trade and military assistance.[49] Gadhia ultimately ended up in federal prison because the money raised actually came from an official in the Indian Embassy in Washington; as modest checks were written by busboys and others, they were handed an equivalent amount of cash.

The largest penalty against a foreign company accused of illegal campaign contributions was an $895,000 fine imposed against a Taiwan-based company in 1993 for laundering $200,000 in donations to officials in Los Angeles and Sacramento.[50] In 1994, the FEC established that twenty-six Japanese businesses, private individuals, and a government entity had made more than $300,000 in illegal contributions to more than a hundred forty political campaigns in Hawaii. The Commission announced $162,225 in fines against the Japanese interests. Congressman Jay Kim (R-California) was found guilty of accepting and hiding $230,000 in campaign contributions, including an illegal $50,000 loan from a Taiwanese citizen.[51]

Bipartisan Campaign Reform Act of 2002 and Its Consequences

Take away soft money and we wouldn't be in the majority in the House and the majority in the Senate and couldn't win back the White House ... Hell is going to freeze over first before we get rid of soft money.
    —Senator Mitch McConnell (R-Kentucky, 1999)[52]

Before and after the stench of the 1996 presidential campaign financing controversies, it seemed as if every politician was for campaign finance reform. During the 104th Congress (1995–1996), members of Congress introduced more than seventy campaign reform measures, then promptly ignored them.[53] During the campaign, Clinton, Dole, and Perot each called for campaign finance reform, deplored the current system, and, especially Dole and Clinton, proceeded to take advantage of its loopholes.

Reform measures sprung up all over. Senator Fred Thompson's investigation of Clinton campaign abuses produced a final report lambasting the involvement of foreign money, but then the committee died off without further action. Many legislators got into the act of producing their versions of reform, some tepid, others more far-reaching.

Some, like Bill Bradley, saw the main obstacle to reform as the Supreme

Court's decision in *Buckley v. Valeo*, which determined that campaign spending is protected by the First Amendment as an element of free speech. *Buckley* permits unlimited spending by candidates on their own campaigns, unlimited spending on soft money, and unlimited spending on issues advocacy. Bradley called for a constitutional amendment to overturn *Buckley*.[54]

The reforms advocated by Senators John McCain (R-Arizona) and Russell Feingold (D-Wisconsin) received the most attention from Congress. Their proposal would ban soft money contributions to national political parties from unions, corporations, and wealthy individuals, would require a disclosure of contributions for last-minute issue ads that target specific candidates, and would ban the use of union and corporate funds for such ads. In early 1998, the McCain–Feingold bill was pulled by Senate majority leader Trent Lott of Mississippi after the Senate, in a fifty-one to forty-eight vote, failed to end a Republican filibuster against the bill—nine votes short of the sixty needed to override a filibuster.

Congress was inundated with proposals for reform, but failed to address campaign finance reform in 1998 and barely addressed reform before the 2000 presidential elections. The track record of Congress has not been good on campaign reform. The nonpartisan citizens group Public Campaign reminded us that over the past decade, the Senate has had twenty-nine hearings, five hundred and twenty-two witnesses, seventeen filibusters, and one hundred and thirteen votes on campaign fundraising reform—and there was no reform in sight.[55]

Finally, in 2002, the legislation introduced by McCain and Feingold in the Senate and representatives Christopher Shays (R-Connecticut) and Martin Meehan (D-Massachusetts) in the House became law. The Bipartisan Campaign Reform Act (BCRA) of 2002 was a comprehensive reform of federal campaign practices. There were high hopes among reformers that big money would finally be driven out of politics and that hidden, unreported, campaign slush funds would be dried up and made illegal. Those lofty goals were not met, but BCRA did make several major reforms.

The first major accomplishment of BCRA was to ban unlimited soft money for national political party committees, restrict the use of soft money by state party committees, and restrict federal candidates and officeholders from raising or spending soft money. This stopped the flow of hundreds of millions of dollars, unreported and unlimited in amount, from labor unions, corporations, advocacy committees, and wealthy individuals going to parties and candidates.

The second major accomplishment was to require "electioneering" communications by labor unions and corporations to be restricted within sixty days of a general election or within thirty days of a primary.[56] Further, the definition of electioneering communications was given a more workable meaning. Earlier, the courts had determined that "express advocacy" communications had to include such words as "vote for" or "vote against." BCRA now considered an advertisement an electioneering communication if it (a) conveyed by broadcast, cable or satellite, (b) targeted to a market of at least fifty thousand persons in a relevant electorate, and (c) named or identified a federal candidate. There was a big gap in this definition of electioneering communication, however; newspapers were not included and, significantly, neither were the growing online communications sources, like websites, blogs, text messaging, or podcasting.

Another reform was to increase the maximum amount of money that individuals and political action committees could contribute to federal candidates. Individuals could now contribute $2,000 (up from $1,000) for each primary, runoff, and general election; within a two-year election cycle, individuals could give up to $37,500 to candidates and up to $57,500 to political action committees and political parties. In all, an individual is permitted to contribute $95,000 in a two-year election cycle. BCRA permitted certain individual funds to be indexed, so for the 2008 presidential cycle, an individual could donate $2,300 and contribute up to a maximum of $108,200 for the two-year cycle. Political action committees would continue with the same maximum contribution of $5,000 to a candidate per election cycle.

Immediately after it became law, Senator Mitch McConnell, the National Rifle Association, and a variety of other interested parties challenged BCRA in federal court. Then in December 2003, a deeply divided U. S. Supreme Court, in *McConnell v. Federal Election Commission*,[57] affirmed the major provisions of BCRA. The two House sponsors of BCRA, representatives Shays and Meehan, later sued the FEC, challenging nineteen of the FEC regulations. A federal district court determined that fifteen of those regulations had to be rewritten.[58]

Several things happened after BCRA was enacted and ruled constitutional by the Supreme Court. First, candidates for office put greater emphasis on collecting money from individuals, who could now give up to $2,300 in the 2008 cycle. However, as discussed below, relatively few people can or are willing to donate that kind of money to candidates. The real news was finding more and more people willing to give less than $200, the small donors who do not have to report money to the FEC. Second, while soft money was severely curtailed, the big soft money donors did not simply take their money and transfer it to other forms of giving.[59] Instead, new advocacy organizations, called 527s, have taken the place of soft money contributions, with many new participants willing to give expansive sums of money.

Section 527 of the Internal Revenue Code allows partisan political organizations to take in contributions without paying taxes on them. In a broad sense, every political committee—from the Democratic National Committee to the Dennis Kucinich for President Committee—is a 527 organization, but the term has come to mean groups that are political organizations for the purpose of the tax code, but are not under the federal campaign finance laws. Campaign finance lawyers Joseph E. Sandler and Neil P. Reiff characterize 527 organizations as those that "thread the needle" between tax law and campaign finance law. They are "political for tax purposes, but not for purposes of campaign finance law."[60] In 2000, Congress passed legislation requiring 527 organizations to file reports with the Internal Revenue Service (IRS) and disclose their contributions and spending. As part of BCRA, Congress forbade party officials and their staff from raising funds for 527s and limited candidates and their staff from raising such 527 funds.

During the 2004 presidential election, 527 groups came into their own and became a bonanza, especially for Democratic causes. Former Clinton White House aide Harold Ickes, Ellen Malcolm of the feminist organization Emily's List, and labor organizer Steve Rosenthal were instrumental in getting Democratic and liberal causes organized to take advantage of 527 status. Democratic-oriented 527s raised $265 million, while Republican-leaning groups raised just $154 million. Altogether, $599.4 million poured into 527 organizations during the 2004 presidential cycle. What was remarkable were the significant contributions by fat cats. Nearly twenty-five individual donors—headed by George Soros ($23.4 million), Peter Lewis ($22.9 million), and Stephen Bing ($13.8 million)— contributed $146 million to 527 groups during 2004. The biggest contributor of all in 2004 (and in 2006) was the Service Employees International Union, which gave some $51.5 million in 2004 alone.[61]

Some of the 527 groups receiving funds for the 2004 cycle included the Media Fund (pro-Democratic, $26.8 million spent), Progress for American

Voters Fund (pro-Republican, $26.4 million), Swift Boat Veterans for Truth (conservative, anti-Kerry, $13 million), and Moveon.org Voter Fund (anti-Bush, $4.7 million). Some 527s were straightforward in their names: Daschle Democrats (to assist Senator Tom Daschle) and Colorado Conservative Voters. For other organizations, it was harder to discern their intentions: Billionaires for Bush (anti-Bush street theatre tactics), Club for Growth (conservative, pro-Republican), and People of Color United (conservative, pro-Bush).[62] The 527 money was spent heavily on media and advertising, direct mail, polling, rent on campaign offices, and salaries for staffers. One of the most important tasks of 527 groups, particularly the liberal Americans Coming Together, was to identify and register voters and get them out to vote.

At the national level, Democrats and Republicans have a fundamentally different approach to fundraising. The Republican Party has a much greater tendency towards centralized control, while the Democratic Party has relied on outside organizations for assistance. The Democrats rely more on superwealthy individual contributors and 527 groups than do Republicans. Senator McCain was one among many Republicans trying to beat back the influence and money flowing from 527 groups, offering legislation that would restrict donors to just $500 annually to 527 groups. Similar legislation passed in the House of Representatives, but Democrats were determined to block it from becoming law. Ken Mehlman, chairman of the Republican National Committee, agreed that there had to be controls on unlimited spending so that "billionaires can't once again use loopholes to try to buy elections."[63]

U.S. District Court Judge Emmett G. Sullivan, presiding in the earlier suit brought by Representatives Shays and Meehan, ruled that there was a "complete failure" by the FEC in its 2004 regulatory efforts, and gave the commission two choices: either issue uniform rules regarding 527 organizations or issue a more complete explanation of why it was dealing with these organizations on a one-to-one basis. In June 2006, just five months before the mid-term elections, the FEC decided it could not make uniform rules and would have to determine 527 controversies on a case-by-case basis.[64]

In the meantime, the 2006 federal campaign season, 527 groups continued collecting and spending money, but not at the furious pace of the 2004 presidential contest. For the 2006 elections, the 527 groups spent more than $426 million.[65]

Most of the activities of 527 groups are aimed at federal contests, but state campaigns are also being affected. In the Florida 2006 gubernatorial campaign, at least five 527 groups had been formed, including supporters of Charlie Crist who created Floridians for a Better and Brighter Future, and quickly donated more than a million dollars. In Colorado, the battle was over control of the state legislature. A pro-Republican group is called the Trailhead Group, while a pro-Democratic 527 is dubbed Clear Peak Colorado. Colorado voters in 2002 had approved a campaign finance reform measure, which limited the amount of money candidates could receive, just $400. But now, with unlimited 527 money flowing in, candidates "are becoming mere pawns in the game."[66]

Who Gives Money? PACs provide enormous help to federal candidates, heavily giving to incumbent members of the House and the Senate. Several union and corporate sources have invested heavily in giving PAC money to candidates. The top donors, from 1989 through 2006, have included the American Federation of State, County, and Municipal Employees (AFSCME), which has given $37.3 million to candidates, almost exclusively to Democrats; AT&T, Inc., which gave $28 million, about two-thirds to Republicans; the National Association of Realtors, which gave $26 million, with slightly more going to Republicans than Democrats. The next six biggest donors are all labor unions and have given a total of more than $144 million, with nearly all the donations going to Democratic incumbents or candidates.[67]

In addition to PAC money, influential organizations also have spent independent expenditure and communication money to influence elections. For the same period of time, 1989 to 2006, the biggest such spenders were the National Rifle Association ($30.5 million), the AFL-CIO ($29.3 million), National Education Association ($19.7), AFSCME ($15.4 million), and the National Association of Realtors ($10.9 million).[68]

Nearly three decades ago, former IRS commissioner Sheldon S. Cohen sketched out a scenario illustrating how a political candidate could skirt the federal tax laws. First, Congressman John Doe would have his supporters create a foundation to promote a public policy agenda consistent with his views. Even better, they would take over an existing but dormant group, thereby avoiding close IRS scrutiny when trying to obtain tax-exempt status for a newly formed organization. The directors of this organization would be key friends and supporters; former staffers would be hired to gear up for the next campaign. Congressman Doe would then solicit donations for the foundation and would appear at events it sponsored. To stay within the letter of the law, the organization would stop short of explicitly trying to influence the outcome of the election.[69]

Much of what Cohen warned about in 1987 became standard practice. Larry J. Sabato and Glenn R. Simpson concluded that the use of tax-exempt organizations for political purposes is becoming a "commonplace and increasingly worrisome practice."[70] Tax-exempt organizations have found ways of using campaign money that is "softer than soft money."[71]

Such organizations fall into one of two categories of independent sector organizations: 501(c)(3) charitable, religious, scientific or educational groups, and 501(c)(4) social welfare/advocacy groups. Their unwieldy designation comes from the section of the Internal Revenue Code that sets the conditions for tax-exempt status. There are approximately 1.4 million 501(c)(3) organizations, including a number of well-known entities like the Brookings Institution, Heritage Foundation, Cato Institute, and the Progressive Policy Institute. They also include organizations with a greater interest in campaigns, such as Americans for Term Limits and Newt Giingrich's Progress and Freedom Foundation. These groups can accept unlimited tax-deductible donations, which are not publicly reported. They cannot give money to candidates, nor can they spend it to influence legislation, and their donor lists are not publicly disclosed. Groups in this category are "absolutely prohibited" from engaging in any political activity or "substantial" lobbying.[72]

There are approximately 140,000 groups designated as 501(c)(4) organizations, including such well-known ones as the National Association for the Advancement of Colored People, the National Rifle Association, and the Sierra Club. These organizations can also accept unlimited donations, but those donations are not tax-deductible and not publicly reported. They cannot give money directly to candidates, but can run issue ads, and the donor lists are not reported to the IRS except during audits. Groups with 501(c)(4) status can lobby for a particular cause, but they cannot push a particular candidate.[73]

Some groups have pushed hard against the limits of the tax code in their political activities. In 1997, Cohen observed that "some of these groups are skating right up to the line. And some are skating right over it."[74] Each year, the IRS audits about fifteen hundred organizations that have 501(c)(3) status and four hundred 501(c)(4) organizations. The IRS has sued the Christian Coalition, which was designed as a 501(c)(4) entity, claiming that it has made illegal and unreported contributions to federal candidates through its "voter guide" activities. The Christian Coalition went so far as to take credit for Republican victories in the 1994 election and created a multimillion-dollar "war room" at the Republican National Convention in 1996.[75] During the 2004 campaign season, the IRS investigated over one hundred organizations for their alleged illegal partisan activities.

Some organizations use more than one vehicle for influencing elections and public policy. A 2006 study by the Campaign Finance Institute[76] showed that a number of high-profile interest groups have deployed three different kinds of organizations: political action committees, 527 groups, and 501(c) advocacy groups. There are three general categories of IRS-defined organizations: 501(c)(4) social welfare organizations, 501(c)(5) labor unions, and 501(c)(6) "advocacy" organizations. These 501(c) organizations are required to pay taxes on their political activities, but unlike 527 groups, they do not have to disclose their contributions and political expenditures.[77] Organizations like AFSCME, U.S. Chamber of Commerce, MoveOn.org, Planned Parenthood, and others, use a combination of PACs, 527s, and 501(c)s.

With the *Citizens United* decision, new independent expenditure committees and organizations sprang up and older ones were able to flourish. Then four years later, in 2014, the Supreme Court went a step further, in *McCutcheon v. Federal Election Commission*, striking down the federal ban on the total amount of money a person could contribute over a two-year cycle to a candidate, party, or political action committee.[78] Now, through *Citizens United*, independent expenditure groups could spend as much as they wanted, and through *McCutcheon*, citizens could spend as much as they wanted in "hard money." These two decisions were a hammer blow to BCRA and the federal campaign finance laws from the 1970s. Justice Steven Breyer, who dissented in *McCutcheon* said "taken together with *Citizens United v. Federal Election Commission*, today's decision eviscerates our Nation's campaign finance laws, leaving a remnant incapable of dealing with the grave problems of democratic legitimacy that those laws were intended to resolve."[79]

Fat Cats and Small Donations: One of the most remarkable facts about money and politics is how few people give money to candidates and campaigns. A study of the 2002 federal elections showed that less than one-tenth of 1 percent of the U.S. adult population gave 83 percent of all itemized campaign contributions during that election cycle. Nearly 237,000 donors (0.08 percent of the adult population) gave $728 million out of the total $873 million given in federal election contributions in

2002. These figures involve not only hard money, but also soft money contributions, and those 237,000 donors averaged $3,071 in giving. The study also showed that Republicans raised more than Democrats from small- and medium-sized donations, while Democrats did much better in luring in deep-pocketed donors.[80] Those who gave, however, were unrepresentative of the population as a whole. They were more toward the political extremes, either more conservative or more liberal, than average voters.[81]

What about those people who give less than $200 and are not recorded on FEC files, or those who give to state and local candidates? In various polls, about 12 to 15 percent of the adult population state that they give to candidates, either directly or in support of the candidates. Survey researchers assume that respondents tend to exaggerate their giving, but we are not clear by how much. One good estimate comes from a study by the Institute for Politics, Democracy and the Internet and the Campaign Finance Institute, which argued that somewhere between 5 and 10 percent of adults gave to presidential and other federal candidates in 2004.[82]

What about the 90 or 95 percent of American adults who do not give to political campaigns? Political strategists and fundraisers for years have considered this an extraordinary potential market. What would happen if 20 percent of the adult population donated to campaigns and candidates; if fifty million adults gave money? This was the fundraiser's holy grail— to reach this great, untapped market. One of the biggest problems, however, was the extraordinary expense of reaching new donors. As seen in Chapter 7, using the tried and true methods of direct mail and telephone solicitations were very expensive and not particularly cost-effective. But that was before the online revolution.

Then came the 2004 presidential elections and fundraising over the Internet. Three or four times as many citizens contributed to political candidates in 2004 as did in the 2000 presidential contest. There was a great surge in donors who contributed small amounts; those who did not meet the $200 cut-off for federal reporting.[83] These new donors were reached largely through the Internet. One-quarter of the recipients had met in small group gatherings or house parties that were arranged through Meetup.com, and were motivated to give money. During the 2003 preprimary season, presidential hopeful Howard Dean's campaign raised an unprecedented $41 million, mostly in small amounts of $25 to $100, using the Internet as both the source for solicitation and payment of campaign funds. Soon, the Kerry and Bush campaigns were reaching out through email and their Internet sites for small donations. Altogether, 37 percent of Kerry's presidential campaign contributions came from donors who gave less than $200; the Bush campaign received 31 percent of its contributions from small donations. However, nothing compares to the online fundraising success that was achieved by Barack Obama in his 2008 and 2012 campaigns. Using social media and a wealth of online communication, the Obama campaign was able to tap into hundreds of millions of dollars coming from both small- and large-amount donations. Clearly, in campaigns to come, online contributions will have the potential to make an extraordinary impact. Online fundraising is far cheaper and more convenient than direct mail or telephone-based contributions. Furthermore, online donors tend to be politically connected, willing to ask others to make donations, and for young people, online contributing is by far the favorite method of donating funds.[84]

Role of Political Consultants: While much of the glamour in political consulting belongs to the media team, pollsters, or the general consultants, none of them could do their work without money in the bank. The political campaign is a hungry beast that has to be fed, and what it devours is money. As the fictionalized senate race in Chapter 3 shows, raising money is always a paramount concern. At nearly every stage in the campaign, the most important job is to raise money. During the heat of the battle, the campaign manager is faced with the starkest of financial realities—the campaign must raise another $75,000 by the end of the week to pay for the next direct mail blitz, it must pay the pollster the $35,000 for the next round of surveys, it must raise $935,000 in four weeks' time in order to make the big splash of statewide television commercials. The money must come in now, not five weeks after it is most needed.

An incumbent senator, just elected, will have six years before she must run again, but precious little time to waste. The most successful will begin fundraising as soon as possible. There may be a debt retirement of $500,000 from the winning campaign, and the prospects of having to raise $10 million for the next race. A newly elected senator would set up a continuing fundraising apparatus, paid for by her campaign, and for the next three hundred and sixteen weeks (until election time in six years) would have to raise an average of $33,000 a week, every one of those three hundred and sixteen weeks, to meet that $10.5 million goal. Many senators wait for a couple of years before beginning their serious fundraising efforts, making it all the more difficult to gather funds.

To raise this kind of money (or in a growing number of cases, much more money) involves an army of professional help. At the core will be the campaign staff that specializes in processing campaign funds. Federal election law is clear about reporting deadlines, complete disclosure of occupation and address of those making the contributions, contribution maximums, and other information. Campaign fundraising staff has to process all this information and electronically submit it to the FEC at specified intervals. Often, campaigns must consult lawyers familiar with the arcane regulations of campaign finance law to make sure they are in compliance. A campaign may also conduct due diligence research: Making sure that campaign contributions do not come from illegal sources or come from individuals or political action committees that would politically embarrass the candidate.

Campaigns rely on event planners and fundraisers who specialize in setting up fundraising events, do all the coordination necessary for a fancy dinner, cocktail reception, or pig roast. Nothing warms the hearts of a donor and spouse more than to have their picture taken with the candidate and a nice letter of thanks sent afterwards. All those details and niceties take time and effort, and are absolutely essential to keep donors happy and willing to come back and give more.

Campaigns also rely on outside help from professional consultants. Direct-mail specialists design fundraising solicitations and send them out to targeted audiences. Telemarketers reach out to similar audiences hoping that the personal touch of a telephone call will solicit campaign dollars. Increasingly, campaigns are using their own websites or email lists to fundraise, particularly to reach the relatively untapped small- and medium-donor market.

Money is a surrogate for political power and activity. When Candidate A has raised $44.9 million and has $22 million cash on hand while Candidate B has raised just $3.0 million with only $0.6 million cash on hand, this is a shorthand way of saying that Candidate A has the power, political muscle, and all the resources she needs to coast to a reelection victory. It says volumes about her opponent, too. The "smart money" in Washington and in the state capital knows that Candidate B does not have a chance and why waste critical funds on a lost cause.

Money is the raw material that provides the energy to run the professionally driven race—to pay for a full range of opinion surveys and focus group analysis, to hire a speech coach, to make the million-dollar television buys, to put up a $50,000 website with all the bells and whistles rather than a barely functioning $3,000 site, to hire twenty-five full-time campaign staffers rather than rely just on volunteers and an overworked staff of two or three, and to buy the smartest, most experienced campaign consultants available, rather than a rookie consultant running his first race.

Notes

1 Daniel Fishert, "Inside the Koch Empire: How the Brothers Plan to Reshape America," *Forbes*, December 5, 2012.
2 Leslie Wayne, "Campaign Finance: Loopholes Allow Presidential Race to Set a Record," *New York Times*, September 8, 1996, 1.
3 Center for Responsive Politics, "Re-election Rates Over the Years," *Open Secrets.org*, https://www.opensecrets.org/bigpicture/reelect.php (accessed February 18, 2015).
4 Center for Responsive Politics, Opensecrets.org campaign finance data, 2014, https://www.opensecrets.org/expends (accessed February 18, 2015).
5 Chris Cillizza, "Kentucky Senate Race Could Top $100 Million," *Washington Post*, August 11, 2013.
6 Anthony Corrado and Molly Corbett, "Rewriting the Playbook on Presidential Campaign Financing," in Dennis W. Johnson, ed., *Campaigning for President 2008: Strategy and Tactics, New Voices and New Techniques* (New York: Routledge, 2009), 126.
7 See Anthony Corrado, "The Money Race: A New Era of Unlimited Funding?" in *Campaigning for President 2012: Strategy and Tactics*, ed. Dennis W. Johnson (New York: Routledge, 2013), 59.
8 Matea Gold and Philip Rucker, "Billionaire Mogul Sheldon Adelson Looks for Mainstream Who Can Win in 2016," *Washington Post*, March 25, 2014; Dan Balz, "The 'Sheldon Primary' Is One Reason Americans Distrust the Political System," *Washington Post*, March 28, 2014. Nicholas Confessore, "Koch Brothers Budget of $889 for 2016 Is on Par with Both Parties' Spending," *New York Times,* January 26, 2015.
9 *Citizens United v. Federal Election Commission*, 558 U.S. 310 (2010).
10 President Barack Obama, Remarks by the President in State of the Union Address, January 27, 2010, White House, http://whitehouse.gov/the-press-office/remarks-president-state-union-address (accessed February 18, 2015).
11 Byron Tau, "Crossroads Groups Fueled by Three Huge Donations," *Politico*, November 19, 2013.
12 Matea Gold, "Liberal Donors Eye New Strategy," *Washington Post*, May 5, 2014, A1.
13 Linda Casey, et al., "An Overview of Campaign Finances, 2009-2010 Elections," National Institute on Money in State Politics, April 12, 2012, http://classic.

followthemoney.org//press/ReportView.phtml?r=487 (accessed February 18, 2015).

14   Michael Barbaro, "Bloomberg Spent $102 Million to Win 3rd Term," *New York Times*, November 27, 2009.

15   Patrick D. Healy, "Pity the Rich in Politics: They Tend to Fare Poorly," *New York Times*, November 13, 2005, 37.

16   Center for Responsive Politics, Millionaire Candidates, 2002 and 2004.

17   On Corzine, Mike Allen, "Multimillionaire Beats Ex-Governor for Senate Nod," *Washington Post*, June 7, 2000, A6.

18   Scott Powers, "It's Official: Rick Scott is the All-Time Big Spender," *Orlando Sentinel*, February 2, 2011; Alexander Burns and Maggie Haberman, "Scott Plans $100M Campaign vs. Crist," *Politico*, February 6, 2013.

19   *Congressional Quarterly's Politics in America*, ed. Phil Duncan (Washington, D.C.: CQ Press, 1993), 618.

20   Mark Dixon, "Money and Incumbency: Advantages in State Legislative Races, 2004," *Institute of Money in State Politics*, 2006.

21   Since 1964, rarely has the reelection rate for House members dipped below 90 percent; in the Senate, however, the return rate has been more volatile. In 1980, just 55 percent of incumbents were returned, and in the mid 1970s, those figures were just 64 and 60 percent. Since the 1990s, however, the reelection rate has been above the 90 percent range. Center for Responsive Politics, "Re-election Rates Over the Years."

22   Institute of Money and State Politics, "2004 Cost Per Vote, Selected States"; Terry Robertson, "A Perfect Story: A Case Study of the Defeat of Tom Daschle by John Thune in the 2004 South Dakota Senate Race," *American Behavioral Scientist*, 49, no. 2 (October 2005): 336–7.

23   Dwight Morris, "Financial Iceberg Not Sinking Moseley-Braun's Campaign", *washingtonpost.com*, June 8, 1998, www.washingtonpost.com/wp-srv/politics/campaigns/money/archive/money060898.htm (accessed February 18, 2015).

24   Moseley-Braun's 1992 campaign was under full audit by the FEC (racking up $558,174 in bills for three accountants); further, there have been several lawsuits and complaints by both the campaign and its consultants, vendors, and landlords. Cited in Morris, "Financial Iceberg Not Sinking Moseley-Braun's Campaign."

25   Cathleen Decker, "Checchi Says Voter Optimism Doomed His Bid for Governor," *Los Angeles Times*, June 11, 1998.

26   Brooks Jackson, *Honest Graft: Big Money and the American Political Process* (New York: Knopf, 1988), 58.

27   Herbert E. Alexander, *Financing Politics: Money, Elections, and Political Reform*, 4th ed. (Washington, D.C: CQ Press, 1992), 20. For early history of campaign finance reform, see Frank J. Sorauf, *Money in American Elections* (Glenview, Ill.: Scott, Foresman and Company, 1988); Alexander Heard, *The Cost of Democracy* (Chapel Hill, N.C.: University of North Carolina Press, 1960); Frank J. Sorauf, *Inside Campaign Finance: Myths and Realities* (New Haven: Yale University Press, 1992); Robert E. Mutch, *Campaigns, Congress, and the Courts: The Making of*

Federal Campaign Finance Laws (Westport, Conn.: Praeger, 1988); and Anthony Corrado, "Money and Politics: A History of Federal Campaign Finance Law," in *Campaign Finance Reform: A Sourcebook*, ed. Anthony Corrado, et al. (Washington, D.C.: Brookings Institution, 1997), ch. 2.

28   W. Clement Stone contributed $2,141,656 (all but $90,000 to Nixon); Richard Mellon Scaife gave $1,068,000 to Republicans ($1 million to Nixon); and Stewart Mott gave $822,592 ($400,000 to McGovern) to liberal candidates and causes. Presidential reporting laws did not become mandatory until April 1972, and Stone was able to give $2 million of his $2.14 million to the Nixon campaign before the deadline. Sorauf, *Money in American Elections*, 33.

29   On the effects of 1974 reforms, see F. Christopher Arterton, "Political Money and Party Strength," in *The Future of American Political Parties*, ed. Joel Fleishman (Englewood Cliffs, N.J.: Prentice Hall, 1982); and William J. Keefe, *Parties, Politics, and Public Policy in America*, 8th ed. (Washington, D.C.: CQ Press, 1998), 161–8.

30   Unless the individual under eighteen years of age controlled the money and the decision to donate.

31   Frank J. Sorauf reminds us that the term political action committee appears nowhere in federal statutes. PACs are "simply a residual category: political committees other than those of political parties." To qualify to give $5,000 per candidate per election, the PACs must be "multicandidate committees:" they must be composed of at least fifty people and give to at least five candidates for federal office. Frank J. Sorauf, "Political Action Committees," in *Campaign Finance Reform*, 124.

32   Trevor Potter, "Where Are We Now? The Current State of Campaign Finance Law," in *Campaign Finance Reform*, 7; and Ross Baker, *The New Fat Cats* (New York: Priority, 1989), 76–7. Many of these PACs went by innocuous, upbeat names like BigTent PAC (Senator Arlen Specter, R-Pennsylvania), Every Republican is Crucial PAC (Rep. Eric Cantor, R-Virginia), Project Freedom (Rep. John A. Boehner, R-Ohio), Rely on Your Beliefs (Rep. Roy Blunt, R-Missouri).

33   424 U.S. 1 (1976).

34   Ibid.

35   An independent expenditure is defined as "an expenditure by a person expressly advocating the election or defeat of a clearly identified candidate, which is made without cooperation or consultation with any candidate, or any authorized committee or agent of such candidate, and which is not made in concert with, or at the request or suggestion of, any candidate, or any authorized committee or agent of such candidate." 2 U.S.C. section 431 (17).

36   116 S.Ct. 2309 (1996).

37   Ruth Marcus, "Reinterpreting the Rules," *Washington Post*, October 26, 1996, Al; and Corrado, "Party Soft Money," 176.

38   An excellent summary of the law and practice concerning hard and soft money is found in Joseph E. Cantor, *Soft and Hard Money in Contemporary Elections: What*

Federal Law Does and Does Not Regulate (Washington, D.C.: Library of Congress, Congressional Research Service, 1997). See also Corrado, "Party Soft Money."

39 Corrado, "Party Soft Money." The FEC opinion was Advisory Opinion 1978–10.

40 Charles R. Babcock and Ruth Marcus, "A Hard-Charging Flood of 'Soft Money'," *Washington Post*, October 24, 1996, A1.

41 Don Van Natta Jr., "The Few, the Rich, the Rewarded Donate the Bulk of G.O.P. Gifts," *New York Times*, August 1, 2000, A1; "Top 1995–1996 'Soft Money' Contributors to the National Parry Committees," *Washington Post*, February 17, 1997, A17; Center for Responsive Politics, "Top Soft Money Donors: 2002 Cycle." The top 2002 soft money contributors were Saban Capital Group (Haim Saban, Los Angeles: $9,280,000; Newsweb Corp (Fred Eychaner, Chicago: $7,390,000); Shangri-La Entertainment (Stephen L. Bing, Los Angeles: $6,700,000); American Federation of State, County, and Municipal Employees (AFSCME, Washington, DC: $6,586,500); and Service Employees International Union (New York local and Washington, DC: $4,862,739).

42 Scott Wilson, "DNC Swaps Funds with Its State Affiliates," *Washington Post*, April 24, 1998, A1.

43 Ibid.

44 Center for Responsive Politics, "Foreign-Connected PACs, 2005–2006," data as of August 7, 2006 FEC reporting; Global Connections (Washington, D.C.: Center for Responsive Politics, 1997).

45 Richard Cooper, James Gerstenzang, and David Willman, "Shield between Politics, Foreign Funds Is Flimsy," *Los Angeles Times*, October 20, 1996, A1.

46 Keith B. Richburg, "Just Business as Usual: Asians Surprised by Fuss over Donations by Indonesians to the Clinton Campaign," *International Herald Tribune*, October 21, 1996.

47 Alison Mitchell, "Clinton Camp Accuses Dole of Hypocrisy on Donations," *New York Times*, October 22, 1996, A23. See also Peter Baker, "Dole Camp Also Got 'Foreign Aid'," *Washington Post*, October 22, 1996, A1. U.S. Senate, Committee on Governmental Affairs, "Investigation on Illegal or Improper Activities in Connection with the 1996 Federal Election Campaigns," Majority Report: Executive Summary, 2. In exasperation, the committee report noted that more than forty-five witnesses either fled the country or refused to cooperate, citing the Fifth Amendment privilege against self-incrimination. According to the committee, "Despite the Committee's request for help, President Clinton took no action whatsoever to persuade such individuals to cooperate."

48 National Republican Senatorial Committee promotional literature.

49 Cooper, Gerstenzang, and Willman, "Shield between Politics, Foreign Funds Is Flimsy," A1.

50 Ibid.

51 Ibid.

52 Terry M. Neal, "Fired-up and Financially Flush, Forbes Prepares to Run Ads in Key States," *Washington Post*, April 11, 1999, A16.

53 For earlier suggested reforms, see David B. Magleby and Candice J. Nelson, *The*

Money Chase: Congressional Campaign, Finance Reform (Washington, D.C.: Brookings Institution, 1990); Fred Wertheimer and Susan Weiss Manes, "Campaign Finance Reform: A Key to Restoring the Health of Our Democracy," *Columbia Law Review*, 94, no. 4 (May 1994): 1126–59. On public financing, see David W. Adamany and George E. Agree, *Political Money: A Strategy for Campaign Financing in America* (Baltimore: Johns Hopkins University Press, 1975). On the failed attempts of campaign reform from 1985 to 1990 in the U.S. Senate, see Greg D. Kubiak, *The Gilded Dome: The U.S. Senate and Campaign Finance* (Norman: University of Oklahoma Press, 1994). Paul S. Herrnson, *Congressional Elections: Campaigning at Home and in Washington*, 2nd ed. (Washington, D.C.: CQ Press, 1998), 250.

54   Bill Bradley, "Congress Won't Act. Will *You?*" *New York Times*, November 11, 1996, A15.

55   Public Campaign Web site (www.publicampaign.org). In July 2000, President Clinton did sign a campaign finance reform measure requiring political action committees under Section 527 of the IRS code to report a variety of data, including contributions, expenditures, and the group's purpose.

56   In late August, 2006, the FEC rejected a proposal that would allow labor unions, corporations and advocacy groups to broadcast ads close to elections that talk about issues, but also identify candidates by name.

57   540 U.S. 93 (2003).

58   Michael J. Malbin, "Assessing the Bipartisan Reform Act," in *The Election After Reform: Money, Politics and the Bipartisan Campaign Reform Act*, ed. Michael J. Malbin (Lanham, Md.: Rowman and Littlefield, 2006).

59   Ibid.

60   Joseph E. Sandler and Neil P. Reif, "The '527' Fuss Explained," *Campaigns and Elections*, August 2004, 40. On 527 groups, see Albert L. May, "Swift Boat Vets in 2004: Press Coverage of an Independent Campaign," *First Amendment Law Review* 4 (2005): 66–106.

61   Center for Responsive Politics, "Top Individual Contributors to 527 Committees, 2004 Election Cycle."

62   Center for Responsive Politics, "Top Contributors to 527 Committees, 2004 Election Cycle"; Federal Election Commission, *Thirty Year Report* (Washington, D.C.: FEC, September 2005), 20, www.fec.gov/info/publications/30year.pdf (accessed February 18, 2015); Derek Willis and Aron Pilhofer, "Silent Partners," Center for Public Integrity, March 25, 2003.

63   Thomas B. Edsall, "'527' Legislation Would Affect Democrats More," *Washington Post*, March 28, 2006, A3.

64   Kate Phillips, "Election Panel Won't Issue Donation Rules," *New York Times*, June 1, 2006, 18; Thomas B. Edsall, "FEC Adopts Hands-Off Stance on '527' Spending," *Washington Post*, June 1, 2006, A4.

65   "527 Group Fundraising Grew More Slowly in First Quarter of 2006 than 2004," Campaign Finance Institute, May 19, 2006; Center for Responsive Politics, "527 Committee Activity, 2006 Election Cycle."

66   Steve Bousquet, "Unofficially, They'll Sway Governor Race," *St. Petersburg (Florida) Times*, July 6, 2006, IA; Peter Blake, "'527s Usurp Campaign," *Rocky Mountain News*, August 2, 2006, 33A.

67   Center for Responsive Politics, "Blue Chip Investors." The six organizations are the National Education Association (93 percent to Democrats), the International Brotherhood of Electrical Workers (97 percent), Service Employees International Union (96 percent), Laborers Union (92 percent), Communications Workers of America (99 percent), and the Teamsters Union (92 percent).

68   Center for Responsive Politics, "Donor Profiles of Independent Expenditures and Communication Costs, 1989–2006."

69   Rebecca Carr, "Ex-IRS Head Gave Early Warning," *Congressional Quarterly Weekly Report*, February 22, 1997, 474.

70   Larry J. Sabato and Glenn R. Simpson, *Dirty Little Secrets: The Persistence of Corruption in American Politics* (New York: Times Books, 1996), 309.

71   Quoting Frances R. Hill, University of Miami, specialist in tax-exempt organizations, in Rebecca Carr, "Tax-Exempt Groups Scrutinized as Fund-Raising Clout Grows," *National Journal*, February 22, 1997, 472.

72   U.S. Internal Revenue Service, "Life Cycle of a Private Foundation: Political and Lobbying Activities," www.irs.gov/Charities-&-Non-Profits/Private-Found ations/Life-Cycle-of-a-Private-Foundation (accessed February 18, 2015); Carr, "Tax-Exempt Groups Scrutinized as Fund Raising Clout Grows," 473.

73   Independent Sector, "Facts and Figures About Charitable Organizations," June 26, 2006 (www.independentsector.org).

74   Carr, "Ex-IRS Head Gave Early Warning," 474.

75   Potter, "Where Are We Now?" 19.

76   Stephen R. Weissman and Kara D. Ryan, "Non-Profit Interest Groups' Election Activities and Federal Campaign Finance Policy," (Washington D.C.: Campaign Finance Institute, 2006).

77   Ibid., 1.

78   572 U.S. ___ (2014).

79   Ibid.

80   Center for Responsive Politics, "Big-Time Donors Small in Number."

81   Joseph Graf, "Small Donors and Online Giving: A Study of Donors to the 2004 Presidential Campaigns," (Institute for Politics, Democracy and the Internet, Graduate School of Political Management, George Washington University, and Campaign Finance Institute, 2006), 6.

82   Costas Panagopoulos and Daniel Bergan, "Contributions and Contributors in the 2004 Presidential Election Cycle," *Presidential Studies Quarterly*, 36, no. 2 (June, 2006), 164–5.

83   Graf, "Small Donors and Online Giving," 6.

84   Ibid., 5.

PART

III

WIDER

REACH

OF

POLITICAL

CONSULTING

9

Ballot Issues, Local Elections, and Consultants

I especially enjoy running initiative campaigns. These campaigns have little relation to politics in any conventional sense. An initiative has no political party, no public record to defend or promote, no personality to charm or disgust the voters. And there are no brothers-in-law who need a job. An initiative is just waiting for you to define it and give it life.

—Political consultant Robert Nelson[1]

If you have $1 million, you can get anything on the ballot.

—Robert Stern, Center for Governmental Studies[2]

Ballot Initiatives

During the hot political summer of 2003, friends of California governor Gray Davis paid $2.1 million to seven signature-gathering consulting firms, not to gather signatures for a ballot initiative, but to keep those firms from being hired by anti-Davis forces. But that tactic proved to be futile. Millions of dollars flowed into a recall effort called "Rescue California," with money coming from labor unions, Indian casinos, state contractors, businesses regulated by the state, wealthy individuals, and California congressman Darrell E. Issa. When it was all over, some estimated that up to $70 million had been spent on the recall and the subsequent new gubernatorial election. Movie actor Arnold Schwarzenegger became the new governor, Gray Davis was booted out of office.

In 1911, California created the recall system. Since then, there had been thirty-two attempts to recall a governor, but the 2003 recall was the first one ever to claim enough signatures to get on the ballot. Despite the efforts of Davis' friends, a professional signature-gathering firm was hired and more than 1.3 million signatures were certified.

The Davis recall was particularly newsworthy, but it was not the last time citizens or special interests tried to boot out a sitting governor. In 2012, Wisconsin governor Scott Walker also faced a recall. Organized labor and other groups were upset with Walker and his fight against state employee unions. A total of $63 million was spent on the recall effort, but the highly contentious attempt to kick Walker out failed. Altogether, $130 million was spent trying to persuade voters in California and Wisconsin to recall their governor. One recall was successful, the other failed; but through it all, political consultants made out like bandits.[3]

At the beginning of the twentieth century, Great Plains and western states, along with several eastern states, enacted legislation and amended their constitutions to permit citizens to have a greater voice in the creation of law and public policy.[4] Direct democracy, through initiatives and referenda, was seen by proponents as a way to "diminish the impact of corrupt influences on the legislature, undermine bossism, and induce legislators to be more attentive to public opinion and the broader public interest."[5] Spurred on by principles of Jeffersonian democracy, reform politics, nineteenth-century populism, and an in-bred suspicion of big government, twenty-two states adopted initiative and referendum mechanisms by 1915.

Today, ballot initiatives are a curious mixture of grassroots civic mindedness, individual entrepreneurship, corporate megabucks influence, and professional political consulting. What was once the province of individual grassroots efforts is now a battleground for contentious policy issues, waged in multimillion-dollar campaigns choreographed by professional consultants.

Twenty-eight states and the District of Columbia have some provision for direct citizen involvement. Twenty states permit direct initiatives—ballot measures created by individuals, citizens groups, or corporate interests and voted on directly by the people. Nine states have indirect initiatives—ballot measures that go first to the legislature for vote; if the legislature fails to pass the measure, it can then be decided by the people. Twenty-three states have adopted the popular referendum—measures passed by the state legislature that must first be ratified by voters before becoming law.[6]

Altogether, eighteen states allow constitutional amendments by citizen initiative, twenty-two states allow statutory amendments by citizen initiative, and sixteen states allow both constitutional and statutory amendments.[7] During the past decade, four overarching issues have appeared on many state ballots: gambling, term limits, gay marriages, and campaign finance reform. Many other issues have been presented to the voters as well: halting bilingual education and advocating "paycheck protection" for union dues in California, banning cockfighting in Arizona, restricting the size of hog farms in Colorado, permitting dental technicians to sell false teeth directly to patients in Florida, limiting black bear hunting in Idaho, allowing medical use of marijuana in Maine, permitting assisted suicide in Michigan, restricting bear wrestling in Missouri, and banning hunting of mourning doves in Ohio.[8]

California and Ballot Initiatives: While ballot issues have played an increasingly important role nationwide during the past decade, California stands out as the state with the biggest, most contentious, and most expensive issue debates. For consultants who specialize in ballot issues, California truly has been the golden state.[9]

For many years, ballot initiatives were seldom used in California. Between 1922 and 1978, there was no year in which more than ten initiatives received enough signatures to qualify for the ballot, and in no decade had more than nine such initiatives ever passed. All that changed with the success of Proposition 13, the 1978 measure spearheaded by Howard Jarvis and Paul Gann that forced property taxes to be cut by half. Proposition 13 spurred tax-cutting proposals throughout the country and encouraged conservative interest groups to use ballot proposals to achieve policy objectives.[10]

Proposition 13 also helped launch the specialty business of ballot issue consulting.[11] Jarvis and Gann hired direct mail consultants William Butcher and Arnold Forde, who built an impressive grassroots mailing list that became the backbone of Proposition 13 support and anti-tax initiatives for years to come. By the early 1980s, their firm, Butcher–Forde, had managed a half-dozen of Jarvis's post-Proposition 13 campaigns, including a drive to reduce the state income tax by one-half, to remove Chief Justice

Rose Bird from office, and to close loopholes in the original Proposition 13. Butcher-Forde, which signed a nineteen-year contract with Jarvis, developed and constantly updated a mailing list of more than a million faithful contributors and petition signers to Jarvis' causes. Even two years after his death, an 800,000-piece mailing, using Howard Jarvis' name and picture, promised a "1987 Property Tax Analysis," and also asked for twenty dollars to help pass a "new Proposition 13."[12]

By the 1980s, political scientists and journalists were commenting on the rapid growth and impact of ballot issues in California."[13] Peter Schrag observed that ballot initiatives were "rapidly crippling representative government" in the state.[14] Similarly, Michael Reese found that initiatives "completely dominate the state's political life. They affect voter turnout, set the tone of campaign debate, and even influence the outcome of local and statewide elections."[15] Larry Berg observed that the rampant use of initiatives "symbolizes the near and total breakdown of government in California."[16]

In 1988, California voters were faced with a total of eighteen ballot initiatives plus twenty-three other matters, such as bond proposals and constitutional amendments, for a total of forty-one ballot questions. A total of $100 million was spent fighting initiative actions, including an estimated $15 million by the tobacco industry to fight antismoking measures and $43 million spent by the insurance industry against measures to cut automobile insurance rates.[17]

Election day became much more complicated for voters, who were now faced with far more decisions on a wide variety of issues. "It's madness," said Kim Alexander, president of the California Voter Foundation, a nonprofit group that tracks campaign spending. "The [ballot measure] ads are designed to scare voters, manipulate voters, do everything but inform voters. I think people are going to wonder whether we have too much democracy in California." In the California 2000 primary elections, interest groups spent $120 million showing thirty-second television commercials to convince citizens to vote for or against insurance reform, Indian gambling, clean water, gay marriages, and a wide variety of other policy issues. The avalanche of ballot initiative commercials all but drowned out the ads of the presidential contenders. For Alexander, who watches elections carefully, and for average California voters, who may pay just marginal attention to politics, there would be over eighty candidates on the ballot and twenty-nine policy decisions for them to make.[18]

Two-thirds of all money spent on California initiatives in 1990 came from business interests, while just 12 percent came from individuals.[19] In 1992, 67 percent of all money donated came in amounts of $100,000 or more, with 37 percent coming in $1 million or greater lumps. In five competing and sometimes overlapping auto insurance initiatives in 1988, $101 million was spent; at the same time, the governor's race cost $29 million. Anheuser Busch spent $8.3 million on two alcohol tax initiatives in 1990; cigarette companies spent $21 million to battle a tobacco tax increase.[20]

During the 1990s, California voters faced even more ballot choices, many of them involving highly controversial public policy, including affirmative action, cutting off public assistance to illegal immigrants, ending bilingual education, medical use of marijuana, and others. California had changed dramatically. Ballot issues, often backed by well-financed special interests and orchestrated by professional consultants, were supplanting a state legislature transformed by term limit restrictions. As Peter Schrag states, California citizens are "in nearly constant revolt against representative government" and the state is now in a condition of "permanent neopopulism."[21]

By 1998, outside interests were joining California issue battles, adding their money to issue advocacy advertising and fueling the debate on contentious issues. For example, five national labor and teachers unions poured nearly $20 million into a successful effort to stop Proposition 226, the so-called paycheck protection issue. The campaign for Proposition 226 started with two outsiders: J. Patrick Rooney, an Indianapolis insurance company owner, gave $50,000 to jump-start the signature gathering campaign, and Grover Norquist of Americans for Tax Reform contributed $441,000 to help pay for a letter sent out by Governor Pete Wilson to gather signatures. Two other organizations, Citizens for a Sound Economy and the National Taxpayers Union, aired issue ads in favor of Proposition 226.[22]

California has been the land of milk and honey for political consultants who specialize in ballot measures. In 2005, there were no candidate elections scheduled in California, but there were eight ballot measures. Altogether, the proponents and opponents of these measures spent an astounding $417.2 million. (By contrast, all presidential candidates in the primaries and general election in 2004 spent $880.5 million). Proposition 78, on voluntary prescription drug discounts, was the most lopsided, with $118.7 million coming from the pharmaceutical industry in support and $0 spent in opposition. Proposition 74, on a waiting period for permanent status for public school teachers, saw a group called Governor Schwarzen-egger's California Recovery Team spend $63.3 million in favor, while teachers' unions spent $14.4 to oppose the measure. Remarkably, all eight ballot initiatives in California went down to defeat despite $255.6 million spent by the proponents.

In 2008, when most of our attention was focused on the presidential election, hundreds of millions of dollars were spent in California on ballot issues. In three Indian casino initiatives, Native American tribes wanting to create their own casinos contributed $108.3 million, while opponents (mainly established race tracks and several other Indian casinos) spent about $64.3 million; altogether, over $172 million was spent trying to persuade voters. Another $106 million was spent on Proposition 8, which added a constitutional provision that restricted marriage to a man and a woman. The Mormon Church invested heavily in pushing this initiative, which passed. However, California state officials would not prosecute under this new constitutional amendment, and a district court ruled Proposition 8 unconstitutional; the U.S. Supreme Court refused to overturn that case. In 2012, two California ballot initiatives—a temporary tax on high-income earners and a prohibition on deducting funds from workers' paychecks for political purposes—each cost nearly $150 million.[23]

Where did all that money go? California is a big state, with 38.3 million people, fourteen media markets, and several distinct political and cultural regions. It takes a lot of money to reach potential voters. The lion's share was spent on television ads, direct mail, billboards, newspaper advertise-ments, and get-out-the-vote drives. On their way to getting the message out to voters, ballot initiative committees hired:

- law firms specializing in ballot initiatives that crafted the exact wording for the measures;
- petition signature firms that gathered millions of signatures;
- media firms that produced and placed television and radio ads;
- coalition builders who lined up groups, celebrities, and public officials to support or oppose the measures;
- door-to-door campaigners who sought voter support in individual neighborhoods;
- polling and focus group firms that tested and gauged the public's mood;
- public relations firms that generated stories and served as the public face for the measures;

- opposition research firms that dug up critical, damaging information about the other side;
- direct mail firms that solicited money to support or to defeat the measures;
- general consultants who oversaw the entire operation for each side of the measures.

The role of consultants: Ballot issues present consultants with a different set of challenges and opportunities from those found in campaign elections. The biggest difference, of course, is that there are no candidates involved in ballot issues, except in cases of recall of an officer holder. Ballot consultants do not have to worry about a candidate's past voting record and performance in office; they do not have to put up with the second-guessing; of a candidate's spouse or former law partners; ballot consultants do not have to contend with a candidate's irritation and fatigue or a candidate who goes off message. Further, political parties generally do not intervene on ballot issues debates.

While there are no candidates in ballot issues, sometimes elected officials stake their reputation on these issues. Increasingly in California, elected officials have played prominent roles in advocating ballot initiatives. In 1990, elected officials played an important role in advocating eleven of the eighteen ballot issues. Pete Wilson, both as senator and as governor, backed several highly charged measures. In 1990, when he was running for governor, Wilson backed Proposition 115, the Crime Victims Justice Reform Act, positioning himself as the conservative, crack-down-on-crime candidate. As governor, Wilson in 1994 backed the divisive and contro-versial Proposition 187, the measure that would deny most state benefits to illegal immigrants.[24] Then in 1996, with his eye on the presidency, Wilson backed the equally controversial California Civil Rights Initiative, Propo-sition 209, to discard affirmative action programs in public education, employment, and contracting. In 1998, Governor Wilson loaned Californians for Paycheck Protection $550,000 from his own political action committee for last-minute television advertising in support of Proposition 226.[25] In 2005, Governor Schwarzenegger put his reputation on the line in the losing effort in a fight waged against public school teachers.

As David Magleby and Kelly Patterson note, in ballot issue campaigns, professional consultants "exercise a tremendous amount of control ... They define the message, construct the ballot wording, and in some cases suggest issues to be placed on the ballot."[26] Consultant Rick Claussen observes,

"With ballot issues, you build your own candidate."[27] Ballot issues give consultants the control and opportunity that many campaign consultants probably wish they had. At some time or another, nearly every campaign consultant has been exasperated with his candidates and has said "If I could only get rid of this candidate, I could really win this election." Ballot issues give consultants that chance. They can take the cynical, candid view of consultant Kelly Kimball and take the money and run. "I've never met a consultant who's in this because he believes in the causes ... The professional consultant world is in this for the dough," he has stated.[28] Or they can be policy entrepreneurs, true believers in issues and causes, ready to bring them directly to the people.

Political gadflies Howard Jarvis and Paul Gann hit a vein of citizen anger and resentment over high property taxes. So, too, did Bill Zimmerman and Harvey Rosenfeld. Their organization, Voter Revolt, fed on the anger of California voters over high auto insurance rates. Despite being outspent thirty-two to one, they prevailed in passing Proposition 103, a radical auto insurance reform referendum in 1988. The measure called for a minimum 20 percent cut in premiums and promised to reduce rates further through later measures. Rosenfeld, a protégé of Ralph Nader, decided in 1986 to take action after he had seen California's car premiums soar by 74 percent from 1982 to 1987, making them the third highest in the United States. Greg Anrig, Jr. described how Rosenfeld, working on his own initiative, wrote much of the language of Proposition 103 on Thanksgiving Day 1987 in his small Santa Monica apartment.[29]

In 1994, California voters overwhelmingly approved Proposition 187, the measure to deny state benefits to illegal immigrants. Proposition 187 was created by a self-appointed committee of ten, calling itself the "Save Our State" campaign. One of the ten was Richard Kiley, a California political consultant who until that year had never managed a major statewide campaign, and his wife, Yorba Linda mayor Barbara Kiley.[30] The Kileys also served as political strategists and advisers for the ballot proposal. The budget for Proposition 187, the illegal immigration measure, was only $700,000, but got a major boost when Governor Wilson decided to spend more than $2 million for two television commercials supporting 187.[31] One of the most provocative of the commercials, produced by media consultant Don Sipple, was shot in black and white, showing people—presumably illegal immigrants—fleeing across the international border into California. In ominous tones, the narrator says, "They keep coming."[32]

Later, Richard Kiley was brought to Orlando, Florida, by Doug Gutzloe, a local political consultant, to help create a possible constitutional amendment to the Florida constitution on illegal immigration.[33] Said Kiley, "If you come into this country illegally, you've already broken laws and shouldn't get any tax dollars. We're going from state to state to make immigration policy align itself with the laws of the land."[34] In Arizona and Florida the initiatives, however, went nowhere because of lack of funds, lack of organization, and the "general failure" to galvanize the voters' interest.[35]

Following in the footsteps of past policy entrepreneurs has been Ron K. Unz, who in 1998 took policy entrepreneurship to a new level. Unz successfully promoted Proposition 227, a statewide initiative in California to halt bilingual education. Bilingual education "struck him as a paradigm of a government program wrapped in lofty theories but miserable results." As reporter Frank Bruni described him, Unz has emerged "as a new force and a new kind of figure in California politics, the ardent ideologue who circumvents the telegenic requirements and messy compromises of a traditional candidacy by working his will through a voter referendum." In fact, so closely was Unz tied to the Proposition 227 that it was called the Unz Initiative. Unz, who owns a software company, had a staff of just two and spent less than $300,000 on commercials and paid promotions for Proposition 227. He relied mostly on free media. Altogether, the initiative cost $1.2 million, of which he contributed $700,000. Proposition 227 was supported by 61 percent of the voters.[36]

The built-in advantage of "no" and ballot wording: Even the most conscientious voter, faced with fifteen or twenty ballot issues couched in complicated and technical language, will not hesitate in voting "no" on every issue on the ballot. Given their choice, consultants prefer managing opposition—or "no"—on a ballot initiative. Consultant Walter Clinton observes, "It is easier to present a negative message than to present a concept."[37] This is accomplished by simply hammering home the point "Vote No," or, in the more artful and persuasive forms of advertising, using fear or self-interest, pointing out the extra tax or bureaucratic burdens, or a whole variety of tactics.

The politically influential Sacramento law firm of Nielsen, Merksamer, Parrinello, Mueller, and Naylor has helped write or defeat forty-one initiatives since 1990. Gene Erbin, of Nielsen, Merksamer, observed that the key to an initiative is "to understand that it's not merely a law. It's also a political document. Voters will read it. So, the proposal can't be too confusing."[38] A proposed ballot issue may undergo a lengthy drafting and refinement of language, so that it not only satisfies the technical, legal language, but also clearly and convincingly summarizes what the ballot issue is all about.

Consultant David Hill noted that most referendum voting takes place "in a virtual vacuum."[39] That is, referenda are usually the last items on the general ballot and are often uninteresting (despite some very high-profile, contentious ballot issues in recent years) and technical in language. Hill stated that pollsters, in pretesting voter reaction to ballot propositions, have to take into account "rolloff"—the tendency of voters to make ballot choices at the top of the ballot (president or governor), but then make fewer choices as they move down the ballot. Pollsters have to measure the salience of down-ballot issues to determine how likely it is that an individual will vote, not simply whether they'll vote "yes" or "no." Hill stated that the way to get around language problems is to plan well in advance: do extensive polls and focus group testing designed to produce ballot language that is "brief enough to avoid troubling voters, but just detailed enough to elicit interest and sympathy."[40] Unless language is clear and persuasive, yet simple and easy to understand, voters will shut off and vote "no" or refuse to vote.

Professional signature gathering: Getting enough valid signatures to qualify a ballot initiative is a very difficult task, and it is almost impossible to gather enough signatures without professional help. David Magleby and Kelly Patterson observed that "few statewide measures in. any state in the 1990s were placed on the ballot without the assistance of paid signature-gathering firms."[41] Their observation applies equally for California initiatives ever since. It is not simply a matter of having the required percentage (from 2 to 15 percent) of qualified voters, but other thresholds also have to be met, such as a geographic distribution—having a sufficient numbers of signatures from a minimum number of counties.[42] Signature collecting became a professionalized business in the late 1960s and was still something of a sideline until direct mail and petition circulation consultants William Butcher and Arnold Forde were hired by Howard Jarvis to raise money for Proposition 13.[43]

In the 1992, 1994, and 1996 election cycles, there were one thousand three hundred and sixteen statewide ballot initiatives circulated throughout the country; altogether two hundred and forty-nine, or 22 percent, were certified for the ballots and were voted on. Richard Arnold, president of National Voter Outreach of Carson City, Nevada, stated that professional signature-gathering firms like his were responsible for 90 percent of the successful petitions during this period.[44]

Petition signature requirements vary throughout the country. Oklahoma has the most difficult requirements, allowing just ninety days and requiring 8 percent of the highest recent vote to qualify a ballot initiative and 15 percent for a constitutional amendment. Arizona also requires 15 percent for constitutional issues and Wyoming requires 15 percent for statutory issues. On the low end, Massachusetts and Ohio require only 3 percent for statutory issues. California requires 5 percent of registered voters in the latest gubernatorial contest for a statutory ballot issue and 8 percent for a constitutional amendment.[45]

The general rule of thumb in the petition-gathering industry is to collect eight raw signatures in order to ensure five valid signatures. This means that to obtain one hundred valid signatures, one hundred and sixty raw signatures must be collected (and paid for).[46]

Just four states (Arkansas, Colorado, Oklahoma, and South Dakota) presume signatures to be valid.[47] Colorado petitions are not considered valid unless signature gatherers obtain 47 percent more signatures than needed. In Oklahoma and South Dakota, signatures will be invalidated only if someone challenges them. Eight states do random sample checks. If a random sample fails, a full check may be executed if time permits. That is what happened in California in a 1994 school voucher initiative. The gathered signatures failed a random sample test, but the initiative was placed on a subsequent ballot after a full check of the signatures deemed them sufficient. Sixteen other states check every signature by comparing them to actual voter registration.

To complicate matters, there is the element of time it takes to validate signatures. In California, about one million signatures are needed to get a measure on the ballot. For the November general election ballot, California elections officials recommended signatures be turned in by February of that year to guarantee enough time to check them prior to certification. If signatures are not turned in by then, the state could not guarantee ballot access no matter how many signatures had been collected.[48]

Got a million? Most states require a filing fee of $200 or $250 to register a ballot initiative with the state board of elections. But then, of course, there is the cost of gathering signatures. In California, with approximately one million signatures needed and a going rate of $1 or $1.50 for each signature obtained, a ballot initiative will cost at least a million dollars, without a dime being spent on lawyer fees, focus group analysis, issue research, television and radio commercials, billboards, or any other element of a successful campaign. The per-unit cost will also vary given other factors—how late the petition gathering begins, how popular or unpopular the cause is, how simple or complex the issue is to explain, and how many competing initiatives are vying for the attention of citizens.[49]

In California, there are about fifty subcontractors who are hired by the five major petition gathering firms.[50] Those subcontractors have their regional coordinators and crew chiefs, who hire petition gathers, many of whom hold other part-time jobs, are college students, real estate and insurance agents, and others. A petition collector may be juggling five to ten petitions at once, trying to get voters to sign up. When a lucrative assignment comes along, it goes to the top of the list. For example, when a coalition of thirty-two Indian tribes in California decided late in the petition process to collect 403,269 valid signatures, they had to pay a premium rate of $1.50 per signature. Following the simple logic of the profit motive, professional signature gatherers gave this petition highest priority.[51] In this simple illustration of petition signing, street-corner democracy has its price and its priorities.

Collecting voter signatures, especially for a price, sometimes leads to shortcuts and even fraud. In 1994, state and local officials in four states—Nebraska, North Dakota, Utah, and Oklahoma—undertook criminal investigations to determine if fraudulent signatures were submitted and petition gatherers from out of state were used illegally in petition drives.[52] Further, the states of Maine and Washington have passed legislation banning the practice of paying petition gatherers for each signature they obtain. However, an earlier ban on paying petition gathers in Colorado was found to violate the First Amendment in a 1988 U.S. Supreme Court decision. Colorado had also enacted legislation curbing petition gatherers by requiring them to be registered Colorado voters and to wear badges identifying themselves by name, and requiring the sponsoring organizations to make monthly and final reports listing the names and addresses of the petition gathers and the amount they received in compensation. In early 1999, the Supreme Court struck down these Colorado restrictions on the petition-gathering process, ruling that they violated the First Amendment's value of uninhibited communication with voters.[53] Fourteen other states, mostly in the West, have rules similar to those that were struck down by the Supreme Court.

In 2002, voters in Oregon overwhelmingly approved Measure 26, the Initiative Integrity Act, making it unlawful "to pay or receive money" based on the number of signatures obtained on an initiative or referendum petition. In early 2006, the U.S. Ninth Circuit Court of Appeals upheld Measure 26, noting that petitions still can be circulated, but that the state could ban payment for signature collections.[54] Currently, three states—Oregon, North Dakota, and Wyoming—prohibit paid petition circulators who get paid for each signature. However, legislators in several states, including California, plan to introduce similar legislation banning paying petitioners by signature.[55]

Despite these challenges, professional petition collecting remains a thriving business. Laws meant to restrict access to the ballot make it difficult to obtain the requisite number of signatures and to comply with state election law hurdles. Booming populations, particularly in California and other parts of the West, make it difficult to obtain the required number of signatures, especially if only volunteers are used. Finally, many people are more willing to pay someone else to get the signatures than sacrifice their own time.[56]

Further, there is the difficulty of obtaining signatures from persons who are increasingly wary of strangers and do not like to be bothered by persons knocking on the front door, just as they do not want them calling to solicit phone business. Finally, it is easier to train paid workers, less expensive, and often more reliable to use professionals to do the grunt work of gaining petition signatures.[57]

The ballot measure business has been very good for many of the traditional political consulting professions, from pollsters who conduct survey research and focus group analysis to media firms who create advertising, direct mail firms who blanket the states or communities with targeted messages, and telephone banks that urge citizens to vote "yes" or "no" on election day. Ballot issues have also have been good business for the professional petition gatherers, the one unique field of political consulting that thrives on initiatives and referenda. In other chapters, we have seen how amateur campaigners are shunted aside or simply do not have the technical skills and experience that count. Here, we find that even the one job that seems so fitted to grassroots involvement—going door to door, gathering petitions—is no place for amateurs. Many grassroots petitions are launched, but few succeed. Only those petition drives succeed that are farmed out to professional petition gatherers with their corps of part-time workers standing in shopping mall parking lots, seven or eight petitions on clipboards dangling from their cut-off jeans, shouting out their pitch like a barker in the circus, gathering signatures at $1.15 a pop.

Yet all this might be changing, thanks to the Internet revolution. Websites devoted to political advocacy and policy issues have enormous potential for rallying like-minded citizens, sending electronic petitions to Congress or state legislators, and coalescing new political forces. MoveOn.org, the online citizen organization established in 1998, has been a major player in electronic citizen activism. It began by generating more than 250,000 telephone calls and a million email messages to Congress to oppose the impeachment of Bill Clinton, and was a major online activist force during the 2004 presidential election. The organization, with 3.3 million members, generated over 500,000 electronic signatures in 2005 to oppose the nomination of Samuel Alito to the U.S. Supreme Court, another 565,000 electronic signatures opposing the war in Iraq, among the many liberal-leaning causes it advocated.[58]

The astounding success of MoveOn shows clearly that in the new age of electronic advocacy, when there is a political vacuum, it can quickly be filled. Others have also come to the electronic advocacy business. One entrepreneur, Alex Sheshunoff, traveled twenty-four thousand miles across the United States on the Grassroots Express, a bus wrapped to look like a giant mailbox. He was promoting a new website called E-thepeople, which dubs itself "America's Interactive Town Hall." Individuals could write their own petitions using E-thepeople, and just after its launching, more than twenty-five thousand visitors to the site signed petitions on over four hundred issues. Many of the petitions have a distinctly local flavor, such as "Remove Family Court Judge Harold J. Lynch," or "Lack of traffic light at Robbins and Walker Streets." Following up on the initial successes of this electronic advocacy vehicle, more than forty newspapers and media affiliates began using E-thepeople's software on their own websites.[59]

Electronic advocacy cuts out the middlemen, the professional consultants, and lets virtually anyone with a web address and a good (or bad) idea get involved. What would truly be extraordinary is if states permitted online petition gathering. Pure democracy, spurred on by its most democratic tool, the advocacy website, may mean that the most ephemeral, mundane, whimsical, or even crackpot ideas could become ballot issues. State election officials in charge of verification of petition signing could be faced with a nightmare of validating addresses and names, and weeding out electronic fraud. Citizens in ballot issue states, accustomed to perhaps eight to ten petitions on their ballots, might find twenty-five or fifty ballot issues they must decide on, no matter how arcane or complex the issue, no matter how much or how little interest they may have in them. Critics rightly worry about the crippling effect that government by ballot initiative has on representative democracy. Online advocacy, bypassing the flawed but traditional forms of representative democracy, might be an even greater cause for concern.

Local Elections and Consultants

They're taking all the patronage out. Electronics has taken all the loyalty out of politics. They go with whoever waves a dollar in front of 'em.

—Jimmy Dean, mayor of Johnston City, Illinois, complaining about political consultants and modern techniques[60]

There's hardly a county council race that doesn't have a consultant involved.

—Consultant Brad O'Leary[61]

For better or worse, an increasing number of candidates for state and local office are spending more time than ever before chasing after campaign funds to pay for professional consulting services. Like statewide and congressional candidates, they are investing in polling analysis, direct mail, candidate and opposition research, and radio and television commercials.

Million-dollar local races: California not only has some of the most expensive statewide candidate races and ballot propositions, it also has some very costly local contests. Figures from the California secretary of state's office indicate how campaign expenses have mushroomed in recent decades. In 2002, twelve candidates for the California Assembly spent over a million dollars each; in 2004, twenty candidates each spent that much money. One 2004 candidate for the Assembly spent $6.6 million, and lost in the primary. In 2012 on average, each member of the California Assembly spent $708,371 and each member of the Senate spent $1,041,537.[62]

In many ways California is unusual. It sets records for campaign spending and for the use of professional consultants. In other states, political consultants are much less of a factor. There is a great variation throughout the states in the amount of funds spent for state legislative and local campaigns. As Gary F. Moncrief writes, a person could "easily spend more on a home computer than what the average candidate spends" to run for the state assembly in Wyoming, Montana, or Maine.[63] In many other states, the average cost of a legislative campaign is no more than $20,000 to $25,000. At this level, professionalized races are far from the norm.

Several party officials in a number of states with small populations and small budgets agreed that professional political consulting was quite limited.[64] One party official in New Mexico observed that while there is more professionalization of campaigns, it still has only a limited extent in his state: "Many state House and Senate candidates don't even have fax machines, let alone political consultants." In Utah, few campaigns use professional consultants. An official at the Utah Democratic Party observed, "Of 399 candidates filing for office in Utah in 1996, I'd be surprised to learn that more than 20 candidates use a professional consultant (outside of Party services). Most of those candidates would be running for statewide and federal office." In Vermont, consultants generally have a difficult time finding business. As one official in the state Democratic Party noted, in a small state like Vermont, "it's a matter of community and economies of scale. 'Outsiders' are not readily welcomed and generally don't know the scene as well. In addition, the amount of money that consultants cost is prohibitive." In Montana, there is an economic disincentive to hiring professional consultants. State politicians, noted an official from the Republican Party, are among the lowest paid in the country, and the legislature serves only ninety days every two years.

State legislatures differ greatly in size, professionalism, length of terms, and other factors. Some state legislatures—especially those in California, New York, Illinois, Oregon, New Jersey, New York, and Wisconsin—are year-round, full-time, and highly professional, with well-paid, full-time legislators, staff, and support services. Others—such as those in Maine, Idaho, Utah, Wyoming, and Montana—are citizen legislatures, which may meet for sixty or ninety days a session, or perhaps every other year, with legislators paid only nominal salaries with no professional staff.[65]

Size of legislative districts, the costs of media, urbanization, and other factors also come into play. In California, for example, the assembly districts each average 475,000 constituents, with many located in expensive urban markets. In Vermont, on the other hand, House districts average three thousand nine hundred constituents in rural or small-town markets.

Altogether, in 2009–2010, all candidates combined for state office spent $2.5 billion, a substantial increase of $300 million over the previous record in 2005–2006. But of that $2.5 billion, just one hundred candidates raised about half of that sum. Not surprisingly, the biggest tab came during the 2010 California governor's race in 2010, when business leader Meg Whitman spent $176.7 million.[66]

California is by no means the only state where political consultants are being widely used in state and local elections. In New Jersey, professional consultants have been working at the local level for well over a decade. Noted one official from the New Jersey Republican Party, "Since 1985, professional consultants have worked on the legislative races and many county races. Their influence is definitely spreading downwards into local races." Here, the influence of professional consultants "seems to feed upon itself. As a consultant builds a relationship with, say, an assemblyman, that assemblyman will often refer or even pay for that consultant to help a local race. It becomes an investment and self-fulfilling prophecy."[67]

In a number of states, the political parties have tried to make their state legislative campaigns more competitive—and more professional. They have brought in pollsters, media advisers, opposition researchers, targeting professionals, and professional strategists to work for the party, groups of legislators, and individual candidates. For example, an official with the Missouri Democratic Party noted that professionalization had "grown dramatically" in Missouri because the state Democratic Party pushes it. "We will not keep a campaign that will not help itself."[68]

Buying professional help: The decision to use professional consultants often boils down to the hard reality of campaign finances. When campaigns have budgets of less than $100,000, it becomes difficult to afford many professional services. For example, a benchmark poll ($12,000 to $20,000), considered a necessity in well-financed campaigns, becomes a luxury for a campaign that has a budget of just $100,000. Typically, a campaign spends about 5 to 10 percent of its budget on polling and voter research, making a benchmark poll very expensive.[69] Yet polling, along with direct mail, is the most sought-after professional service for local campaigns. To save on expenses, small-budget campaigns will share a poll with other campaigns or piggyback questions onto a poll paid for by the party, the legislative caucus, or a well-funded campaign. This shared approach is definitely a compromise—the campaign may not get more than one or two questions on the poll and the poll may not be conducted at the optimal time for the campaign.

An alternative to a shared poll is a stripped-down version of a political poll. One such example is offered by two Republican firms, Spalding Group and Hill Research Consultants, who created ExpressPoll, which advertises affordable polling services for Republican candidates for countywide, legislative, and state races. This service (and inevitably others will join it) targets races that in past years would not have used professional consultant services. The unique aspect of ExpressPoll is its flat, publicly disclosed price of $2,495, making it well within the budget of many smaller campaigns.

Candidate and opposition research, while generally not an expensive professional service ($8,000 to $15,000) becomes unaffordable for campaigns with budgets of less than $100,000. Many campaigns will not be able to afford media consultants and will rely on less-expensive and better-targeted direct mail or telephone banks to get out their messages. Others will try innovative, but inexpensive, communications through email, a basic campaign website, blogs, and other online formats.

Who uses professional services? Congressional Quarterly's *Campaign Insider* each week lists political consultants together with their newly signed clients. Along with the sign-ups of congressional, senatorial, and gubernatorial candidates are a growing variety of other statewide and local candidates. Here is one week's sampling from a recent campaign cycle: A Harris County (Houston) commissioner candidate, a candidate for Florida secretary of state, a candidate for Texas Supreme Court justice, and a candidate for Norfolk County (Massachusetts) district attorney all chose media consultants. Candidates for the San Francisco Superior Court, the California board of equalization, the South Carolina agriculture commission, and a sheriff candidate in Massachusetts all hired consultants.

As an example of local campaign consulting, Repper, Garcia and Associates, a general consulting practice in Florida, listed seven Florida state legislative races; two judicial circuit court races; a candidate for Pinellas County court; two candidates for Hillsborough County commissioner; county commissioner candidates in Martin, Pinellas, and Manatee counties; a candidate for Hillsborough tax collector; and two candidates for the Pinellas County school board.[70]

There is no fully accurate, complete listing of which local candidates have hired consultants. A compilation from the *Campaign Insider* and

Campaigns and Elections' annual "won–lost" for consulting firms gives the most accurate listing available. Most often, professional consulting is used by candidates for state House (or assembly) and state Senate races, followed by statewide offices (other than governor, attorney general, and lieutenant governor)—state supreme court, state treasurer, and secretary of state, plus local races, such as mayor, city council, sheriff, and even school board.

Fueling more professionalization at the state legislative level is the push by both political parties to coordinate funds and use legislative caucuses to coordinate campaign finances and the hiring of consultants. Partisan competition in state legislatures is a driving force, and the availability of state soft money is another. In state after state, legislative caucuses are raising funds to develop professionalized services for legislative candidates. Daniel Shea has noted that in the early years of state legislative caucuses, their principal role was to collect money from political action committees and channel it to caucus members.[71] But, in recent years, the role of the legislative caucus campaign committees has gone from just parceling out money to incumbents and challengers to giving them a wide variety of campaign assistance, from seminars on running campaigns and computer assistance to the services of professional consultants.

The Republicans were first to aggressively use legislative campaign committees, and Democratic caucuses were sometimes slow to catch on. But, in recent election cycles, state House and Senate caucuses have been much more active in recruiting professional consultants to assist the caucuses and their candidates.

For example, in 1996 Democrats in the North Carolina Senate organized their first campaign committee to help candidates implement "modern, effective campaigns." During the 1998 election cycle, the North Carolina Senate Committee was to implement a comprehensive campaign plan with a budget of $1.5 to $2 million targeted to approximately ten races. The North Carolina Senate Committee sent out a "Request for Proposal" to Democratic consulting firms, seeking bids from professionals for these services:

- **Polling**: Firms to bid on an eight-hundred sample statewide issues poll, a minimum of five polls with four hundred samples, a fifteen-minute benchmark poll, and a minimum of five ten-minute tracking polls.
- **Opposition research**: Ten research assessments on vulnerable Republicans.

- **Direct mail**: Proposals to produce eight mail pieces for a minimum of five campaigns, to average 25,000 households (a total of one million mail pieces).
- **Media**: Proposals for producing a minimum of nine radio and nine TV spots for three campaigns with a three-week saturation media buy.
- **Telephone banks**: Proposals for persuasion and GOTV calls.[72]

North Carolina Senate Democrats, like many other state legislative caucuses, were willing to raise the funds to bring a level of professionalism that was unknown in recent years.

High-stakes local elections: Sometimes local elections take on great importance, especially when the control of the state legislature is at stake. Under such circumstances, professional consultants are soon at center stage.

When long-time Virginia state senator Virgil Goode was elected to the U.S. House of Representatives in November 1996, the vacancy created in the Virginia State Senate led to a flurry of activity, with political consultants rushing to the rural backwaters of southwest Virginia for a five-week special election that would determine which party would win control of the Virginia Senate. Democratic lawyer and eventual winner Roscoe Reynolds and his Republican opponent Allen Dudley, a small-town banker, managed to spend nearly $400,000 in a hard-fought battle over the 20th Senate district. Professional consultants came from Richmond, Washington, D.C., and Raleigh, North Carolina, "unleashing their attack ads, opinion polls, response tests, telephone banks, and voter-turnout models."[73] For the first time in eleven years as an elected official, Roscoe Reynolds and his campaign bought television commercials, his pollster tested responses to Reynolds's and his opponent's ads, and a Chicago direct mail firm blanketed the 20th district with fliers that stated in harsh terms: "When our children needed Allen Dudley, he just wasn't there," and "Don't let politicians like Allen Dudley sell out our families."

Professional consulting had come to the small cities of Rocky Mount and Martinsville and rural Henry and Franklin counties. This is a region of the state unaccustomed to persistent telephone calls from professionally organized phone banks, attack ads on local television, and celebrity appearances by the governor, the Republican senator, and Oliver North. The rhetoric was sharp, the charges were flying, and a small voter turnout backed Reynolds. In probably any other election not a single professional consultant would be found in far southwestern Virginia, but with the legislature's balance of power at stake, this became an expensive, divisive battleground.

Alabama, trial lawyers, and tort reform: When powerful interest groups clash, the stakes can be quite high. Inevitably, professional consultants are brought in, and many times the contests turn bitter and negative. In Alabama, the fight pitted trial lawyers against business and corporate interests. As Dale Russakoff noted, Alabama politics has "fallen into the grip of a national showdown between two of the country's most powerful interest groups, trial lawyers and business groups, whose money now overwhelms elections for once-obscure offices" in Alabama.[74]

Since the mid-1980s, Alabama has been a battleground between trial lawyers and business interests. It turned increasingly political as wealthy trial lawyers tried to get friendly candidates elected to the state supreme court. In 1986, many legislators were elected with the help of generous amounts of probusiness money. As one business lawyer said about the 1986 election, "You can't buy legislators here, but you can rent them. In 1986, business rented a lot of them." In 1987, a tort reform package became law, significantly reducing the amount that could be awarded for punitive damages to $250,000—a damages cap that threatened the livelihood of trial lawyers.

The following year, the trial lawyers struck back. The head of their state association, Ernest "Sonny" Hornsby, was elected chief justice over a business-backed candidate. Candidates spent an unprecedented $800,000 and were engaged in a battle between the interest groups. With Hornsby as chief justice, the Alabama Supreme Court struck down most of the major 1987 tort reform legislation and unleashed several major punitive-damage cases, including the infamous BMW judgment. A local jury had slapped BMW with $4 million in punitive damages because the carmaker had sold as "new" a car on which paint damage had been repaired, but not disclosed to the buyer. The actual damage had been $4,000. The U.S. Supreme Court ultimately decided that the $4 million damages, which were cut down to $2 million by the Alabama Supreme Court, were "grossly excessive."

In the next election, Hornbsy was defeated in a contest so close it ultimately had to be decided by a federal court. The federal court invalidated some two thousand absentee ballots that were not properly notarized or witnessed. The Alabama Supreme Court, including justices who had contributed to Hornsby's campaign, had earlier voted to count the contested ballots that would have given Hornsby the victory.

In amounts normally reserved for a Senate race in a major state, the Alabama 1996 campaign for Supreme Court justice reached more than $5 million, and state legislative races approached $500,000, unprecedented figures in Alabama. The challenger in the 1996 Supreme Court race, Republican Harold See reportedly raised more than $3 million and retained veteran political consultant John Deardourff. The incumbent, Associate Justice Kenneth Ingram, spending approximately $2 million, hired Democratic media consultant Hank Sheinkopf.

Harold See was subjected to blistering attacks on his personal life and his record. One ad, sponsored by the so-called Committee for Family Values, and financed by a number of trial lawyers, accused See of having a "secret past," saying that he had "abandoned his wife and two children, had a love affair ... and fled Illinois for Alabama" twenty years earlier. See and his former wife vehemently denied the characterization in these campaign commercials. Despite all this, Harold See was able to win with 53 percent of the vote.

In 1998, the terms for three of the nine justices were up, along with that of the governor and lieutenant governor—a sure bonanza for political consultants fighting for both the trial lawyers and probusiness groups, though some were having second thoughts about subjecting judges to popular approval. Alabama Bar Association president Warren Lightfoot has called for an end to election of judges in favor of merit appointments, stating, "Our courts will not be able to function if justices have to engage in this kind of campaigning."[75]

In 2000, campaigns for top state judgeships were even more expensive and nastier. Candidates for a seat on the Ohio Supreme Court spent an estimated $12 million, and judicial elections in Illinois, Michigan, Alabama, Idaho, and elsewhere brought charges of influence peddling, race baiting, and dirty politics.

As Dale Russakoff observed, "As Washington gives more power to states to regulate issues from the environment to banking to welfare, well-financed groups are pouring resources into political races in capitals from Albany, New York to Sacramento."[76] The National Institute on Money in State Politics in 2014 noted that there were two dominant trends in judicial elections: they were getting to be more expensive and they were nastier. The Institute noted that "many of these judicial races seemed alarmingly indistinguishable from ordinary political campaigns—featuring everything from Super PACs and mudslinging attacks to millions of dollars of candidate fundraising and independent spending."[77]

During the 2011–2012 election cycle, approximately $56.4 million was spent on judicial races, with about $15.4 million coming from independent expenditure groups, like the conservative Americans for Prosperity (the Koch brothers), the progressive America Votes, and the Law Enforcement Alliance of America (linked with the National Rifle Association).[78]

Local or national consultants? Local campaigns are often faced with the question of whether to go with local- or state-based consultants or with national consultants. Many state party professionals prefer using local or statewide talent whenever possible.[79] For example, an official with the Texas Republican Party observed that locally based consultants are better than nationally based "in just about every way. They are much more responsible to campaign needs, more accessible, more understanding of Texas, better able to tap human and capital resources in Texas." Nationally based political consultants are better "only when a campaign needs to tap national resources," such as the Republican National Committee. An official of the Utah Democratic State Coordinated Committee was even more emphatic. Locally based consultants were better in "damn near every way—cost less, know what's going on, know the players, understand the composition of the electorate, work harder for the specific campaign, and have closer proximity to the campaign and the candidate."

A South Carolina Republican Party official noted that in addition to having a better feel for the state and state issues, locally based consultants "won't skip town if the race is lost or screwed up. They live here and have to see you for the rest of their lives!" As one party executive director from the middle South stated, "The bias that local candidates have for national political consultants and managers is unfortunate. They think by hiring nationally, they are obtaining an advantage when, in fact, in many cases all they are obtaining is a very hefty monthly consulting fee."

The better-financed campaigns are able to afford national political consultants, who tend to charge higher fees. In 1992, Tom Cole, the executive director of the National Republican Congressional Committee (and later a member of Congress), noted that local and regional consulting firms charge "70 percent of what a national firm would charge," and campaigns, in addition, "don't have to pay travel costs."[80]

Local, state, or regionally based consulting firms have been successful in exploiting their built-in advantages: they generally know the states, regions, and players better than nationally based firms, and they are able to hold their costs to a competitive advantage.

Using volunteers: Why not use volunteers instead of professionals? That is the question candidates inevitably ask at campaign training seminars. I have attended enough of these seminars to see the predictable answer, If you cannot afford professionals, then go ahead and use volunteers, but if you want to win, you are better off with professionals. These are usually self-serving answers given by campaign professionals to worried candidates who have not raised a lot of money. But, very often the professionals are right-if you want to win, go with pros, if you want to feel good about democratic participation, go with volunteers. This attitude particularly irks political bloggers and other online political activists who feel free to comment on elections, direct funds to candidates, and do their best to get people to vote.

Probably not even the hardest-bitten professional would deny that volunteers are important at some level of campaigning. But pros would argue that volunteers have no place in the specialist and certainly not in the strategic category of campaign services. Let the candidate's law firm partners devote their energies to raising money from friends, but do not let them get near campaign strategy. Let the local college professors write campaign position papers, but make sure those papers never see the light of day during the campaign, unless they are right on message and are cleansed of anything that will offend important interest groups and snare the campaign. Let the candidate's brother-in-law and other well-meaning supporters carry mail sacks down to the post office, but don't let them design the direct mail pieces. Volunteers are fine for answering the telephone, licking envelopes (as long as there are not ten thousand that need to go out the next day), driving people to the polling booth, and other last-minute activities that require a lot of hands. But, professionals would say, keep them away from the important strategic activities.

As seen in the earlier chapters, the modern campaign depends on the use of sophisticated technology and advanced social science techniques. Campaign specialists, like opposition and candidate researchers, direct mail writers, focus group moderators, voice-over artists, speech and debate preparers, targeting and voter file specialists, and more have the information, know the techniques, understand the language, and have the experience to run campaigns. These skills and levels of experience cannot be readily picked up by the volunteer or campaign amateur.

Two examples show how volunteers can be detrimental to a campaign. Many professionals would keep volunteers away from the telephones, especially when trying to conduct telephone polling. A campaign might, however, be tempted to cut the cost of administering a poll by using volunteers to make telephone calls instead of hiring a professional phone bank. However, this can lead to serious problems.

Problem of accuracy: The individuals answering the telephone often want to please the interviewers. When the volunteer interviewer is excited about the candidate, as an amateur often is, that enthusiasm can creep into the conversation through subtle voice cues. Democratic pollster Mark Mellman and his colleagues observed that this problem is "difficult to detect, but can produce significant bias, and you'll never know how wrong your polling might be."[81] Because professional callers usually are from out of state and have no commitment or built-in empathy toward the candidate, they are much less likely to produce interviewer bias.

Burnout and lack of discipline: Telephone work, especially trying to administer a complicated ten- to fifteen-minute poll, is wearing business. To complete a benchmark poll, a team of ten to fifteen volunteers must be trained and prepared to devote three to seven nights in a row at a telephone bank. Few volunteer campaigns can do this; people drift in and out, and it becomes very difficult to administer the poll to the minimum of three hundred or so voters needed to make the poll accurate.

Another example illustrating the difficulties of relying on volunteer and untrained help came in the embarrassing 2002 reelection campaign for Anthony Williams, mayor of Washington, D.C. The Williams campaign hoped to collect ten thousand signatures, well over the two thousand needed to qualify for the ballot. But volunteers could not do the job, panicked, forged signatures, and added obviously bogus names (like Kofi Anan and Tony Blair). The District of Columbia elections board kicked Williams off the ballot and later fined his campaign $250,000. Williams, who was a virtual shoo-in for reelection, eventually won, but only as a write-in candidate. No reputable professional signature-gathering firm would have made such monumental blunders.[82]

The committed grassroots campaign: Campaigns can be successful without the domination of professional consultants, but they must have the key ingredient of committed volunteer support. Often, those best able to sustain the level of grassroots volunteer commitment come from the energized religious right or from organized labor. The Republican primary election for attorney general in Virginia provides a good example. Three of the four Republican candidates for the 1997 primary for the Virginia attorney general's race hired a battery of professional consultants and purchased television advertising. The winning candidate, State Senator Mark Earley, hired no professional consultants and bought no advertising time. Earley, the candidate of the Christian Coalition, counted on four things: a field of multiple candidates, low voter interest and voter turnout, a corps of true believers, and a concerted effort to get out his supporters. In the primary, only 5 percent of Virginia registered voters turned out—the lowest figure since 1949. Earley relied on Christian Coalition supporters and like-minded fundamentalists, who believed fervently in his anti-abortion, antipornography, procharter schools campaign. There were no billboards, no news conferences, and no rallies. Instead, Earley relied on some 600,000 pieces of direct mail (through a direct mail firm) to religiously conservative supporters, and a network of three thousand preachers to spread his candidacy. Earley's own pastor, the Reverend A. George Sweet of Atlantic Shores Baptist Church in Virginia Beach, sent an endorsement script to fellow ministers. Careful of the Internal Revenue Service restrictions for tax-exempt organizations, the script read: "The IRS guidelines say I can tell you who I am going to vote for and why, as long as I don't tell you how to vote. I am voting for Senator Mark Earley, who has been our true pro-life, pro-family standard-bearer."[83]

Earley won the primary, but there was considerable speculation that he could not duplicate that success in the general election. "You can't run a general election campaign underground," observed Mandy Grunwald, Democratic media consultant. "The true believers are not going to win it for you. There just aren't enough of them."[84] That general principle, so true in many other contests, did not apply here. The Republicans swept the three top statewide elections, including Mark Earley's win in the attorney general's race.

When former Arkansas governor Mike Huckabee ran for the Republican presidential nomination in 2008, he had a secret weapon in the Iowa caucuses: a massive data file of email addresses of Christian conservatives. An Alabama-based organization called Redeem the Vote had compiled a list of some seventy-one million individuals. The Huckabee campaign pared it down to 414,000 potential voters in Iowa. Huckabee, a former Baptist minister, was able to energize the religious conservatives in Iowa and come in a surprising first place.[85]

The Tea Party, Religious Right, and like-minded organizations are not the only ones pursuing grassroots election mobility. As seen in Chapter 7, interest groups and the national political parties have heightened their grassroots efforts, spending millions to recruit, mobilize, and above all get supporters to the polls.

Notes

1   "Media and the Initiative Campaign," *Campaigns and Elections*, January 1992, 35.

2   Dan Morain, "Making of a Ballot Initiative," *Los Angeles Times,* April 16, 1998, A1.

3   Thomas B. Edsall, "Recall Loopholes in Campaign Finance Law," *Washington Post*, September 25, 2003, A8; John Wildermuth, "Schwarzenegger's GOP Rivals Quitting," *San Francisco Chronicle*, August 8, 2003, A1; Matea Gold and Tom Hamburger, "Wisconsin Gov. Scott Walker Suspected of Coordination with Outside Groups," *Washington Post*, June 19, 2014.

4   On ballot initiatives as a western phenomenon, see Charles M. Price, "The Initiative: A Comparative State Analysis and Reassessment of a Western Phenomenon," *Western Political Quarterly*, 28 (June 1975): 243–62; and Claes H. de Vreese and Holli A. Semetko, *Political Campaigning in Referendums: Framing the Referendum Issue* (London: Routledge, 2004).

5   Thomas E. Cronin, *Direct Democracy: The Politics of Initiative, Referendum, and Recall* (Cambridge, Mass.: Harvard University Press, 1989), 53.

6   In most states, sponsors of popular referenda are given a shorter period of time to collect signatures than permitted sponsors of initiatives. Because of this, relatively few popular referenda become law. Richard Braunstein, *Initiative and Referendum Voting: Governing Through Direct Democracy in the United States* (New York: LFB Scholarly Publishing, 2004), 6.

7   Kenneth Mulligan, "Statewide Measures on the 1996 General Election Ballot," unpublished report (Washington, D.C.: Free Congress Foundation, 1996). Voters in fifteen states and the District of Columbia can also *recall* elected officials; thirty-six states permit the recall of various local officials. Cronin, *Direct Democracy*, 3.

8   See David S. Broder, "The Ballot Battle: Collecting Signatures for a Price," *Washington Post*, April 12, 1998, A1.

9   On California ballot initiatives, see Peter Schrag, *Paradise Lost: California's Experience, America's Future* (New York: New Press, 1998); Charlene Simmons, *California's Statewide Initiative Process* (Sacramento, Calif.: California Research Bureau, 1997); Charles M. Price and Charles Bell, *California Government Today: Politics of Reform* (Belmont, Calif.: Wadsworth, 1996); Ken DeBow and John Syer, *Power and Politics in California*, 5th ed. (Needham, Mass.: Allyn and Bacon, 1997); California Commission on Campaign Financing, *Democracy by Initiative: Shaping California's Fourth Branch of Government* (Los Angeles: Center for

Responsive Government, 1992); and E. Morgan Young, "Government by the People: The Evolving Impact of Citizen Initiatives on Public Policy and Government Advocacy in California," unpublished master's thesis, Graduate School of Political Management, George Washington University, Washington, D.C., 1997.

10   John E. Mueller, "Voting on the Propositions: Ballot Patterns and Historical Trends in California," *American Political Science Review*, 63 (December 1969): 1197–212; Cronin, *Direct Democracy*, 3. See also David O. Sears and Jack Citrin, *Tax Revolt: Something for Nothing in California*, enlarged ed. (Cambridge, Mass.: Harvard University Press, 1985), 261; and David Lowery and Lee Sigelman, "Understanding the Tax Revolt: Eight Explanations," *American Political Science Review*, 75 (1981): 963–74.

11   On Proposition 13, see Schrag, *Paradise Lost*, 142ff.

12   Peter Schrag, "Initiative Madness," *New Republic*, August 22, 1988, 18.

13   Larry L. Berg and C. B. Holman, "The Initiative Process and Its Declining Agenda Setting Value," paper presented at the American Political Science Association annual meeting, New Orleans, LA, August 1985, 31–2, cited in Cronin, *Direct Democracy*, 223. On ballot issues, generally, see David B. Magleby, *Direct Legislation: Voting on Ballot Propositions in the United States* (Baltimore: Johns Hopkins University Press, 1984). On the use of consultants in ballot initiatives, see David B. Magleby and Kelly D. Patterson, "Consultants and Direct Democracy," and Dave McCuan, Todd Donovan, and Shaun Bowler, "Grassroots Democracy and California's Political Warriors: Campaign Professionals and the Initiative Process," both papers delivered at the American Political Science Association annual meeting, Washington, D.C., August 1997; and David B. Magleby and Kelly D. Patterson, "Campaign Consultants and Direct Democracy: The Politics of Citizen Control," paper delivered at conference, The Role of Political Consultants in Elections, American University, Washington, D.C., June 19, 1998; Elisabeth R. Gerber, Arthur Lupia, Mathew D. McCubbins, and D. Roderick Kiewiet, *Stealing the Initiative: How State Government Responds to Direct Democracy* (Upper Saddle River, N.J.: Prentice Hall, 2001).

14   Schrag, "Initiative Madness," 18. See also Peter Schrag, "California's Elected Anarchy: A Government Destroyed by Popular Referendum," *Harper's*, November 1994.

15   Michael Reese, "Profiles of a Promised Land: Is This Any Way to Run a State," *Newsweek*, July 31, 1989, 27.

16   Ibid; also John Haskell, *Direct Democracy or Representative Government: Dispelling the Populist Myth* (Boulder, Colo.: Westview Press, 2001); David S. Broder, *Democracy Derailed: Initiative Campaigns and the Power of Money* (New York: Harcourt, 2000); Richard J. Ellis, *Democratic Delusions: The Initiative Process in America* (Lawrence: University Press of Kansas, 2002).

17   Ronald Grover, "In California, They're Voting on Nearly Everything," *Business Week*, October 31, 1988, 30.

18   Peter Marks, "Fierce Ad Wars on Ballot Measures in California," *New York Times*,

March 5, 2000, 23. Oregon voters must have also felt the frustration of ballot initiative mania. During the 1994 and 1996 elections, Oregon citizens were asked to vote on thirty-two constitutional amendments and laws and, in 1998, ten more had been certified for the ballot, ranging from marijuana regulation, mandatory jail terms, union political dues check-off, and adoptees' birth records. In 1996, there were sixteen voter initiatives, and the voters' pamphlet, containing paid advertisements from backers and opponents of the measures, was 248 pages long. Observed Oregon secretary of state Phil Keisling, "It was almost as long as *War and Peace,* but with less of a discernible plot." David S. Broder, "In Oregon, Critics See a Good Idea Gone Bad," *Washington Post*, August 1, 1998, Al.

19   David B. Magleby, "Direct Legislation in the American States," in *Referendums around the World*, ed. David Butler and Austin Ranney, (Washington, D.C.: AEI Press, 1994), 243. See also David B. Magleby, "Ballot Access for Initiative and Popular Referendums: The Importance of Petition Circulation and Signature Validation Procedures," *Journal of Law and Politics*, 2 (1985): 287–311.

20   Magleby, "Direct Legislation in the American States," 242–3. There have been expensive ballot issues in other states as well. For example, in 1988 the National Rifle Association spent $8 million in Maryland in a losing effort to oppose a handgun registration measure; in Maine, the paper industry spent more than $5 million, an unprecedented sum for Maine campaigns, to defeat successfully a proposed ban on clear-cutting ten million acres of northern Maine forest land. Occidental Petroleum Corporation reportedly spent as much as $5 million to promote a citywide ballot measure to drill for oil near Pacific Palisades, an expensive beachfront community near Los Angeles. See Ronald Pear, "In California, Foes of Affirmative Action See a New Day," *New York Times*, November 7, 1996, B7; and Grover, "In California, They're Voting on Nearly Everything," 30.

21   Schrag, *Paradise Lost*, ch. 1.

22   Morain, "Making of a Ballot Issue." John Berthoud, president of the National Taxpayers Union, stated that his organization spent "over $1 million" on issue ads favoring Proposition 226.

23   Data compiled from "California 2005 Ballot Measures," Institute on Money and State Politics, http://classic.followthemoney.org//press/ReportView.phtml?r=279&ext=3 (accessed February 28, 2015).

24   Reid Wilson, "The Most Expensive Ballot Initiatives," *Washington Post*, May 17, 2014.

25   California Commission on Campaign Financing, *Democracy by Initiative*, 275; and Dan Bernstein, "Initiatives Are at Top of Politicians' Lists of Favorite Things," *Sacramento Bee*, August 5, 1996. See Schrag, *Paradise Lost*, 229–34, and Young, "Government by the People," ch. 4; Morain, "Making of a Ballot Issue."

26   Magleby and Patterson, "Campaign Consultants and Direct Democracy," 21.

27   Morain, "Making of a Ballot Initiative."

28   Quoted in Magleby and Patterson, "Campaign Consultants and Direct Democracy."

29   Greg Anrig, Jr., "The Flamboyant Force behind California's Auto Insurance Revolt," *Money*, July 1989, 145. Altogether there were five separate, sometimes overlapping, propositions on auto insurance in 1988. Some $80 million was spent by special interests promoting or opposing these five measures. Schrag, *Paradise Lost*, 197. Schrag also notes that the changes brought about through Proposition 103 were blocked by auto insurance company litigation for four years, then Charles Quackenbush, a friend of the industry, was elected as insurance commissioner, further blunting the intent of the reform.

30   "Politics '94: A Behind-the-Scenes Look at Orange County's Political Life," *Los Angeles Times*, November 13, 1994, B3; and Paul Feldman, "Figures behind Prop. 187 Look at Its Creation," *Los Angeles Times*, December 14, 1994, A3. Peter Schrag observes that Alan C. Nelson, former head of the Immigration and Naturalization Service (under Reagan) and California lobbyist for FAIR, the Federation for American Immigration Reform, was the principal writer of Proposition 104. Schrag, *Paradise Lost*, 229.

31   Dave Lesher and Bettina Boxall, "Proposition 209: Hot-Button Issue Fails to Attract Big Money on Either Side," *Los Angeles Times*, September 19, 1996, A3.

32   This advertisement and the whole issue of curbs on illegal immigrants outraged many. "From a moral and ethical perspective, it was heinous," said Antonio Gonzalez, president of the Southwest Voter Registration and Education Project in Los Angeles. "I think it did long-term damage to the social fabric of California society." Sipple has stated that his work is an accurate, if vivid, portrayal of a legitimate issue. Dave Lesher, "Meet a Very Laid-Back Maniac," *Los Angeles Times Magazine*, August 11, 1996, 18.

33   Gutzloe specializes in opposing tax referenda in Florida through his Ax the Tax Committee, of which he is the chairman. According to his promotional literature, the Ax the Tax Committee has not lost any of the nine campaigns it has waged in two states and has saved taxpayers over $4.1 billion in tax proposals since its founding in 1982. Ax the Tax advertisement in *Campaigns and Elections*, June 1998, 59.

34   Reena Shah Stamets, "Seeds Planted to Pass Florida 'Proposition 187'," *Tampa Today*, January 11, 1995, 8B.

35   Patrick J. McDonnell, "Anti-Illegal Immigration Proposition Fails to Qualify for Arizona Ballot," *Los Angeles Times*, July 15, 1996, A3.

36   Frank Bruni, "The California Entrepreneur Who Beat Bilingual Teaching," *New York Times*, June 14, 1998.

37   Magleby and Patterson, "Consultants and Direct Democracy," 20.

38   Morain, "Making of a Ballot Initiative."

39   David Hill, "Wording Ballot Issues," *Campaigns and Elections*, August 1995, 28.

40   Ibid.

41   Magleby and Patterson, "Consultants and Direct Democracy," 8.

42   Ibid.

43   Schrag, *Paradise Lost*, 147–8 and 210–1; and Magleby and Patterson, "Consultants and Direct Democracy."

44   Broder, "The Ballot Battle," A6.

45   Council of State Governments, *Book of States* (Lexington, Ky.: Council of State Governments, 1996).

46   Arnold, "Taking the Initiative: Step-by-Step Tips on How to Put an Issue on the Ballot," *Campaigns and Elections*, June/July 1993, 23.

47   Richard Arnold and Susan Johnson, "Validating Signatures," *Campaigns and Elections*, June 1997, 41.

48   Ibid.

49   Broder, "The Ballot Battle," A6.

50   The five major firms are Kimball Petition Management (Fred and Kelly Kimball), National Voter Outreach (Richard Arnold), American Petition Consultants (Michael Arno), Progressive Campaigns (Angeo Paparella), and Masterton and Wright. Broder, "The Ballot Battle," A6.

51   Morain, "Making of a Ballot Initiative."

52   Ibid.

53   The 1988 decision was *Meyer v. Grant,* 486 U.S. 514, and the 1999 decision was *Buckley v. American Constitutional Law Foundation,* 525 U.S. 182.

54   *Prete v. Bradbury* (2006).

55   Andrew M. Gloger, "Paid Petitioners After *Prete*," *IRI Report*, Initiative and Referendum Institute, University of Southern California, Los Angeles, May 2006.

56   Jennifer Mears, "Proponents Turn to Paid Circulators to Get Initiatives on Ballot," Associated Press Political Service, July 14, 1995.

57   For example, Richard Arnold estimated that in the 1992 Colorado petition drive to pass the Colorado Education Voucher Initiative, it cost an average of 82 cents for each signature obtained by a professional petition-gathering firm, and 90 cents per signature obtained by volunteers. Morain, "Making of a Ballot Initiative."

58   MoveOn website (www.MoveOn.org).

59   E-thepeople website: http://ethepeople.org/our-affiliates (accessed February 19, 2015).

60   Quoted in Chris Meyer, "Ten Years in the Making," *Campaigns and Elections*, April/ May 1990, 41.

61   Ibid., 40.

62   California 2002 and 2004 data available on www.followthemoney.org. Rosie Cima, "The Cost of a Seat in the California State Legislature," *Maplight*, December 11, 2013, http://maplight.org/content/73318 (accessed February 19, 2015).

63   Gary F. Moncrief, "Candidate Spending in State Legislative Races," in *Campaign Finance in State Legislative Elections*, ed. Joel A. Thompson and Gary F. Moncrief (Washington, D.C.: CQ Press, 1998), 56. See also Gary F. Moncrief, "The Increase in Campaign Expenditures in State Legislative Elections," *Western*

Political Quarterly, 45 (1992): 549–58.

64   Survey of Party Professionals on Political Consulting, April 1996.

65   Joel A. Thompson and Gary F. Moncrief, "Exploring the 'Lost World' of Campaign Finance," in *Campaign Finance in State Legislative Elections*, 11.

66   Linda Casey et al., *An Overview of Campaign Finances: 2009–2010 Elections*, National Institute on Money in State Politics, April 12, 2012, http://classic.followthemoney.org//press/ReportView.phtml?r=487 (accessed February 20, 2015). Anthony Gierzynski, "A Framework for the Study of Campaign Finance," in *Campaign Finance in State Legislative Elections*, 19; Robert E. Hogan, "The Cost of Representation in State Legislatures: Explaining Variation in Campaign Spending," *Social Science Quarterly*, 81 (4) (December, 2000), 944.

67   Survey of Party Professionals.

68   Ibid.

69   Mark Mellman et al., "Benchmark Basics and Beyond," *Campaigns and Elections*, May 1991, 22ff.

70   *CQ Campaign Insider*, August 6, 1998, 1.

71   Daniel M. Shea, *Transforming Democracy: Legislative Campaign Committees and Political Parties* (Albany, NY: State University of New York Press, 1995), 26. See also Anthony Gierzynski, *Legislative Party Campaign Committees in the American States* (Lexington, Ky.: University Press of Kentucky, 1992).

72   North Carolina Senate Committee, "Request for Proposal," October 8, 1997.

73   Mike Allen, "Small Town, Va., to Determine Control of the State Senate," *Washington Post*, December 16, 1996, B1.

74   Dale Russakoff, "Legal War Conquers State's Politics," *Washington Post*, December 1, 1996, Al. Much of what follows comes from Russakoff's article on politics, money, and Alabama judgeships.

75   Ibid.

76   Ibid., and William Glaberson, "Fierce Campaigns Signal a New Era for State Courts," *New York Times*, June 5, 2000, A1.

77   Linda Casey, "Courting Donors: Money in Judicial Elections, 2011–2012," *National Institute on Money in State Politics*, March 18, 2014, http://classic. followthemoney.org//press/ReportView.phtml?r=505 (accessed February 19, 2015).

78   Ibid.

79   Survey of Party Professionals.

80   Jerry Hagstrom, "Where the Action Is," *National Journal*, October 31, 1992, 2483.

81   Mellman et al., "Benchmark Basics and Beyond," 30.

82   Yolanda Woodlee and Craig Timberg, "Panic Led to Dubious Signatures," *Washington Post*, July 19, 2002, BI.

83   Mike Allen, "In GOP Primary, Earley's Focus on 'Friends' Prevailed," *Washington Post*, June 15, 1997, B8.

84   Ibid.

85   Chris Cillizza and Shailagh Murray, "The Man Who Helped Start Huckabee's Roll," *Washington Post*, April 16, 2012.

10

Citizens, Voters, and Democratic Choice

I will not indulge in any activity, which would corrupt or
degrade the practice of political campaigning.

—First article in the Code of Professional Ethics, American
Association of Political Consultants[1]

[Politics] is a world of taunts, jeers, jabs, pointed fingers and
mudslinging... . Fear, anger, envy, indignation and shame are
powerful emotions in the political arena... . Negative campaigning is rarely pretty. Sometimes it doesn't feel very good
either. But once you've made the decision to inform the voters
of your opponent's shortcomings, stick to your guns... .
Remember, you're playing to win.

—Political consultants Richard Schlackman
and Jamie "Buster" Douglas[2]

The Uneasy Relationship between Candidates
and Consultants

One of the quotations that began this book comes from Bill Clinton,
who was chewing out his consultants, Dick Morris and Doug Schoen,
warning them not to undermine his presidency. When the Dick Morris
scandal erupted during the summer of 1996, frustration with celebrity
political consultants had reached a boiling point. Senator Jay Rockefeller

278

expressed what many elected officials felt about high-profile consultants. "I don't like it," he said, "they've become the interpreters of everything. They get on TV shows and reveal how they tell the politicians where to go and what to do."[3] Senator Patrick Leahy also weighed in, saying, "I think it's wrong. It's the people who elect the candidate, not the consultants. If their egos become so great, it can lead to the sort of trouble we're seeing here [with Dick Morris]. I don't think necessarily you should fire them. Maybe just draw, quarter, and behead them."[4] Even former political consultant Lyn Nofziger was in the mood to get rid of them all. "You'd think that the nation had never gotten along without them. But I will tell you this, we'd still have elections, and someone would win and someone would lose if we assassinated every one of the consultants, and the country might be better off."[5]

Most irritating were the few consultants who would publicly gloat about their importance in the campaign or, worse, disparage their clients. Former political consultant Ed Rollins, ever willing to burn his bridges, was one of them. He trashed candidate Michael Huffington and his high-profile wife, Arianna, and bragged about his own political acumen. "I had star quality," boasted Rollins, "and I had people interested in meeting me as much as meeting the candidates." Rollins wrote that George Nethercutt, another of his clients, "could never have beaten Tom Foley in 1994 without me and the professionals I put around him. And Speaker Foley, even after winning fifteen previous elections, would not have made it competitive without his imported hired guns." Consultant Ray Strother in 2003 lambasted his former client. "I'm sorry I ever met Bill Clinton. He was a dream killer, who ended our relationship by damaging my business and adding my body to those he climbed over to reach the White House."[6] Many consultants have felt the same way as Rollins and Strother, but few have had the audacity to name names and proclaim it in print.

Bob Dole's consultants in the 1996 presidential campaign could not keep quiet about their client's shortcomings. What was consultant Don Sipple able to convey to Bob Dole? "Virtually nothing," Sipple wrote. "The cosmetics of modern campaigning is something Dole thinks should not make a difference. The appreciation for the picture, the aesthetics of the road show, the lighting, the sound. He didn't think it should *count*."[7] Mike Murphy, Dole's media consultant, had the temerity to write an open letter to Dole, giving him campaign advice, after having resigned just two months before the election.[8] Open criticism, unsolicited advice, and candidate trashing further irritate the inherent tensions between candidate and handlers.

Notoriously uncommunicative with both staff and consultants, Bob Dole had a particularly difficult time during his runs for the presidency. In 1988, Dole abruptly fired his two senior consultants, David Keene and Donald Devine, literally tossing them off the campaign plane. As Scot Lehigh observed, "It was a case of wheels down, consultants off, wheels up."[9] In 1996, Dole's first set of senior consultants, Bill McInturff and Bill Lacy, were replaced during the primaries by Don Sipple and Mike Murphy, who lasted until early September, then were replaced by Greg Stevens, Alex Castellano, and Chris Mottola, who themselves were discarded in the waning days of the campaign.[10] Little wonder that the 1996 Dole campaign has been described by Evan Thomas and his colleagues as "one of the most hapless campaigns in modern political history."[11]

It was rough going for Al Gore's 2000 presidential campaign. Nearly all of Gore's trusted long-time senior staff and top loyalists were brushed aside, and a battery of high-priced consultants came in, often giving conflicting advice. The campaign wasted precious time trying to gain its footing, define and then redefine Gore's image, and figure out just what Gore stood for. During much of the preprimary stage, the Gore camp was acting a lot like the dysfunctional crew of the Dole campaign four years earlier. By contrast, George W. Bush's campaign, under the guidance of the low-profile, but highly effective consultant Karl Rove, was doing everything right: raising enormous amounts of money, lining up key Republicans, developing its strategy and message in preparation for the crucial first primaries. The John Kerry 2004 campaign also had its rocky stages before settling down with a consistent message and a stable consulting team. Hillary Clinton's 2008 presidential bid was marred by infighting and second-guessing among rival consultants and political operatives. Newt Gingrich and Rick Perry, both trying to gain the 2012 Republican nomination, had the same troubles: dysfunctional campaigns, conflicts with the candidates, and in the end, campaigns going nowhere.

Candidates are sometimes at odds with their consultants, complaining that they charge too much money, manipulate candidates to say and do things they instinctively would not do, and give advice that backfires and hurts the campaign. But it works both ways. While candidates are sometimes leery of consultants, consultants often wish they did not have to put up with candidates. In a provocatively titled report, "Don't Blame Us," the

Pew Research Center found that political consultants "have a mixed view at best of their own clients." Fifty-two percent rated their clients as either good or excellent, but 48 percent rated their clients as poor or fair. Forty-two percent of the consultants felt that candidate quality was slipping, and 44 percent of the consultants who helped elect candidates to office were later sorry to see them serve.[12]

Once in a great while the shoe is on the other foot, and a political consultant will run for public office. Veteran Democratic consultant Clinton Reilly ran unsuccessfully for mayor of San Francisco in 1999, proclaiming that he was "not your ordinary candidate," but was someone who had a "thirty-year track record of fighting progressive causes against the political machine." Tom Cole and his consulting firm helped a number of Republicans win seats in Congress. Later, Cole became chief of staff of the Republican National Committee, and since 2003 has been a member of Congress and deputy majority whip of the House. Another consultant who ran for office was Phil Noble, long-time opposition research specialist before turning to international consulting and Internet political services. He ran unsuccessfully for lieutenant governor of South Carolina in 1994. Like Reilly, Noble ran on a populist theme, tweaking elected officials all the while. One of his direct mail pieces touted his plans for the state and proclaimed, "Politicians Think I'm Stupid."[13] What better way to run for office than to ridicule politicians or rage against the political machine? Bill De Blasio, mayor of New York City, was campaign manager for Hillary Clinton's 2000 successful senate race in New York.

While there have been abuses and certainly a natural tension between consultants and clients, most consultants do not behave badly. Consultant Gary Nordlinger, chair of the American Association of Political Consultants' (AAPC) Ethics Committee, observed that "the overwhelming majority of consultants are ethical, respectful of both their clients and the process, and truly put their clients' interests before their own. When they fail to, the marketplace often puts them out of business."[14]

The political consulting industry gets a bad reputation because of the abuses and missteps of a few. While Nordlinger may be a little too optimistic about the forces of the marketplace, he is right about the behavior of political consultants-most respect their clients and serve them well. They remain behind the scenes and out of the campaign spotlight and focus on getting their client elected. Political consultants are no more and no less ethical or moral than any other professionals. The very nature of their work—the battleground of public opinion, policy, and person-ality—invites controversy and confrontation. Certainly, like lawyers or athletes, they are aggressive and competitive. Consultants are often highly partisan, believing strongly in their political party or its underlying ideology. While they work for clients who are not always the best of candidates, rarely do consultants operate strictly as hired guns, working for anyone who will pay the bills.[15]

Some political consultants at times suffer the same lapses as other profes-sionals: conflict of interest, overbilling or other financial irregularities, failure to deliver promised services, breaches of confidentiality, or poor performance and shoddy work." These are lapses not endemic to the political consulting profession. Yet political consultants are particularly vulnerable because they and their clients communicate with the public in a most fundamental way.[16] While political consultants may employ many of the marketing techniques of Madison Avenue, there are deep underlying differences. Consultants are not selling soap or mouthwash, they are com-municating to the public about the character, reputation, and principles of very human candidates. They are also criticizing, sometimes ridiculing, the foibles and character flaws of opponents. They are sharpening the lines of debate on issues and policies that matter to voters. Political consultants are not participating in an end-of-the-season used car sales campaign, they are injecting themselves and their candidates into the sometimes messy process of democratic choice. To a considerable extent, consultants and their clients set the tone of elections. What voters see on television, what they receive in their mailboxes, what unsolicited voices say to them over the telephone are the end products of consultants' work.

What particularly tarnishes the reputation of the profession is the win-at-any-cost attitude and practice of some consultants—those who engage in character assassination or guilt by association. Worse still are those consultants who attempt to suppress voter turnout by discouraging people to vote through vicious media attacks or last-minute telephone or direct mail solicitations.

In truth, the public does not focus on individual consultants or their tactics. They do not hold consultants responsible, even the occasional celebrity consultant. A *New York Times*/CBS News poll taken a week after the Dick Morris sex-tabloid affair found that 86 percent of voters said the information they heard about Morris had not influenced their opinion of President Clinton; only 9 percent said the affair made them think worse of

Clinton. Some 37 percent of voters said that the Dick Morris scandal made them more likely to vote for Clinton.[17] James Carville, who has probably dusted up as much controversy as any political consultant, rightly observes that consultants simply do not factor into voter decisions. When Dole's last round of consultants departed in 1996, Carville observed, "Find an exit poll where someone says, 'Gee, I didn't vote for Bob Dole because they fired Don Sipple.'"[18] It simply is not going to happen.

Only within the small fraternity of the consulting industry, and perhaps only for a brief time, will people remember the consultants responsible for Al Checchi's hugely expensive, disastrous defeat in the California gubernatorial primary or recall the consultants in the nasty fight between George W. Bush and John McCain in the 2000 South Carolina presidential primary. The creators of the infamous Willie Horton commercial, the ads linking congressional candidates to Polly Klaas's murderer, the character assassination of John Kerry by the Swift Boaters—none of these consultants are held accountable by the public or even by the consulting industry itself.

Campaigning can be a very tough business, and fighting electoral battles year in, year out wears down even the best of consultants. In talking with many consultants over the years, I have gotten the sense that for them much of the joy of campaigning seems to have been lost, the campaign is more of a business than a crusade, and bonds of loyalty and trust between consultants and candidates have been loosened. Many consultants have seen it all—candidates who have let them down, the tides of politics over which they have no control, strategies that have backfired, and messages that have fallen on the deaf ears of voters.

But consultants can also take heart from the fact that they are indeed appreciated by most candidates, and their services and professionalism are acknowledged and respected. A recent survey of state and local candidates found that they welcomed the advice and professional experience of their consultants.[19] Celebrity political consultants make the news and enjoy the talk show circuit, but the real story is the important role that the relatively anonymous consultants play in making modern campaigns work.

Ethics and Campaign Consulting

A few years ago, a magazine posed this question: "How moral are political consultants?" For some political consultants, that question really has no bearing on what they do. Consultant Dan Schnur responded, "It's an irrelevant question. Political consultants are supposed to win campaigns, not have morals." Other consultants defended their craft and their colleagues. Thomas M. "Doc" Sweitzer responded, "We're certainly more honest than the legal profession. And we're definitely more honest than the advertising profession. I don't sell cigarettes to kids." Senior adviser for the Gore for President campaign, Carter Eskew, whose client list included tobacco companies, insisted, "Certainly [political consultants are] more moral than used-car salesmen, pro athletes, and most local police."[20]

The AAPC, the principal professional association of campaign consultants, requires each of its members to sign and adhere to a code of conduct. Yet, there is little enforcement of the code. Gary Nordlinger, once the chair of the ethics committee, observed that enforcement of the AAPC code of ethics "doesn't happen very much because not very many people file complaints with us. I guess they tend to be very happy with the conduct of our members."[21] A poll taken in 1994 backs up Nordlinger's point, at least when it is confined to consultants themselves. Eighty-four percent of the political consultants surveyed rated their own profession's ethics as either "fairly high" or "very high."[22]

Others consider the code unworkable or irrelevant. "We've never come up with anything that is workable," said one of the AAPC's founders, the respected veteran Joseph Napolitan; this is a sentiment shared by many consultants. In the 1998 poll "Don't Blame Us," nearly two-thirds of the consultants were familiar with the AAPC's code of ethics, but 81 percent said the code had "little or no" effect on their conduct or the conduct of others in the profession,[23] while 62 percent in the 1994 poll said there was no need for a well-enforced code of professional ethics.

Consultants can get testy and defensive when asked about campaign conduct. In the 1998 study, nearly all of the consultants surveyed (97 percent) believed that negative advertising was not wrong and that consultants were not to be blamed for the public disillusionment with the political process, and a majority of those surveyed did not believe that campaign tactics like those that "suppress turnout, use scare tactics, and take facts out of context are unethical" although they may be considered "questionable."[24] They did draw a clear line on certain activities. Consultants almost unanimously believed that making statements that are factually untrue is "clearly unethical," and the great majority felt that push-polling was clearly an unethical practice.[25]

The survey results, according to Andrew Kohut, director of the Pew Research Center, gave an "in-your-face response to the consultants' critics. They were sort of like hired guns. They were saying, 'Don't blame us for the level of violence. We're just doing a job.'"[26] Professor James Thurber took issue with the consultants, arguing that they need to take "some of the blame, stop pointing the finger elsewhere, and to try to improve the quality of campaigning so that we may have better governance and improve our democracy."[23]

When campaign abuses do occur, consultants certainly can and should be blamed, but the ultimate responsibility falls on the shoulders of the candidate. Every negative advertisement, every line of print in direct mail pieces, every emailed message is, in the end, the responsibility of the candidate. Office seekers have a public duty to own up to that responsibility.[28] Yet, as veteran political writers Jules Witcover and Jack W. Germond observed, candidates are often "content to let the professionals run their campaigns as they see fit. After all, they are paying big money to these experts. If something goes too far, you can always take responsibility, replace the consultant, and move on. Nobody will blame you, and the consultant can always find another candidate looking for someone with good ideas.[29]

One candidate who did own up to a mistake was Senator John Warner, a Republican from Virginia. In his hard-fought contest for reelection, Warner demonstrated clearly and decisively the sometimes forgotten principle that the candidate ultimately bears the responsibility for the decisions and judgments of the campaign. During the latter weeks of his senate reelection contest against Democratic challenger Mark Warner, John Warner's media team, Greg Stevens and Company, doctored a photograph of President Clinton, former Virginia Governor Douglas Wilder, and Senator Charles Robb that was used in a campaign television commercial. Senator Warner quickly fired his media advisers and the next day took full responsibility for the action and apologized to his opponent, stating, "although I had nothing to do with it, knew nothing about it [beforehand], I accept the responsibility, and extend an apology to all Virginia voters, including Mark Warner."[30] Yet, this example also shows the validity of Germond and Witcover's observation. John Warner was embarrassed and his campaign slightly damaged, but his fired media firm, its reputation just slightly dented, soon moved on to other contests. Few consultants ever suffer permanent damage to their reputations because of past misdeeds.

States and Communities Respond

E. J. Dionne, Jr. has written that Americans hate politics because liberal and conservative politicians offer voters false choices that have no connection with most Americans' values or concerns.[31] He stated that Americans hate politics as it is now practiced, "because we have lost all sense of the public good," and that "politics these days is not about finding solutions. It is about discovering postures that offer short-term political benefits."[32] What Dionne wrote in 1991 is just as true today, and modern campaign tactics have pushed the American voter's patience even farther.

A mid-1998 survey conducted for the Project on Campaign Conduct indicated strong support for campaign codes of conduct as ways to improve the quality of elections.[33] In this survey of sixteen hundred registered voters in Ohio and Washington, over three-quarters of the respondents said they would have more respect and would be more likely to vote for a candidate who signed and abided by a campaign pledge, and that negative, attack-oriented campaigning produces "leaders who are less ethical and trustworthy." As part of a code, voters wanted candidates to agree not to make personal attacks on their opponents, not to use any language or images that define other candidates based on their race, sex, or personal characteristics, and not to question publicly an opponent's honesty, integrity, or patriotism.

One key focus for election reform is the meager television coverage of state and local campaigns, which are often overshadowed by crime reports and other more sensational news. Former journalist Paul Taylor, who headed Alliance for Better Campaigns, observed, "The culture we run into on the news side is that politics is boring, politics is bad television, people don't care. And the candidate culture says that anything that's unscripted is risky. They're more comfortable in a world of thirty-second ads." Taylor's group, funded by the Pew Charitable Trusts, worked with ten state civic organizations in an effort to press local news directors to devote more resources to politics.[34]

Thus far, states and localities have focused on laws and restrictions on campaign spending and communications. One city, however, has placed before voters the activities of consultants themselves. San Francisco citizens in two successive years considered ballot measures affecting the activities of political consultants. In 1996, they passed an "honest elections" proposal requiring consultants to refrain from lobbying their former political clients.

Mayor Willie Brown, however, vetoed this measure. Then, in 1997, voters considered Proposition G, a measure that would require consultants operating in San Francisco and making more than a $1,000 per year running campaigns to register, pay a fee, endorse a code of conduct, and file a quarterly disclosure statement that names the consultant's clients and how much they are paying. The ballot issue—both modest and flawed—failed, while political consultants from throughout the country poured in $67,500 to defeat it.[35]

More states and communities will doubtless attempt to pass campaign finance and good campaigning laws. They may have some success in reining in campaign costs, though the biggest hurdle remains the Supreme Court's interpretation of the First Amendment's protection of unlimited campaign spending by candidates and advocacy interests. Laws attempting to impose codes of conduct and standards of good campaigning by most candidates will be more problematic. One of the voluntary codes is the Minnesota Compact, which sets out the responsibilities of the candidates, media, and citizens in the electoral process. During the 1996 Minnesota elections, two hundred and eighty-three candidates for state and local office endorsed the compact and promised to abide by its principles. First analyses of the compact suggest that voters rejected television ads aired by Senate candidate Rudy Boschwitz that were perceived as "unfair," and that newspaper coverage provided more coverage of issues and less on the horse-race components of the Senate race.[36]

Ohio went further by passing a "campaign truth squad" law that made it illegal to publish or broadcast "a false statement concerning the voting record" of a candidate. The Ohio state elections commission was given the power to decide the truth or the falsehood of the advertisement. Minnesota had a similar law trying to stop false political ads. But, in September 2014, a federal judge struck down the Ohio law (and earlier the Minnesota law was stricken as well). The federal judge, Timothy S. Black ruled that "we do not want the government (i.e., the Ohio Elections Commission) deciding what is political truth—for fear that the government might persecute those who criticize it. Instead in a democracy, the voters should decide." Judge Black also quoted Frank Underwood, the shady fictional character in the Netflix show, "House of Cards": "There's no better way to overpower a trickle of doubt than with a flood of naked truth."[37]

Voluntary codes may help, but they can only go so far. Laws forbidding "political lies" run into the very heart of free speech and expression. Such laws or codes invariably bump up against the very nature of campaigning. Political communication should be robust, even contentious. It should draw clear distinctions between candidates and issues; legitimate candidate shortcomings should be brought to the attention of voters. Good campaigning demands it and constitutional protections of free speech ensure nothing less. Candidates willingly enter the political spotlight and have to expect scrutiny and criticism of their positions, background, character, and promises. This inevitably leads to sparks, contention, and cries of unfairness.

The greatest restraint on the perceived harshness of campaign activities will not come through legislation or through volunteer codes, but by a public that no longer tolerates abusive commercials, personal insults, character assassinations, and fear-mongering. But, that is a tall order. We have seen in the last decade a citizenry numbed by frontal assaults of the coarser side of popular culture and political discourse.

Consultants will state, without flinching, that their role is to do their best to help their clients win. For many, the question of morals is irrelevant. The ultimate test is what the electorate will believe and what the electorate will bear. This is an era in which politics is an extension of entertainment, where the foibles of politicians provide the laugh lines. Many citizens believe that all politicians are liars, and many others have tuned out of politics and civic life altogether. If we are not appalled by the corrosion of popular culture, where is the sustained anger and outrage that will rid our airwaves and mailboxes of the shocks of modern campaigning? What penalties do candidates and consultants pay for playing hardball—or gutter ball?

The Wired Citizen and Electronic Advocacy

I've got news for you politicians and business people and anyone else who has let your fear of technology keep you from understanding and embracing the Internet. This is the dominant technology—not of some distant future—but of tomorrow, of next week, of now.

—Joe Trippi, Howard Dean's presidential campaign manager, 2004[38]

The digital revolution has incredible potential for campaigns, elections, and, most of all, citizen participation. For those truly interested in politics and public policy, there can be no better time than right now and in the electronic years to come. For those who are pure political junkies, the Internet is a virtual candy store of information. There is now almost unlimited access to campaign information, policy issues, voting records, and fundraising information. Many state governments are now requiring electronic filing and online disclosure of candidate and contribution information, and that information is available to the public on the web. Bill Jones, the California secretary of state, has been a leading proponent of online disclosure, and the Political Reform Division of his office has published invaluable online reports on lobbying expenditures and campaign contributions. Online disclosures of federal campaign finance data are found on sites of the Federal Election Commission, the Center for Responsive Politics, and Public Disclosure; the National Institute on Money in State Politics and the Campaign Finance Information Center provide information on state campaign finances.[39]

Digital Sunlight, a project of the California Voter Foundation, has been at the forefront of electronic disclosure and provides helpful links to a variety of other online sources. Through the California Voter Foundation website, citizens in many California jurisdictions can simply type in their zip codes, and the website will display all candidates and ballot issues for the next election.

In 2004, the League of Women Voters Education Fund and a private business, Capitol Advantage, supported DNet, an Internet-based election program that covered 25,000 candidates in over 5,800 primary and general elections. DNet provided detailed candidate biographies and issue statements, information on ballot initiatives, voter registration forms, fundraising and volunteer links, election calendars, and other pertinent information. Further, Capitol Advantage's Capwiz Election Tool and DNet received 25 million page views on election day 2004 and were linked to over 200 websites and portal sites like Yahoo!, AOL, C-SPAN, and MSNBC.[40]

Through Project Vote Smart, voters could obtain information on thousands of candidates and elected officials, including their biographies, positions on issues, voting records, campaign finances, and the evaluations of special interests. Children can learn more about democracy and the voting process through Kids Voting USA, a website that encourages students to vote and sponsors a recommended civics educational curriculum for primary and secondary students. The Young Voter Strategies project at the George Washington University coordinated the registration of more than five hundred thousand young voters in 2006, using a variety of online technologies, including websites, text messaging, and instant messaging.[41]

With the wealth of information now available, there is simply no excuse for citizens to be uninformed about candidates, issues, and voting. There are many more websites available for the interested citizen; several of them are listed in the "Citizens' Internet Resource Guide," found in the Appendix.

The Internet provides incredible amounts of information about politics and candidates, giving citizens the opportunity to interact with campaigns, sign up as volunteers, give money to candidates, and act on their own as electronic advocates. Yet, the Internet is no cure-all for the ills of citizen apathy, poor voter turnout, and general disinterest in politics. Indifferent citizens will have no incentive to reach out to the many information-rich websites and politics-oriented blogs, apathetic nonvoters will not click on a website to see who will be on the ballot during the next election, and unconcerned individuals will have no more incentive to sign an electronic petition than a paper petition on a clipboard thrust at them in front of the neighborhood grocery store.

Electronic democracy shows us clearly the great divide in American politics. On one side of the divide are those citizens who have access to the Internet, participate, and vote, and on the other side are those who have limited access to online resources and do not vote. Those with better educations and higher incomes are more likely to vote; they are also more likely to have access to the Internet and have an interest in web-related campaign and advocacy sites.[42] Those on the other side of the divide, by and large, will neither vote nor bother with campaign and advocacy websites. The digital divide is narrowing and more citizens have access to laptop computers, tablets, and smart phones. In 2013, 85 percent of American adults used the Internet; 70 percent had access to broadband; and 56 percent owned a smart phone. When taking broadband access and smart phones together, some 80 percent of whites, 79 percent of African Americans, and 75 percent of Hispanic Americans had access to these devices. Those citizens who were not invested in digital communication tended to be more rural, older, and poorer.[43]

At all levels of campaigning and electioneering, there is a need for citizen involvement. The vast majority of campaigns at the local level depend on volunteers; the hundreds of thousands of local contests could not be held without friends, neighbors, and loyalists willing to roll up their sleeves and help. Local ballot initiatives springing up from grassroots movements would never get off the ground without volunteer activism. Candidates for the presidency depend heavily on grassroots support and volunteer organization. Armed with new tools of electronic advocacy, citizens can exert their voices in extraordinary new ways. All that is needed is the interest in politics and a willingness to become involved in elections.

Despite the enthusiasm of Joe Trippi and others for web advocacy, electronic democracy will not supplant old-fashioned, professionally run political campaigning. Over the years, professional campaigns have added the thirty-second television spot, direct mail, demographic and computer aided targeting techniques, focus group analysis, dial meter research, and online database research to their arsenals. Now they have added the worldwide web, text messaging, blogs, online advertising, and social media messaging. Smart, aggressive, professionally run campaigns have co-opted the digital information and are making campaign websites, email, and other electronic tools integral parts of their communication strategies.

Professional campaigns and the political consulting industry will flourish in the decades to come. Candidates for public office—both incumbents and challengers—will not hesitate to raise increasingly larger sums of campaign funds to pay for professional consultants and their services. Despite the occasional outburst from elected officials or the public, candidates need, want, and, for the most part, appreciate the assistance they receive from professional consultants. We may see profound changes in campaign financing, communications, and technology. Through it all, professional consulting will endure, adapt, and prosper. Professionals have become indispensable players in modern campaigns.

Notes

1   American Association of Political Consultants, Code of Professional Ethics, article 1, adopted unanimously by AAPC members at the annual meeting in Las Vegas, Nevada, January 28, 1994, www.theaapc.org/default.asp?content ID=701 (accessed February 20, 2015).

2   Richard Schlackman and Jamie Douglas, "Attack Mail: The Silent Killer," *Campaigns and Elections*, July 1995, 25.

3   Lloyd Grove, "Taken under Advisement," *Washington Post*, August 31, 1996, D1.

4   Ibid., D3.

5 Ibid.

6 Charles S. Clark, "Political Consultants," CQ *Researcher*, October 4, 1996. Francis X. Clines characterized Rollins as a "cantankerous" Republican strategist who had been "twice read out of politics, but manages to survive as a wisecracking talking head on the celebrity rim" of the 1996 election season. Francis X. Clines, "In Dick Morris Specter, a Vision of Marley's Ghost," *New York Times*, October 20, 1996, A20. Second quote from Ed Rollins with Tom DeFrank, *Bare Knuckles and Back Rooms* (New York: Broadway Books, 1996), 339.

7 Roger Simon, *Showtime: The American Political Circus and the Race for the White House* (New York: Times Books, 1998), 310. Emphasis in original.

8 Mike Murphy, "How to Win," *Weekly Standard*, October 21, 1996, 18.

9 Scot Lehigh, "Fired! When Famous People Get Canned, Our Interest Is More than Casual," *The Boston Globe*, October 6, 1996, D1.

10 During the Republican convention, on the eve of Dole's acceptance speech, "feuding among staff members was so fierce" that the campaign manager was forced to step in, fearing that the press would catch wind of the bitter fighting. Elizabeth Kolbert and Adam Nagourney, "Staff Turmoil Seems a Staple of Dole's Management Style," *New York Times*, September 15, 1996, 1. As Scot Lehigh observed, "If Dole wanted to banish the man truly responsible for his problems, the GOP might suddenly find itself without a standard bearer." Lehigh, "Fired!" D1.

11 Evan Thomas et al., *Back from the Dead: How Clinton Survived the Republican Revolution* (New York: Atlantic Monthly Press, 1997), xiii.

12 Pew Research Center for the People and the Press, "Don't Blame Us: The View of Political Consultants," Andrew Kohut, director, June 17, 1998. Two hundred political consultants were surveyed in late 1997 and early 1998. Additional commentary in James A. Thurber, Candice J. Nelson, and David A. Dulio, "The Consultants Speak: An Analysis of Campaign Professionals' Attitudes," unpublished paper for conference, The Role of Political Consultants in Elections, American University, Washington, D.C., June 19, 1998.

13 Reilly campaign website: www.clintreilly.com/Your Mayor. See Noble advertising in *Campaigns and Elections*, September 1994, 32. It is unusual for a political consultant to shed the role and actually run for elected office. Gary Hart, who managed George McGovern's 1972 presidential campaign, but who wasn't really a professional campaign consultant, was elected as U.S. senator from Colorado and then became a presidential candidate. One successful consultant turned elected official was Ron Faucheux, who was elected to statewide office in Louisiana and later became editor of *Campaigns and Elections* magazine.

14 Gary Nordlinger, "Ethical Responsibilities," *Campaigns and Elections*, April 1998, 63.

15 Dick Morris has been the notable exception, working for both Democrats and Republicans. He has worked for Democrat Bill Clinton but also for Republicans Trent Lott, William Weld, and Jesse Helms. In a bit of premature political repentance, Dick Morris is reported to have said to an aide of Republican Senator

Dan Coats of Indiana, "Look, I've gone both ways. I realize that was my mistake. I will never, never work for a Democrat again." Richard L. Berke, "Adviser Who Has President's Ear Thrived as Anti-Clinton Strategist," *New York Times*, October 23, 1995, A20.

16 On ethics and professional responsibility, see F. Christopher Arterton, "Professional Responsibility in Campaign Politics," unpublished paper for Conference on Professional Responsibility and Ethics in the Political Process, sponsored by the American Association of Political Consultants, Williamsburg, Va., March 24, 1991.

17 Richard L. Berke, "The Voters: Majority Give Clinton Credit on the Economy, Poll Finds," *New York Times*, September 6, 1996, A1; and Ernie Freda, "The Road to Washington: Campaign Notes," *The Atlanta Journal and Constitution*, November 8, 1996, 12A.

18 James Bennet, "The New Campaign Story," *New York Times*, September 9, 1966, A14.

19 Ron Faucheux and Paul S. Herrnson, "See How They Run: State Legislative Candidates," *Campaigns and Elections*, August 1999, 25.

20 Liza DePaulo, "The Scandal Sheet," *George*, December 1996, 102.

21 Eliza Newlin Carney, "Gold-Plated Guns for Hire," *National Journal*, June 6, 1998, 1296.

22 Cited in Peter Levine, "Consultants and American Political Culture," *Report from the Institute for Philosophy and Public Policy*, 14, no. 3/4 (summer/fall 1994): 5.

23 Pew Research Center, "Don't Blame Us."

24 Ibid. Forty-six percent of consultants considered suppressing voter turnout "clearly unethical," while 22 percent found this tactic "acceptable," and 29 percent found it "questionable." Fourteen percent found the use of scare tactics about an opponents' positions "clearly unethical," while 36 percent found this tactic "acceptable," and 46 percent found it "questionable." Twenty-six percent found the tactic of making statements that are factually true, but taken out of context "clearly unethical," while 13 percent found this "acceptable," and 60 percent found it to be a "questionable" practice.

25 Ibid. Ninety-eight percent felt that making statements that are factually false was "clearly unethical." Seventy percent considered the use of push-polls "unethical," while only 7 percent considered them "acceptable."

26 Bill McAllister, "Consultants' Ethics," *Washington Post*, June 18, 1998, C2.

27 James Thurber, "Are Campaign Pros Destroying Democracy?" *Campaigns and Elections*, August 1998, 56.

28 As Linda Fowler has written, "individuals who hide behind their subordinates are unworthy of the public trust." Linda L. Fowler, "Campaign Ethics and Political Trust," in *Campaigns and Elections: American Style*, ed. James A. Thurber and Candice Nelson (Boulder, Colo.: Westview, 1995), 212.

29 Jack W. Germond and Jules Witcover, "The Curious Case of the Consultant and the Migrating Head," *Baltimore Sun*, October 16, 1996, 17A.

30 Spencer S. Hsu, "John Warner Fires Consultant Who Altered Challenger's Photo in Ad," *Washington Post*, October 11, 1996, B1. Challenger Mark Warner fired back: "Is doctoring a photograph and taking one person's head and putting it on another person's body the Virginia way? I don't think so ... and I don't think voters are going to think that your way, John, is the Virginia way." For many elections, the concept of the "Virginia way" still has resonance with many Virginia voters—a mark of civility and fair play.

31 E. J. Dionne, Jr., *Why Americans Hate Politics* (New York: Simon and Schuster, 1991).

32 Ibid., 332.

33 The Project on Campaign Conduct is led by the Institute for Global Ethics in Camden, Maine, and is funded by a grant from the Pew Charitable Trusts. Reported in *Campaign Insider*, July 23, 1998, 10.

34 Howard Kurtz, "Adversaries Join Campaign to Improve Coverage of State, Local Politics," *Washington Post*, May 28, 1998, A4.

35 "Circle the Wagons," *San Francisco Chronicle*, November 3, 1997.

36 Joseph N. Cappella and Mark Brewin, "The Minnesota Compact and the Election of 1996," Annenberg Public Policy Center, University of Pennsylvania, April 1998; and Paul Taylor, "Case Study: The Minnesota Compact," Alliance for Better Campaigns, Washington, D.C., June 1998, cited in Task Force on Campaign Reform, "Campaign Reform: Insights and Evidence," Woodrow Wilson School of Public and International Affairs, Princeton University, Larry M. Bartels, chair, September 1998, 44.

37 Josh Gerstein, "Judge Strikes Down Ohio Law on Political Lies," *Politico*, September 11, 2014.

38 Joe Trippi, *The Revolution Will Not Be Televised: Democracy, the Internet, and the Overthrow of Everything* (New York: HarperCollins, 2004), 4–5.

39 Federal Election Commission Web site: www.fec.gov; Center for Responsive Politics: www.opensecrets.org; Public Disclosure: www.public disclosure.org; National Institute on Money in State Politics: www.follow themoney.org; Campaign Finance Information Center: www.campaign finance.org.

40 League of Women Voters: www.lwv.org.

41 Project Vote Smart (www.vote-smart.org) and Young Voter Strategies project (www. youngvoterstrategies.org).

42 The one big exception to this generalization is the elderly population. Older citizens tend to vote far more regularly than other groups, yet the elderly, as a group, use the Internet the least frequently. But time might take care of this: citizens who were in the prime working years back at the beginning of the online revolution, are now entering retirement years, and many are fully comfortable using the latest tool and digital toys. Pew Research Center for the People and the Press, "On-Line Polling Offers Mixed Results," January 27, 1999, www.people-press.org/1999/01/27/online-polling-offer-mixed-results (accessed February 20, 2015).

43   Kathryn Zickhur, "Who's Not Online and Why," Pew Research Internet Project, Pew Research Center Internet, Science and Tec, September 25, 2013, www.pewinternet.org/2013/09/25/whos-not-online-and-why (accessed February 20, 2015).

Appendix

Citizens' Internet Resource Guide

The Internet now provides a rapidly growing list of sites that give information about candidates, elections, campaign financing, voter registration,
and public policy. Voters have never before had so much solid, objective,
nonpartisan (and fervently partisan) information available to them.

California Voter Foundation www.calvoter.org

The California Voter Foundation is a nonprofit, nonpartisan organization that provides a database to help California voters track campaign
money and provides an online voter guide, news, and links to other
relevant sites. In many California jurisdictions, voters can type in their
ZIP codes and the site will display all candidates and ballot issues for
the next election.

Campaign Finance Institute www.cfinst.org

Nonpartisan, nonprofit organization that conducts research related to
campaign finance and national election law.

Campaign Legal Center www.campaignlegalcenter.org

A nonpartisan, nonprofit organization working in the fields of campaign
finance, communications, and government ethics. The organization is
interested in administrative and legal proceedings at the Federal
Election Commission, the Federal Communications Commission, and
the Internal Revenue Service.

Center for Responsive Politics www.opensecrets.org

A nonpartisan, nonprofit research group specializing in the study of
Congress and the role money plays in its elections and actions. The
center conducts computer-based research on campaign finance issues for
the news media, academics, activists, and others interested in Congress.

The site includes a do-it-yourself congressional investigation kit, ways to track donations to election officials and those running for office, a list of potential presidential candidates, and a database of those who have slept at the White House or attended Clinton fundraising coffee mornings.

CNN's All Politics www.cnn.com/politics
Covers state, local, national, and international political issues as well as campaign coverage; "Political Ticker" links to *Congressional Quarterly* and *Time*, in addition to political cartoons.

C-SPAN.ORG www.cspan.org
Clearinghouse for information on policy and politics. Political news links to newspapers throughout the United States, listing of major political blogs, and listing of policy organizations, as well as full coverage of Congress.

Daily KOS www.dailykos.com
Founded by Markos Moulitsas Zúniga ("Kos"), this liberal and progressive leaning site features campaign and policy news, with Democratic elected officials contributing regular columns as well as trenchant comments from other contributors.

Digital Sunlight www.digitalsunlight.org
This site is provided by the California Voter Foundation, giving visitors detailed information on campaign financing for California candidates and ballot issues, and an online voter guide.

Drudge Report www.drudgereport.com
This news aggregation site first became well known during the Monica Lewinsky scandal in 1998. Bare bones site that links to other news sources, gossip, and unsubstantiated rumor. Very heavily viewed site, particularly with conservative and anti-Obama/anti-Clinton themes.

FiveThirtyEight.com www.fivethirtyeight.com
Site developed by Nate Silver to look at the prospects of presidential candidates. Five thirty-eight refers to the number of electoral votes up for grabs every for years. Now reaches much wider into many other aspects of politics, economics, science, even sports.

Huffington Post Politics www.huffingtonpost.com/politics
Lively reports on politics from a variety of reporters, guest columnists, and regularly featured opinion writers.

Kids Voting USA www.kidsvotingusa.org
Kids Voting USA is a nonprofit, nonpartisan "grassroots organization dedicated to securing democracy for the future by involving youth in the election process today." The site includes a list of sponsors, a recommended K-12 curriculum, online activities for students, and information for students and teachers on contacting their local branch of Kids Voting USA.

League of Women Voters www.lwv.org
The site includes a connection to the League of Women Voters Election Central, providing information on registering to vote and becoming involved in voting and elections at the local level.

National Journal Group Policy Central www.nationaljournal.com
The site covers political news and current hot-button issues, but also includes information on upcoming elections and campaigns, including political advertisements. Also listed are a congressional calendar and a news archive. The site is subscription-based.

New York Times Politics www.nytimes.com/pages/politics
Comprehensive look at politics, elections, and public policy.

PBS Online www.pbs.org
An online version of the public television network that provides links to its election site, which allows visitors to learn about the candidates and positions, how to view political advertisements with a critical eye (one area of the site shows how television spots have changed American politics), how to speak out through PBS political polls, and how to receive classroom materials and other election resources.

Pew Research Center for the People and the Press www.peoplepress.org
This site is operated by the Pew Charitable Trusts and features its studies on attitudes toward the press, politics, and public policy issues. Visitors to this site can express their opinions on issues, look at recent survey results, and answer a questionnaire to determine how they fit under certain political typologies.

Politics1 www.Politics1.com

Comprehensive links to all the presidential, gubernatorial, U.S. Senate, and congressional candidates and political parties across the spectrum, and includes election results and news throughout all fifty states.

Politico www.politico.com

A must-read for all things political in Washington; one-stop site for columnists, blog, daily information on Washington policy, elections, and politics.

Project Vote Smart www.votesmart.org

This site provides facts on thirteen thousand candidates and elected officials, including biographies, addresses, issue positions, voting records, campaign finances, and evaluations by special interests.

RealClearPolitics www.realclearpolitics.com

Aggregation site of news about politics, elections, public policy, world events; particularly good for assembling public polling data.

Roll Call www.rollcall.com

Roll Call is a newspaper devoted to covering Congress. This site provides election coverage, news and commentary, policy briefings, and a guide to Congress.

Salon www.salon.com

Covers politics, news, entertainment, sustainability and other topics, from a progressive point of view.

Slate www.slate.com

Daily coverage of politics, elections, policy, many other issues, from progressive point of view.

Taegan Goddard's Political Wire www.politicalwire.com

Up-to-date political and election news, with a Democratic bent.

TechPresident www.techpresident.com

Sponsored by the Personal Democracy Forum, this site focuses on how presidential and other candidates are using online communication.

TownHall.com www.townhall.com

Go to site for conservative news, opinion, blogs, and information. Good links to other conservative and like-minded political sites.

Washington Post Politics www.washingtonpost.com/politics/
Comprehensive look at politics, elections, and public policy, including
Chris Cillizza's "The Fix."

Index